BAKING AT HOME

with *The Culinary Institute of America*

BAKING AT HOME

with *The Culinary Institute of America*

WILEY

JOHN WILEY & SONS, INC.

THE CULINARY INSTITUTE OF AMERICA
Vice President, Continuing Education: Mark Erickson
Director of Marketing and New Product Development: Sue Cussen
Editorial Project Manager: Mary D. Donovan

JOHN WILEY & SONS, INC.
Vice President and Publisher: Natalie Chapman
Senior Editor: Pamela Chirls
Marketing Manager: Adrianne Maher

WELDON OWEN INC.
Chief Executive Officer: John Owen
President and Chief Operating Officer: Terry Newell
Creative Director: Gaye Allen
Associate Publisher and Project Editor: Sarah Putman Clegg
Associate Publisher: Val Cipollone
Designer and Photo Director: Kyrie Forbes
Production Director: Chris Hemesath
Color Manager: Teri Bell
Co-edition and Reprint Coordinator: Todd Rechner

A WELDON OWEN PRODUCTION
Weldon Owen Inc.
814 Montgomery Street
San Francisco, CA 94133

Published by John Wiley & Sons, Inc., Hoboken, New Jersey.

Library of Congress Cataloging-in-Publication Data is available.

Photographs by Quentin Bacon.
Food Styling by Alison Attenborough.

Set in Adobe Garamond and Berthold Akzidenz Grotesk.

Color separations by Embassy Graphics.

Printed and bound in China by Midas Printing, Ltd.

First printed in 2004.

10   9   8   7   6   5   4   3   2   1

THE CULINARY INSTITUTE OF AMERICA wishes to thank the faculty, students, administration, and staff for their support and assistance throughout the development of this book, especially our recipe testers, Lisa Lahey, Margaret Otterstrom, and Lynn Tonelli. We also gratefully acknowledge the assistance of Chef Thomas Gumpel, Associate Dean of Baking and Pastry Arts, and the entire Baking and Pastry faculty.

JOHN WILEY & SONS and WELDON OWEN wish to thank the following people for their generous assistance and support in the production of this book: Editor and Writer Mary Donovan; Consulting Editor Ann Martin Rolke; Copy Editor Sharron Wood; Photographer Quentin Bacon; Photographer's Assistant Amy Sims; Food Stylist Alison Attenborough; Art Director Joseph De Leo; Prop Stylist Joe Maer; Food Stylist's Assistants Craig Thompson and Sean Coyne; Food Stylist's Assistants and Hand Models Maureen Grady and Eliza Watt; Proofreaders Carrie Bradley, Desne Ahlers, and Arin Hailey; Production Designer Joan Olson; and Indexer Ken DellaPenta.

CONTENTS

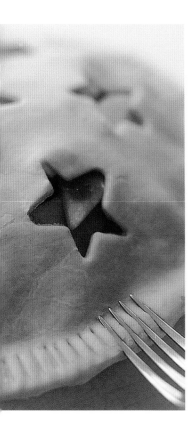

Introduction

As the public's appetite for high-quality baked goods and fine pastries grows, so too does the demand for bakers and pastry chefs trained specifically in those disciplines. During the 1980s, the Culinary Institute of America began offering a thirty-week certification course. Today, we offer two full-fledged degree programs in baking and pastry. The faculty for the baking and pastry arts program has developed a wide-ranging program that covers all aspects of baking, from yeast breads and pies to pastries and confections.

In the creation of this book, we have drawn extensively from the school's first-ever professional text for bakers, *Baking and Pastry: Mastering the Art and Craft,* a book developed by the school's faculty for its students. In preparing this book for the home baker, we concentrated on teaching the same skills and techniques employed by professionals, but carefully adapted to work in the home kitchen.

Ingredients for baking

Great baked goods begin with the best-quality ingredients. The recipes in this book were developed and written with commonly available ingredients in mind. We hope that when you visit your market, you will occasionally find a special flour, a European-style butter, heavy cream that hasn't been ultrapasteurized, or deluxe chocolates. If you find these luxury ingredients, try them for yourself to see what all the excitement is about. In the past, bakers often had to search far and wide, or even rely on mail-order sources, to find bread flour or high-quality chocolate, but most stores across the country are now stocking a larger assortment of flours, sugars, syrups, chocolates, nuts, and extracts than ever before. Fresh fruits, both local and seasonal options like strawberries and exotic, tropical offerings like mangos and passion fruit, are much easier to find. The freezer case holds quick-frozen berries with no added sugar, puff pastry, phyllo, and other dessert basics. Experimenting with ingredients is a great way to become even more expert at appreciating great quality. While this is true for any cooking, it is more apparent in baking, since you typically work with a smaller group of basic ingredients. Learning how to choose the best "basics" is an important skill for any baker or pastry chef.

Learning the techniques

The CIA's baking and pastry faculty teaches our students the basic mixing methods that translate into a dazzling display of breads, cakes, cookies, custards, tortes, and confections. These basic techniques are the building blocks for every type of baked good, from simple muffins to complex tortes. Practicing the fundamentals over and over is the only path to mastery, of course; the learning curve, although long, is delicious and rewarding. Bakers learn, however, that technique, all by itself, is not enough. You need to become thoroughly familiar with your kitchen, your stove top, your oven, your pans, and the variables, such as weather, that can affect what you make.

Our recipes offer you a chance to get plenty of practice as well as get familiar with your baking environment. Eventually, you will be able not just to read the recipe, but also to consider the conditions or ingredient choices that might affect your baking: a hot, humid day or a cold, dry one, vanilla extract or a vanilla bean, large eggs or medium eggs, a hand mixer or a stand mixer, and so forth.

We've included suggestions and substitutions for several key recipes to give you a sense of how bakers might introduce a different fruit or nut, substitute one chocolate for another, or add a special twist by pairing a sauce or a pastry with something as simple as a custard to make a spectacular plated dessert. You'll find a discussion of basic ingredients and tools, as well as four key mixing methods in the beginning of the book. Then, in each chapter that follows, we focus on using those techniques to create each category of baked goods and pastries.

This book gives you the opportunity either to concentrate on a particular technique and test your skills or to take your baking and pastry skills to a higher level. Bread bakers looking for a challenge might try such classic bread-baking endeavors as sourdoughs, *biga*s, or brioche. A simple but perfect butter cake gives testimony to perfectly executed technique, but a filled, iced, and decorated torte stretches not just your technical expertise, but also the artist within. Similarly, once you master producing ice cream, you might try to make a Baked Alaska.

Baking at Home also provides an entry point for some advanced recipes, especially chocolates and confections. Some candies are actually quite simple to prepare, giving you a head start on the sugar and chocolate skills that lead up to making gelées and hard candies or tempering chocolate to enrobe a truffle.

Nearly everyone loves a good dessert, but some of us have a special passion for baked goods or pastries. Whether you adore rich chocolate layer cakes or European-inspired pastries, cookies for dunking or elegant desserts for a special dinner party, *Baking at Home* has both the basic information and the mouthwatering recipes to help you succeed and to share your best efforts with your friends and family.

ABOUT BAKING

Although they share many similarities, baking and cooking are fundamentally different activities. While a soup, a stew, or even a sauté can be adapted or changed at virtually any stage of preparation, most breads, cookies, muffins, cakes, or custards need to be put together exactly as a recipe describes before you bake, chill, or freeze them. Once a batter is ladled into the pan or a custard ice-cream base is cooling, it may be too late to adjust the amount of salt or change the texture. Another important distinction between baking and cooking is that many of the dishes you cook for your family and friends are meant to be served straight from the pan or the oven, still piping hot, while most baked goods and desserts require a little more advance planning. Cakes need to cool and be frosted, parfaits and mousses need to chill and firm up in the refrigerator, and yeast breads need plenty of time to rise.

Far from being seen as a drawback, this thoughtful approach to preparing food holds special appeal for most dedicated bakers. Today, home bakers see their craft as a way to break from a rush-rush routine and settle into a rhythm that typically can't be hurried—one that invites you to slow down and enjoy the process of creating good food.

Mystery or science?

The fact that yeast makes a stiff dough light and airy, or that gelatin makes liquids firm enough to slice, or that a trace of grease prevents egg whites from whipping up properly, or that baking powder turns blueberries green can be mysterious or even perplexing if you don't understand some of the science of baking. The ingredients used in baked goods interact in specific ways, often on the chemical level. If you approach baking as an experiment that you can use to learn more about the way everyday ingredients work together, you'll come away with more than just a sweet treat at the end of a session in the kitchen.

Try to approach baking in a systematic, methodical way. Before you begin baking, gather all the equipment and measure out the ingredients called for in a recipe. Chefs call this preparation *mise en place,* or "putting in place." Read your recipe carefully; you may need to sift dry ingredients together, melt and cool some ingredients, or permit others to warm slightly at room temperature. Be sure to plan ahead so that your frozen desserts are perfectly chilled and set when you want to serve them, pastry doughs are ready to roll out when your filling is complete, and cakes are adequately cooled before you start to frost and decorate them.

Measuring

Baking and pastry recipes combine ingredients in exact amounts, in a specific proportion to one another. Professional bakers focus carefully on the proportion of ingredients both to develop new recipes and to improve ones that do not turn out well. Sometimes even a small deviation in an ingredient amount can have a big impact, especially with ingredients like baking soda, baking powder, yeast, or salt. There are three basic ways to measure ingredients: by weight, by count, and by volume. Most recipes in this book, as well as in other cookbooks, use a combination of these methods.

For consistent measurements using volume measures, you will need to use the right measure for the type of ingredient and fill the cup or spoon properly (see page 21). Some ingredients, such as raisins or brown sugar, may need to be packed into the measuring cup, while others, like flour, should be aerated before measuring. Be sure to consult your recipe to determine how best to measure an ingredient. Always using the same method for measuring each ingredient will ensure more consistent results.

Baking temperature and time

The right cooking temperature is important for turning out golden, crisp cookies, softly set custards, or a chewy caramel candy. But every stove and burner can behave a little differently. Great bakers know how important it is to measure temperature accurately, but they are also skilled at using other clues—the color of a crust, the way something smells, and how a mixture feels when you stir it—to determine whether it has been cooked properly. Each recipe you make adds to your store of experience, making you a better judge of the next one.

The oven is one of the most important pieces of equipment any baker uses. Most modern ovens require at least 10 minutes to preheat properly, and older ones may need longer. Having the oven at the right temperature before you slide in a tray of cookies or a custard in a water bath means that items start to brown and bake properly right away. Whether the oven is gas or electric, set the racks near the center for the most even color, unless a recipe specifies some other arrangement. If you are baking with multiple pans, you will most likely need to place the racks in the upper and lower thirds of the oven, but to ensure even baking, switch the pans from one rack to another, usually about halfway through the total baking time. Use an oven thermometer to double-check your oven's thermostat; it isn't uncommon for the actual temperature to be 25 or more degrees above or below the temperature at which it is set. Adjust the dial accordingly.

Using a liquid measure.

Measuring by weight

Recipes for professionals tend to rely on weight measurements, for greater precision and more consistent baked goods. Although weight is the most accurate method for measuring ingredients, most American home cooks and bakers are not accustomed to working this way. Instead, they use wet and dry volume measures. (For conversions, see pages 288–89.)

The proof is in the pudding

Bakers can learn a lot by eating their own baked goods. You may be inclined to focus mainly on the way a recipe differs from what you expected or remembered, but be sure to also notice what you like so that you can make it happen again. You might even jot down notes on your recipe to refer to the next time you make it.

Opposite: *Pouring batter into a pan; whisking; rising dough.*

Measuring flour accurately.

INGREDIENTS AND THEIR ROLES

Ingredients function in specific ways to help determine the final texture, flavor, and color of baked goods. Good bakers know how each ingredient affects the outcome.

Flours, meals, and grains

These ingredients are made by processing the seeds of a wide range of cultivated grains, including wheat, rice, oats, rye, and corn. The whole grain may be used virtually intact, as in the case of wheat or rye berries; slightly milled, as in cracked wheat or cornmeal; or ground to a fine flour. The amount of starch and protein in a flour determines how it will behave in a recipe.

Flour gives structure to a wide range of baked goods. Wheat flour is especially useful because it contains the right amounts and types of certain proteins (glutenin and gliadin) to give structure and resiliency to yeast-raised doughs. When wheat flour is moistened and then kneaded, the proteins combine to make gluten, a network of long, stretchy strands that trap carbon dioxide given off by yeast or other leaveners. This interaction between gluten and gas is what allows bread to rise.

Whole-grain and stone-ground flours

Whole-grain flours are milled to leave some of the bran intact. Stone-ground flours have been milled using stone mill wheels; they are usually produced in small batches. They are not heated during the milling process, so they retain more oils and are more flavorful.

The more bran and germ in a grain, the more perishable it is. Whole-grain and stone-ground flours are best stored in the refrigerator after opening so that their oils don't turn rancid.

Additionally, all flours contain starches that both thicken when heated and absorb liquids to produce homogenous batters and doughs. Different flours contain different types of starch, and the results you get when you cook or bake them differ greatly; for example, cornstarch-thickened puddings have a different look and feel from flour-thickened ones.

Consult specific recipes for guidance when selecting flours, meals, and grains. All-purpose flour is a blend of "soft" (low-protein) and "hard" (high-protein) wheats and is called for in the majority of the baked goods in this book. Bread flour has more protein and is considered "stronger," making it appropriate to use in most yeast bread recipes. Cake flour has less protein and is "softer" than either bread or all-purpose flour. It is used in most cake and many cookie and muffin recipes for a less chewy, more tender result.

Self-rising flour

Flours labeled "self-rising" contain a chemical leavener such as baking powder. Note that none of the recipes in this book uses self-rising flour. It should not be substituted for other types of flour unless you also intend to reduce the amounts of the other leaveners that may be indicated in a recipe.

To store opened packages of flour, transfer the contents to an airtight container or a large resealable plastic bag to keep out moisture, dirt, and pests, as well as to prevent opened bags or boxes from spilling in the cupboard. Unopened packages of white flour keep for up to 2 years in a cool, dry cupboard. Once opened, they should be used within 8 months. Store whole wheat, potato, rice, rye, oat, and corn flours in a cool, dry cupboard and use them within 2 or 3 months after opening—or keep them in the refrigerator for up to 6 months. For long-term storage, keep whole grains in the freezer.

Opposite: Sifting dry ingredients.

Fermenting yeast.

Yeast types

Dry yeast is commonly available in packets of about 2½ teaspoons each or in 4-ounce vacuum-sealed jars. Active dry yeast is readily available to the home baker and is the yeast used in this book's bread recipes. Instant dry yeast, the preference of many professional bakers since it has a higher percentage of "live" yeast cells, is usually unavailable in the supermarket but may be purchased at specialty baking shops. (For best results, avoid rapid-rise yeast.)

Unopened dry yeast can last as long as a year in the cupboard; check the "use-by" date on the envelope or label, or "proof" the yeast by combining it with the warm liquid in a recipe and verifying that it foams within a few minutes. Once jars of yeast are opened, refrigerate them for up to 6 months.

Fresh yeast is quite moist and is sold in small cubes; refrigerate for up to 6 days or keep for up to 6 weeks in the freezer. To use fresh yeast, substitute 1 cube for every packet (or 2½ tsp) called for in a recipe. Crumble it into the mixing bowl and dissolve it in the liquid before adding the flour.

Leaveners

Bakers rely upon three basic types of leaveners—organic leaveners, chemical leaveners, and physical leaveners —to raise breads, cakes, and cookies.

Yeast, a tiny single-celled organism, is known as an "organic" leavener because it must be living to do its work. Commercially produced yeast is made from the strain known as *Saccharomyces cerevisiae,* while sourdough starters trap wild yeasts from the air. Like any living organism, yeast needs the right environment in order to thrive. When the conditions are right, yeast cells grow and reproduce, giving off carbon dioxide in the process. This carbon dioxide increases the volume of a dough during rising and again when exposed to the heat of the oven, resulting in bread's spongy texture. In order to grow and reproduce, yeast requires moisture, to hydrate the yeast cells and bring them in contact with their food source; food, in the form of sugar, whether added or naturally present in flour; and warmth. Yeast grows most rapidly between 60 and 90°F. Cooler temperatures slow the yeast down, although they don't kill it. Yeast is destroyed when the temperature of a baked good reaches 200°F.

Chemical leaveners—baking soda and baking powder—react rapidly to leaven a baked good when they are combined with moisture, heat, and, in the case of baking soda, an acidic ingredient. When these leaveners are blended with liquid in a batter, a chemical reaction produces a gas that forms bubbles. As the batter settles into a firm structure during baking, these pockets give the baked item a spongy, springy texture, sometimes known as its "crumb." If baking soda and baking powder are not properly blended into the batter, the bubbles may be too large, resulting in tunnels or big air pockets. Recipes often call for the chemical leaveners to be sifted with the flour and other dry ingredients to break up any clumps and make sure that they are well dispersed.

Physical leaveners include steam and air. Cakes made using the creaming mixing method (layer cakes and pound cakes, for instance; see page 31) and the foam mixing method (sponge cakes, angel food cakes, and chiffon cakes; see page 33) get their distinctive textures from physical leaveners, as do soufflés. When moisture in a batter from butter, eggs, or other liquid is heated, it turns into steam. The steam takes up more space than water, since water expands when you heat it. Air also expands when it is heated, thereby leavening a batter. Creaming butter or whipping egg whites incorporates air into a batter, and as items such as cakes or soufflés bake in the oven, the pockets of air are trapped while the batter dries enough to take on a relatively firm structure. The trapped pockets give baked goods height as well as a soft, spongy crumb.

Eggs

Eggs contribute proteins, fat, and moisture to baked items. They can also provide structure and texture in a dish. As eggs are agitated (stirred or whipped) and/or heated, their protein coils unfold and then recombine. This creates a web or network that traps liquids or air, resulting in a texture that can range from a soft foam like a meringue to a sliceable custard such as a quiche. Other ingredients in the recipe, as well as the way you mix and cook egg-rich dishes, can give a variety of results.

When eggs are stirred over direct heat, as when making a custard sauce, the agitation keeps the protein strands short enough to prevent a solid network from forming, producing a smooth, spoonable consistency. When a custard is baked in the oven, however, the mixture is not stirred as it cooks, so longer strands of protein can settle into a firm structure that holds its shape. When eggs are whisked, they can trap enough air to make a foam, giving lightness to dishes like mousses and soufflés. Adding eggs to batters and doughs gives the dough some moisture to help it cohere, as well as additional protein for a firmer and drier dish after baking. The water in eggs expands when you bake cakes and muffins, helping them to rise.

Egg yolks add a rich golden color to any dish that includes them, from sponge cake to challah bread to vanilla sauce. Brushing the tops of breads and pastries with an egg wash—a mixture of egg and water or milk—before baking gives a glossy sheen. Egg washes that include only the whites become very shiny, while those that include the yolks give a brilliant golden hue.

Eggs are an enormously versatile ingredient, but they are also a potential source of pathogens such as *Salmonella*. Once the shell is broken, those pathogens can invade the interior of the egg. Eggs in the shell are inspected and graded for wholesomeness, freedom from cracks, and size. Check eggs before purchase for cracked or dented shells. The carton should be clean and dry, and the sell-by date should not have passed. Large grade AA eggs are the size used in the recipes throughout this book. (To substitute other sizes, see page 290.) Eggs can be refrigerated in their carton for 3 to 5 weeks after the sell-by date. Controlling the temperature of eggs as you cook, cool, and store them is one of the most important ways to keep eggs wholesome. Eggs should be refrigerated at about 38°F. Cooking eggs to a safe temperature (165°F) also helps prevent illness by killing any pathogens. Cool egg-based batters like pâte à choux or pastry cream quickly to keep them from sitting too long in the temperature range between 40 and 140°F, most hospitable to the growth of bacteria.

Egg wash for brushing.

Pasteurized eggs

Pasteurized eggs have been heat-treated and can be used to guarantee food safety in those recipes that call for uncooked or semicooked eggs that are not cooked to the safe temperature of 165°F. This is especially important when preparing food for the very young, the elderly, pregnant women, or anyone with an impaired immune system. You can buy pasteurized eggs in the shell, shelled and packaged in pourable cartons, or sold as just yolks or just whites.

Egg substitutes

Egg substitutes can often be found in the freezer case of supermarkets, as well as in the dairy case near the fresh eggs. They are useful when you want to control the amount of cholesterol in a recipe. Most can be refrigerated in unopened containers for 10 days; use them within 3 days once open. Egg substitutes (powdered or liquid) may be substituted for fresh eggs in most cases; however, some sources suggest that substitutes should not be used for more than 3 eggs. There will be some differences in the flavor, color, and texture of baked goods made with egg substitutes.

Dicing cold butter for pastry.

Butter styles

Butter contains fat, moisture, and milk solids. It browns at relatively low temperatures compared to other fats, because of the presence of these milk solids—which are also responsible for butter's creamy taste. Butter can be unsalted or lightly salted. Unsalted grade AA butter is used in the recipes in this book. If you substitute a European-style butter, which has a slightly higher butterfat content and less moisture, in a baking recipe, you may need to add a bit more liquid.

Hydrogenation

Most shortenings and margarines contain substances known as trans fatty acids, by-products of the hydrogenation process, which turns a liquid fat such as vegetable oil into a solid. If you are concerned about "trans fats," look for products that specify that they are free of them. In the future, all food labels will be required to show the amount of trans fats on the label along with the other nutrition information.

Opposite: *Adding liquid fat; creaming butter; cutting in butter.*

Butter, oils, and shortening

Fat is critical to flavor. It lingers on the palate, imbued with the flavors of a dish, allowing you to experience their richness. Some fats—namely, butter, lard, and certain oils, such as nut oils—contribute their own special flavors to baked goods. Other fats, such as vegetable oil, margarine, and shortening, are chosen specifically for their lack of flavor, to allow the flavors of other ingredients to come to the fore.

Fats also determine the texture of baked goods. Depending upon the type of fat you use in a baked good and the way it is worked into a batter or dough, the resulting texture may range from meltingly smooth to flaky and brittle. The more fat in the recipe, the softer the batter or dough. Baked goods that are made from softer batters or doughs have a tendency to spread out while they bake. The way batter spreads is important, for example, to making cookies of the right size and color. The fat in a batter or dough also helps to encourage browning on crusts and edges; this extra color translates as extra flavor on the palate. It also produces a delightful texture contrast, as the outer edges become crisper than the middle of the baked good. Finally, the fat in a baked good also improves its texture and extends its life by holding in moisture, delaying staling.

Solid fats

Some fats, including butter, shortening, margarine, and lard, are solid at room temperature. The texture of these solid fats permits them to be rubbed, cut, or creamed into a dough or a batter. Butter is made from cream and lends good flavor and flakiness to pastry or biscuits; lard, refined pork or beef fat, has a unique flavor and makes a very flaky pastry. You can substitute it in equal amounts for the shortening or butter in most pie dough recipes; it is especially good when used to make the pastry for savory dishes. Vegetable shortening is vegetable oil that has been processed (hydrogenated) to keep it solid at room temperature. Margarine is produced in a similar manner. Vegetable shortening performs the same functions as butter and lard, but it contributes relatively little flavor of its own and extraordinary flakiness.

Store solid fats such as butter or lard in the refrigerator for up to 2 months or in the freezer for 7 to 8 months. Since these ingredients tend to absorb odors easily, keep them well wrapped and away from strongly flavored cheeses, meats, or produce. Unopened shortening keeps in a cupboard for up to 1 year. Once opened, it will keep properly wrapped in a cool cupboard or in the refrigerator for 4 to 5 months. Store margarine in the refrigerator and take note of the use-by date.

Liquid fats

An oil is a pure fat that is liquid or pourable at room temperature. Some oils have a neutral flavor: canola, corn, and safflower are examples. "Vegetable oil" on a label generally indicates that a blend of oils was used. These oils keep well in a cool, dry cupboard for 5 to 6 months. Other oils—walnut, peanut, sesame, almond, and extra-virgin olive oils, for instance—have distinctive flavors. These oils are more perishable than vegetable oils and should be purchased in small quantities. Once bottles are opened, they can be held in the refrigerator. (The cold of the refrigerator may cause the oil to cloud, but this does not affect its flavor or use.) Cooking sprays made from canola and corn oils are extremely useful for coating pans lightly and evenly. Smell all opened oils before you use them and discard them if the aroma is unpleasant or rancid.

Mixing methods for fats

The mixing method used for a batter or dough often dictates the form a fat must take when it is blended with the other ingredients in a recipe. Cakes and quick breads made using the straight mixing method (page 30) require a fat in liquid form, either an oil or melted butter or shortening, which is added in alternation with the dry ingredients. This produces a baked item with a somewhat coarse texture. These baked goods are sometimes described as having a large crumb.

The creaming mixing method (page 31), used for some cookies and cakes, requires a softened solid fat such as room-temperature butter or shortening; as the fat is creamed, or beaten, air is worked into it and trapped in the batter, producing a smaller crumb and a lighter texture. Cookies, which typically call for a relatively short creaming time, are crisper and denser than cakes, which require more creaming for more added air. Cakes turn out soft, tender, and light when the fat in the batter is well creamed and emulsified throughout the entire batter. When using the creaming method, it is important to keep the butter or shortening from becoming too warm; if the fat melts, the air will be released too quickly and the baked item might turn out flat and heavy.

Blending solid fat into a dough as layers or pockets produces a flaky or crumbly texture; biscuits, scones, and pie crusts all owe their texture to this blending technique, known as the rubbing mixing method (page 32). Butter, shortening, or lard may be rubbed or cut into flour, distributing small, discrete pieces of fat throughout a dough. When these doughs are baked, the fat releases its moisture, and the puffs of steam create a crisp, flaky pastry that shatters or breaks easily.

Sweeteners

Granulated sugar, brown sugar, and confectioners' sugar, as well as a range of syrups—including molasses, honey, maple syrup, and light and dark corn syrups—not only give baked goods flavor, but also add moisture and keep baked items fresh longer. Granulated sugar, or ordinary white sugar, is refined from sugar cane or sugar beets. Thick, dark molasses, a by-product of sugar manufacture, is combined with white sugar to make flavorful and moist brown sugar. Honey ranges in color from very light to almost as dark as molasses and is often identified by the flower from which the bees gathered nectar. Maple syrup is the boiled-down sap of maple trees.

In addition to flavor, sweeteners also give baked goods a light texture and a good rich color. When you cream sugar and butter together, the sugar's granular shape traps some air in the batter, which helps raise the baked good and improves its texture after baking. Like salt, sugar and other sweeteners attract moisture, making baked goods softer and longer lasting than those with little or no sugar. Sugars and syrups develop a rich brown color when heated, an effect known as caramelization. This process adds appealing color as well as delicious flavor.

Sugar also interacts with other ingredients on a chemical level. When combined with liquids, sugar raises the temperature at which the liquid will boil. Adding sugar makes eggs less prone to overcook, even over direct heat. Different sugars behave differently when they are mixed and baked, so use the type specified in a recipe.

Store sweetening ingredients in a cool, dry cupboard. Unopened jars and bags typically last at least 2 years. Once opened, use within 6 to 8 months.

Acids

Citrus and other fruit juices, wine, vinegar, yogurt, buttermilk, honey, and salt are some of the acids used in baked goods. Acids change the structure of proteins, an effect known as denaturing. When an acid is added to proteins, the strands that compose the protein either tighten or loosen, depending on the specific proteins the foods contain. By changing the amount and type of acid in a recipe, you can create different textures, from the light, frothy consistency of a sabayon to a dense lemon curd. Fermenting yeast cells give off alcohol—another acid—to produce a good flavor and texture in breads. The alcohol relaxes the gluten strands enough for them to stretch again while the dough proofs and bakes. Acidic ingredients are also added to batters leavened with baking soda in order to start the leavening action.

Sprinkling coarse sugar for a caramelized finish.

Superfine sugar

Superfine sugar, sometimes called baker's sugar, is granulated sugar that is more finely ground so that it dissolves more easily. Superfine sugar can be made in a pinch by grinding regular sugar in a food processor or blender.

Maple syrup styles

Maple syrup is graded according to color, body, and flavor. Grade B is richer in flavor than grade A and is suggested for baking.

Salvaging crystallized syrup

If honey or molasses crystallizes and becomes solid, you can liquefy it by warming it briefly in a microwave.

Opposite: *Sweetening a batter with honey.*

Salt, an essential flavor enhancer.

Pectin

Pectin, which works much like gelatin to thicken a liquid, is a substance naturally found in high concentration in certain fruits, especially apples and citrus fruit. Commercially available pectin is refined from the pectin in these fruits. Unlike gelatin, pectin does not usually require chilling to reach its full thickening potential, making it well suited for fruit preserves and confections. Also unlike gelatin, pectin requires the presence of both a liquid and the correct amount of acid to thicken properly. Pectin is sold in powdered or liquid form, which are not interchangeable, so use the type specified in a recipe. Powdered pectin is mixed with an unheated liquid, whereas liquid pectin is added to a cooked liquid and sugar mixture immediately after it is removed from the heat.

Tapioca

Quick-cooking or instant tapioca is made from the cassava root, a starchy tropical tuber. Since it contributes no flavor of its own and imparts transparent gloss to fruits, it is often used to thicken fruit pie fillings in a two-crust pie as well as to make pudding.

Salt

Salt is a powerful flavor enhancer and seasoning, even for sweet dishes. In small amounts, it does not actually add an identifiable flavor to a dish. Instead, it seems to balance other flavors and make them more vivid. As you add salt in larger quantities, it begins to contribute its own distinctive flavor.

Salt is important in baking because of the way it reacts with other ingredients. Salt controls the activity of yeast, keeping it from overfermenting and thereby ensuring a bread's good texture. If the yeast is not controlled, the bread may rise rapidly at first, only to deflate.

Table salt is assumed for use in the recipes in this book, but kosher salt may be substituted. Table salt has finer grains than kosher salt and contains additives to keep it flowing freely, even when the humidity is high. It may also be fortified with iodine. Kosher salt may taste less salty than table salt because it has coarser, flakier grains. Most kosher salt contains an anticaking ingredient, but additive-free salt is also sold. To substitute kosher salt for table salt, increase the amount called for in a recipe by about 25 to 50 percent, depending on its flavor (some brands taste saltier than others). Coarse salt and sea salt are used as a topping for breads. Salt keeps almost indefinitely in dry storage.

Thickeners

Thickeners give body to liquid mixtures. Cornstarch, a fine, powdery flour made from corn, as well as arrowroot, made from the starchy portion of the arrowroot plant, are often blended with cold liquid before being added to a simmering pudding or pie filling as a thickener. You can substitute an equal amount of arrowroot for cornstarch in most recipes. Both of these thickeners last for up to 8 months on the shelf.

Gelatin is a protein processed from the bones, skin, and connective tissue of animals. It is used as a gelling agent to thicken and stabilize foams or liquids. Gelatin is widely available in granulated or powdered form, in either tins or individual packets (1 package equals 2¼ teaspoons and weighs ¼ ounce). When substituting the less widely available gelatin sheets, use the same weight as you would powdered gelatin (refer to the package information; different types of gelatin sheets may have different weights). Packages of powdered gelatin desserts contain flavorings and sweeteners in addition to gelatin and cannot be used in place of unflavored powdered gelatin in a recipe.

TYPES OF EQUIPMENT

The quality of the equipment you use for baking has a distinct effect on the quality of your baked goods. A good rule of thumb is to always use the right tool for the job.

Tools for accurate measuring

Scales can accurately measure both dry and liquid ingredients. When you weigh ingredients, be sure that you are taking the measure of the ingredient only, and not the container holding the ingredient as well. Set an empty container on the scale, then set the scale to zero (known as tare) before adding the ingredient to be weighed.

Graduated measuring cups are commonly used to measure liquids and pourable ingredients such as milk and honey. The cups are marked with lines to show amounts. Glass or plastic measures in 2- and 4-cup capacities are the most useful.

Dry or nested measuring cups are used for ingredients such as flour, sugar, cocoa powder, and rice. A standard set includes ¼-, ⅓-, ½-, and 1-cup measures.

Measuring spoons typically include measures for 1 tablespoon and 1, ½, and ¼ teaspoons. Fill the spoons to the rim with both dry and liquid ingredients.

Rulers or tape measures make rolling dough to the proper thickness and dimensions easier. They are also useful when you need to determine the dimensions of a baking pan or mold. (For more about substituting baking pans, see page 293.)

Timers keep track of time as you bake. The classic timer works by counting down the time, but some digital timers give you the option of counting time down or up. Some timers allow you to keep track of the baking times for as many as four different items, which is a very helpful feature when you are making multiple batches or a variety of different baked goods. Many digital timers have a cord or clip so that you can carry them with you if you leave the kitchen.

Thermometers play several roles in baking. An instant-read thermometer consists of a long stem with a head that indicates the temperature. Candy and deep-fat thermometers are clipped to the side of a pan so that you can easily monitor the temperature of liquid contents. Refrigerator and freezer thermometers ensure that your refrigerator and freezer keep food at the right temperature, while an oven thermometer is critical to ensure that your oven's thermostat is accurate so that biscuits, breads, and cakes will rise properly, become brown without burning, and finish baking in the appropriate amount of time.

Dry and liquid measures.

Measuring savvy

When measuring, be sure to use the right tool for the job. A clear glass or plastic graduated measuring cup is used for liquids, while nested metal or plastic measuring cups are for dry ingredients. After you pour a liquid into a graduated measuring cup, check the amount with the cup held at eye level to ensure an accurate reading. Dry ingredients throughout this book were measured using the scoop-and-sweep method: Whisk the dry ingredient to aerate it if necessary and then scoop it into the measuring cup. Overfill the measuring cup or spoon and then level it off with a knife. Flour should not be packed into a measuring cup, whereas brown sugar should be.

To get sticky things like honey, molasses, shortening, or peanut butter out of a measuring cup easily, coat the cup with cooking spray before filling it.

When filling measuring spoons, it's good practice to avoid pouring over your bowl of ingredients, in case you accidentally overpour and spill.

Tools for cutting, peeling, and juicing

Knives are used in baking for a variety of chopping, slicing, and mincing chores. A basic set of knives should include a chef's (or French) knife with a blade about 8 to 10 inches long. A utility knife is a smaller version of a chef's knife used for lighter cutting chores. The blade is generally 5 to 7 inches long. A paring knife has a 2- to 4-inch blade, useful for paring and trimming fruits and vegetables. Serrated knives are good for slicing breads and cakes without tearing them.

Slicers have very long blades with a round or pointed tip. The blade may be flexible or rigid. The long, thin blade is perfect for slicing cakes into layers and cutting decorated cakes neatly without marring the frosting.

Kitchen shears or scissors are made of heavy-duty stainless steel and are useful for a variety of cutting tasks, including portioning dough, trimming pastry, and candy making. Some scissors come apart for easy cleaning.

Bench scrapers or bench knives have rectangular steel blades, usually 6 inches wide, capped with a wooden or plastic handle. The steel blade has a dull edge but is thin enough to cut through doughs. You can use a bench scraper like a knife to cut soft ingredients like butter or soft cheese or to lift and turn soft or wet doughs as you knead them, as well as to transfer ingredients like chopped nuts from your work surface to the mixing bowl. They also make short work of cleaning off a work surface.

Graters have flat stainless-steel surfaces with many small perforations that create cutting edges used to zest, grate, shave, and shred. A box grater has four sides and at least two different surfaces for different size shreds. Nutmeg graters and ginger graters are designed to handle these specific ingredients. Microplane graters (or rasps, as they are sometimes known) work well to finely grate citrus zest, chocolate, or hard cheese.

Pastry blenders or pastry knives have a crescent-shaped loop of thin wires attached to a handle and are used to mix fat into flour when you make a pastry dough. If you don't have one, substitute two table knives to cut the fat into the flour.

Corers are short metal tubes attached to a handle. Some have a serrated edge to cut through an apple or a pear as you twist the tube into it, then pull it out to extract the core. Alternatively, use a knife or melon baller to core the fruit after slicing.

Zesters are small hand tools with a cutting head designed to detach the outer layer of the peel from citrus fruits in long, thin shreds.

Reamers have a bulb-shaped end with a sharp point and deep ridges for juicing lemon and other citrus. This tool is traditionally made out of nonporous wood, but may also be glass, metal, or plastic. Some juicers are essentially reamers mounted in a bowl; the juice runs down the reamer and collects in a bowl. Electric juicers have a rotating reamer to release the juice as the citrus is pressed down on the point. Lever-operated juicers exert a great deal of pressure on the halved fruit, pressing out most of the juice.

Cherry or olive pitters have a plunger that pushes the stone from olives and cherries, leaving the fruit whole. If you don't have a pitter, you can use a clean paper clip to fish out the pit. Unfold the smaller end of the paper clip, then insert the larger end along the pit. Hook the end around the pit and pull it out, leaving the olive or cherry intact. If you are chopping the fruits, you can crush them with a mallet or a small clean frying pan in order to extract the pit before chopping.

Biscuit and cookie cutters are made of thin metal sheets or molded plastic. The edges are sharp enough to cut through pastry or cookie dough cleanly. Biscuit cutters may have straight or scalloped edges; 3-inch cutters (the size used in our biscuit recipes) are a good basic size. Cookie cutters are sold in a variety of shapes and sizes; we used a 3-inch-diameter round cutter for our rolled and cutout cookies.

Swivel-bladed peelers are used to remove thin layers of peel from fruits before preparing fillings or compotes. They are also useful for removing thin strips of citrus zest to either mince or candy, while leaving behind the bitter white pith. Replace peelers when the blades become dull.

Tools for mixing and transferring foods

Wooden spoons and spatulas made of tight-grained, unfinished woods do not conduct or transfer heat, so there is no threat of burning your fingers or changing the critical temperature of a mixture when using one. Hardwoods such as boxwood, beech wood, and olive wood are highly regarded because they are less likely than others to split or crack. Wash wooden utensils by hand and avoid prolonged soaking.

Metal spoons—solid, slotted, or perforated—are used to scrape, scoop, and serve baked items. Avoid using them with nonstick cookware and bakeware. Use slotted spoons to lift large pieces from poaching liquids or frying fat; a spider is essentially a large flat spoon made of wire, resembling a web, making it perfect for lifting items out of liquids or fat and allowing them to drain adequately.

Citrus reamer.

Work surfaces

Wood surfaces are excellent for kneading bread dough. Wood is relatively warm, compared to marble, metal, or even plastic materials. This warmth creates a hospitable environment for yeast.

Marble surfaces

Marble is a cool, smooth stone that is very useful if you like to make chocolates and confections such as fudge or caramel. It is also very good for rolling out delicate pastry doughs and cookies; you can work them more easily with less chance of their warming up and getting too soft.

Opposite: *Paring knife; bench scraper; Microplane grater.*

Icing a cake with an offset icing spatula.

Getting the scoop

Ice-cream scoops with a one-piece construction, as well as those with a thin, curved blade and a thumb-release spring mechanism, may be used not only to serve frozen desserts, but also to portion batters and doughs. A 2-ounce scoop is a good size for shaping cookies, but you can also buy 1-ounce scoops, which are excellent for making truffles.

Melon ballers consist of a small bowl attached to a handle; some have only 1 bowl, while others have 2 of different sizes. The metal bowl is used to scoop small balls of fruit, soft doughs, or ganache, and to neatly core halved apples and pears.

Opposite: *Ladling sauce.*

Wire whisks can have as few as two wires and as many as twenty. The thickness of the wires determines the flexibility of the whisk and its function. Balloon whisks, which have a very round shape, incorporate a great deal of air; their wires are generally flexible. Sauce whisks are flat, less flexible, and used to blend and smooth sauces and other dishes as they simmer. Coiled whisks (which look like springs) blend ingredients well without incorporating as much air as a balloon whisk. Some whisks available today have ball-bearing ends instead of wire loops for easier cleaning and better performance.

Rubber spatulas are available in many lengths and widths. Narrow heads make it easy to scrape foods from jars or tins with small openings. Spatulas with wider heads are good for stirring and folding batters. Some spatula heads have a pointed edge useful for getting into pan corners and a notch on one side to clean bowl edges. (Bowl scrapers are another tool that serve this purpose.) Spatulas with silicone heads can withstand temperatures up to 600°F, making them perfect for stirring sauces as they cook or flipping crêpes.

Tongs have two arms attached by a spring. They are usually made of stainless steel, although bamboo and wooden tongs are also available. They make it easy to lift and turn foods as they cook or bake.

Ladles help scoop and measure liquids. Those constructed of a single piece of stainless steel last the longest and are easiest to clean. A slight angle in the handle is a sign of good design. Two- and 4-ounce ladles are the most helpful to have on hand, although other sizes, ranging from 1 to 12 ounces, are widely available.

Metal spatulas and palette knives have long metal blades with blunt edges. The handle may be offset (angled) to make it easier to lift baked goods from the pan or turn them as they cook on a griddle; such tools are generally referred to as spatulas. Palette knives are long, narrow, and often blunt and rounded. Small palette knives with offset handles are good for spreading fillings, icings, and glazes without accidentally dragging your hand in the food. Large palette knives are also used to decorate cakes and pastries, as well as to spread batters and doughs into an even layer before they bake. Some palette knives have a serrated edge for slicing cakes into layers.

Tools for straining and draining

Colanders, sieves, and sifters are essential for draining foods, sifting and combining dry ingredients, and even puréeing soft foods. Well-made colanders have handles and a foot to keep them steady; some have a cone shape. Sieves may be bowl shaped or flat, with

Puréeing through a food mill.

Specialized bread-baking equipment

Peels are large flat wooden or metal paddles used to slide breads onto baking stones or tiles and to retrieve them when they are done. If you don't have a peel, you can use a cookie sheet that has no sides.

Baking stones or tiles are unglazed ceramic pieces used to line an oven rack. The stones or tiles help develop a crisp crust on breads and pizza by holding and transferring the oven's heat evenly. The stones need to preheat along with the oven for best results.

Pan finishes

The surface of a pan has an effect on how items bake. Darker pans produce baked goods with a deep crust color, while those with nonstick surfaces tend to produce goods with a lighter color; the total baking time may also be longer when using nonstick pans. Doubled or insulated cookie sheets require you to bake cookies for longer, and the cookies may not develop as deep a golden color as those baked on other types of cookie sheets. Insulated sheets are ideal for cookies that shouldn't brown, like macaroons or shortbreads.

or without handles; ingredients may be pushed through with a spoon. Sieves also function well as sifters. Sifters have a crank that pushes ingredients through the mesh.

Food mills or Foley mills are used to purée soft foods and strain out skins, seeds, and fibers. A flat, curving blade is rotated over a perforated disk by a hand-operated crank. Some models have interchangeable disks with holes of varying size.

Cheesecloth is a gauze that can be used to strain foods. Before use, rinse out cheesecloth first in hot and then in cool water. This removes loose fibers, as well as to make the cheesecloth cling better to the sides of a bowl or colander as you strain through it, and keeps the cheesecloth from absorbing too much liquid from the food being strained.

Appliances

Mixers make baking tasks like creaming, whipping, and kneading easier and more efficient. Stand mixers are heavy-duty machines capable of mixing and kneading even heavy yeast doughs. They typically have a variety of attachments, such as a whisk, a paddle, and a dough hook. Some stand mixers rotate the bowl, while others move the attachment in an elliptical orbit inside the bowl for thorough and even mixing. Handheld mixers are usually not as sturdy as stand mixers and are best for lighter mixing jobs, such as whipping cream.

Food processors have powerful motors, a work bowl that holds the food, and a blade that rotates in the bowl. Different blades and attachments enable the machine to perform different functions, such as chopping, puréeing, some mixing jobs, grating, and slicing. A midsize model is large and powerful enough for most tasks in the home kitchen. Mini-processors are used to chop small amounts of nuts, spices, or herbs.

Blenders consist of a base, which houses the motor and displays speed control settings, and a removable lidded jar with a propeller-like blade in its bottom. Blenders are excellent for puréeing and liquefying foods. Immersion or handheld blenders have a motor in the handle and a blade on the other end. They are used to purée sauces and batters directly in their cooking pot or mixing bowl, without having to transfer the food to another container. This is particularly helpful when puréeing hot foods.

Baking pans and molds

Loaf pans or tins are rectangular pans used for simple cakes and quick breads. Mini loaf pans are available for making small loaves. You can buy loaf pans in metal, glass, and ceramic, with or without a nonstick coating.

Pie pans or tins have sloped sides and are made from aluminum, glass, or earthenware. The sides of the pan may be up to 3 inches tall; the deeper the pan, the more filling you need. The pies in this book were baked in a standard 9-inch aluminum pie pan with sides that are 1½ inches tall. If you prefer to use glass pie pans, lower the oven temperature by about 25 degrees and the baking time by 5 to 10 minutes. Glass conducts heat efficiently, so the edges and bottom of your pie may brown too rapidly.

Tart pans are made of tinned steel or ceramic; have short, often scalloped sides; and usually have a removable bottom. They may be round, square, or rectangular. Some pans have a nonstick coating. Tartlet pans are simply small tart pans, sized to make individual pastries.

Cake pans are manufactured of tinned steel, aluminum, glass, or silicone; they may have a nonstick coating. Many cake recipes in this book call for an 8-inch round cake pan.

Springform pans consist of a hinged ring that clamps around a removable base. These pans are used for baking delicate cakes that might otherwise be difficult to unmold.

Tube pans have a center tube of metal that conducts heat through the center of the batter, which helps to bake heavy batters evenly without overbrowning the outside of the cake. The tube pan also works well for those batters that need to bake quickly, such as angel food cake. They are typically made of thin metal with or without a nonstick coating. They come in a range of sizes, and the sides may be fluted, molded, or straight.

Baking sheets provide a flat baking surface. A standard cookie sheet measures 13 by 16 inches and has one or more edges without sides to make it easier to slide baked items from the pan to cooling racks. A jelly roll pan has four sides ½ to ¾ inch tall to support a sponge cake batter as it bakes, but may also be used to bake cookies.

Sauté pans, skillets, saucepans, and pots are available in a number of sizes and styles. Choose nonreactive materials, such as stainless steel, enameled cast iron, or anodized aluminum, to preserve the delicate color of cream- and egg-based dishes. Saucepans and pots should have tight-fitting lids. Their sides may be straight or sloped. Pans with high-quality nonstick, enameled, or stainless-steel interiors help avoid scorching when cooking milk- and cream-based items; they are also easier to clean. Use pans with flat, level bottoms; warped pans develop hot spots and cook unevenly. A level, heavy-gauge bottom is vital when cooking sugar; use pans with a light-colored surface like stainless steel to better gauge the color of a caramel.

Unlatching a springform pan.

Substituting cake pan sizes

Refer to the pan dimensions chart on pages 294–95 if you want to use a pan of a size different from the one called for in a recipe.

Parchment for baking

Parchment paper is a grease-resistant, nonstick, heatproof paper used to line baking sheets and pans. The paper is coated with silicone on one side, allowing baked goods to spread properly and release from the paper easily. It comes in rolls, or precut for particular uses such as parchment cones or cake pan liners. Rectangular sheets can also be used to create cones to fill with icings and glazes to decorate baked goods such as cookies and cakes.

Silicone for bakers

Silicone can withstand temperatures up to 600°F. Flexible mats, sold in several sizes, give baking pans a nonstick surface and provide a heat-resistant surface for candy making. Baking pans and molds made of the same material are available in a variety of sizes.

Double boilers are used to cook delicate dishes like custard sauce and to melt chocolate. Some double boilers are essentially two nested pots. The upper pot holds an ingredient or mixture suspended over water simmering in the lower pot. For some recipes, it may be easier to prepare your own double boiler by setting a glass or metal mixing bowl on top of a pot filled with an inch or two of simmering water. Using a bowl permits easier mixing and whisking as the mixture heats.

Soufflé dishes, custard cups, and pudding molds are ovenproof ceramic, glass, or earthenware dishes used to bake a variety of dishes. Soufflé dishes have straight, smooth sides that are typically as high as the dish is wide and come in a range of sizes, from 2 ounces to 2 quarts. Custard cups can have straight or sloped sides and come in a variety of sizes. *Petits pots* are custard cups that may have lids. Gratin or crème brûlée dishes may be oval or round; they have relatively short sides. Pudding molds may have smooth or patterned sides for a special appearance when the pudding is unmolded.

Tools for pastry, decorating, and confections

Rolling pins stretch doughs and pastries into thin sheets. Ball-bearing pins have a steel rod that extends through the pin and is fixed to the handles. Ball bearings on each end of the rod make it easy to roll the pin. These rolling pins may be made of wood, marble, metal, or a synthetic material. Straight (or French) pins look like oversized dowels; they have no handles. Tapered rolling pins are good for rolling dough into circles because of their shape. Marble pins stay cool, a boon to the pie baker or pastry maker. Specialty rolling pins have grooves or patterns to imprint the dough as you roll. Wooden rolling pins should never be soaked in water, and soap should never be used on them, as they will absorb moisture and become distorted. Simply wipe wooden pins well with a moist towel and dry them thoroughly.

Pastry brushes are used to apply egg wash, brush loose crumbs from cake tops, and butter pans. They are made with soft, flexible nylon or unbleached hog bristles. The bristles should be blunt cut and flexible. Unlike brushes used for paint, pastry brushes have no reservoir in the handle, so they are easy to clean completely after each use. Soak the brush briefly if necessary to loosen anything dried on the brush, but avoid prolonged soaking. Let the brush air-dry as soon as it is clean to keep the bristles in place longer. A 1- to 1½-inch-wide brush is suitable for most uses. Brushes used for pastry work should be kept separate from those used to apply barbecue sauces, marinades, and other savory ingredients.

Pastry wheels are round blades mounted on a handle. As you roll the blade over pastry doughs, they make a single, clean cut. The blade may be straight or scalloped to make a decorative edge, particularly nice for lattices on pies. You can also use a sharp paring knife or scissors to cut pastry.

Pastry bags and tips are used to add fillings to pastries such as éclairs and profiteroles, to make delicate cookies like macaroons, and to apply decorative finishes to cakes and pastries. Bags are made of nylon or plastic; some are considered single-use. Tips may be held in place using a coupler, consisting of a tip holder and screw-on ring. Plain round and star tips of medium size are the most versatile, but you can buy specialty tips to make leaves, roses, and other shapes. If your bag is reusable, wash it well in warm soapy water inside and out, rinse thoroughly, and air-dry completely before storing.

SAFETY

Whenever you cook or bake, keep foods like eggs and uncooked fruits or vegetables separate until you actually start to cook or bake them. Pathogens on the surfaces of foods are easily transferred to your hands, knives, cutting boards, and containers, or from one food to another. Clean your tools and work surfaces whenever you switch from one type of food to another, and wash produce thoroughly before preparing it.

Protect your hands with oven mitts or hot pads when you lift pans from the oven. Damp towels provide no insulation because they conduct heat, and should never be used in place of mitts. To lift a dish from a hot water bath, twist a clean kitchen towel into a rope and wrap it around the exterior of the dish. Tongs, especially those used to lift preserving jars from a hot water bath, are also useful.

Adding liquids to hot sugar can cause the sugar to splatter or foam up. To lessen the chances of burning yourself, take the pan away from the heat before you add the liquid. Wear oven mitts to protect your hands when you add the liquid, and keep your face partially turned away. Even if the mixture doesn't spatter, the steam can scald you.

MIXING METHODS

Whether you are making muffins or cream puffs, you are likely to use one of the basic mixing methods on the following pages. You will find more details about how each technique is modified to make a range of baked goods in every chapter of this book, from Yeast Breads to Icings, Glazes, and Sauces.

Using a pastry bag.

Specialized cake tools

Cake combs are used to create a decorative edge on iced cakes and tortes or to give texture to a chocolate coating or glaze. A cake comb is a triangular or rectangular piece of metal or plastic with serrated edges. The teeth vary in their size and shape, giving you a choice of three or four different effects.

Turntables, although not essential, make it easier to decorate cakes. You can easily turn the cake with one hand while the other is free to wield the palette knife, pastry bag, or cake comb.

First aid for bakers

Burns are the most common baking hazard. The first line of defense is to concentrate on your work. Should you get too close to a hot pan or fall victim to spattering hot sugar or oil, however, immediately flush the affected area with cool water. Keep a cool compress on the area until it feels more comfortable, and then apply a bandage.

Opposite: *Using a double boiler; making a collar for a soufflé dish; rolling out dough with a straight pin.*

The straight mixing method is one of the most common techniques for mixing quick breads and simple cakes.

1 Combining the dry ingredients
The dry ingredients—such as flour, salt, and baking powder or soda—are evenly blended by either sifting or whisking them together.

2 Combining the wet ingredients
Wet ingredients commonly include milk, buttermilk, cream, water, fruit juice, oil, and melted butter. Eggs are also considered a liquid. All of these ingredients should be properly measured and, when necessary, warmed enough to blend easily with the other wet ingredients. Batters blend most evenly when the liquid ingredients are all close to room temperature. Use a whisk or a table fork to blend the wet ingredients together until they are smooth.

3 Combining the dry and wet ingredients
Most batters made with the straight mixing method are best mixed by hand. They are usually not heavy enough to make stirring difficult, and a short mixing time produces the most tender baked goods. Combine the wet and the dry ingredients all at once. Use a wooden spoon or a spatula to stir and fold the batter until the dry ingredients are evenly moistened. For some batters, such as pancake batter, the presence of a few small lumps in the batter is acceptable. As soon as the batter is mixed, transfer it to prepared pans and bake at once (unless a recipe directs otherwise). If the batter sits for too long after mixing, the chemical leaveners can lose their leavening power.

The creaming mixing method is used to make cakes with a fine texture and a moist, dense crumb, as well as to make cookies.

1 Creaming the butter and sugar
Beat together butter and sugar until the mixture is very smooth and quite light in texture. This incorporates small air pockets into the mixture, which expand in the oven's heat and give cakes an appealing texture. The technique is used for certain cookies and quick breads, but when making cakes you want to incorporate more air, so the creaming time is generally longer, producing a finer crumb.

2 Adding the eggs
Be sure any eggs or other wet ingredients are at room temperature. If they are very cold, they may cause the butter to harden into little flecks; if this happens, keep mixing until the flecks disappear before adding more ingredients. Add the eggs one at a time and continue to mix until the mixture is quite smooth and emulsified before adding more eggs or starting to add the dry ingredients.

3 Alternating dry and wet ingredients
For cookies and pastry doughs, you may not add any wet ingredients (besides eggs). For these batters, add the dry ingredients all at once. Cake batters often include a liquid ingredient such as milk. For these batters, add about one-third of the dry ingredients and blend by hand or on low speed just long enough to make an evenly moist batter. Next, add one-third of the wet ingredient(s) and mix until smooth again. Continue alternating wet and dry ingredients. Increase the mixing speed slightly to finish with a smooth, light batter. Scrape down the bowl with a rubber spatula at each stage of mixing.

The rubbing mixing method is used for some biscuits and scones, pie doughs, and even some cookies. The fat, usually butter, is kept cold so that it will not blend readily with the flour.

1 Combining the dry ingredients
To ensure the even distribution of the dry ingredients (such as salt and flour), sift or whisk them together before cutting in the fat.

2 Tossing the cut-up fat with flour
Keep the fat chilled until ready to use, then cut the fat into pieces and add to the flour, tossing to coat. On warm days, chill the mixing bowl and use a marble board for rolling out the dough, if available.

3 Cutting in the fat
You may be instructed to cut in the fat until it is reduced to very small pieces; the resulting mixture is often described as looking like a coarse meal. Other recipes may instruct you to leave the fat in larger, pea-sized pieces. In both cases, these small pockets of fat melt as the dough bakes, producing a flaky or very crumbly texture in the finished baked good. If using a food processor, use a series of short pulses. With a pastry blender, use a cutting and tossing motion. With two table knives, make slicing motions in opposite directions to cut in the fat.

Once the fat is cut in, add just enough ice-cold water to moisten the dough so that it will hold together. Use as little liquid as possible. After the dough is mixed together in a rough mass, knead it two or three times to pull it together into a ball. Now the dough can be patted into an even layer or rolled out. If you cut out shapes, try to create as few scraps as possible. Scraps can usually be gathered up and gently pressed together to roll out and cut again, but they won't be quite as tender as those cut after the first roll.

The foam mixing method gives angel food and sponge cakes their delicate, light texture.

1 Whipping the eggs

The cold foam mixing method, used primarily for angel food cakes, calls for eggs (whole or separated) to be whipped with sugar until they make a thick, relatively stable foam. The warm foam mixing method, typically used for sponge cakes, calls for the eggs and sugar to be warmed to about 110°F in a bowl over simmering water. As they warm, the eggs should be stirred until they are evenly blended with the sugar. Once the eggs are warm, whip them until they double or triple in volume and are very thick.

2 Folding in the dry ingredients

Once the foam is prepared, work quickly to keep as much air in the foam as possible. Scatter the dry ingredients over the entire surface of the batter. Use a smooth, circular motion to fold the batter together: sweep a rubber spatula down along one side of the bowl and toward the center, then lift the spatula up through the center of the batter. Give the bowl a quarter turn periodically as you fold to mix the batter evenly.

3 Adding fat without losing volume

Adding a small amount of melted butter or oil to a foam provides moisture and tenderness, but as you add these ingredients you want to avoid weighing down the foam so much that it collapses. Both the foam batter and the fat should be at room temperature. Add a few dollops of batter to the fat and fold them together before adding the tempered fat mixture back into the batter, folding swiftly and carefully.

1 Yeast Breads

Ever since humans learned to harvest cereal grasses and make them into simple unleavened cakes, bread has been one of our most important foods. Although the earliest breads weren't much like the loaves we enjoy today, they marked a significant improvement in our ability to stave off hunger during the long winter or on long journeys. Historical records dating from the time of the ancient Egyptians demonstrate just how important bread was. Bakers were also among the first professionals to organize; the *Collegium Pistorum,* or Baker's Guild, was established in Rome around 168 BCE.

Almost any cereal grain can be ground, moistened, formed into a cake or loaf, and baked. But it is wheat, with its stretchy proteins, that made it possible for loaves to be leavened with yeast. At first, bakers simply relied upon the yeast in the air, letting their dough sit out until it rose. Later, bakers learned to capture and control the yeast by saving some dough from the previous day and mixing it into a new batch, thereby "seeding" it with yeast.

Today, yeast breads are easier to master than ever before. You can choose from a number of different flour types. Commercially processed yeast provides consistent results. Heavy-duty mixers permit you to mix and knead the dough in just a few minutes. And refrigerators and freezers help you control the timing of your bread baking to suit your schedule.

As far as we may have surpassed Stone Age bakers with their simple grinders and heavy wheat-and-barley cakes, though, the basics of bread baking remain the same. Great yeast-raised breads demand good—though generally inexpensive—ingredients: wheat flour, pure water, and salt are enough to make a delicious loaf when combined with yeast. Unlike making a salad or stew, however, which simply asks that you throw everything together in a bowl or a pot, baking bread demands special techniques for mixing, kneading, and shaping. This chapter offers a selection of both classic and contemporary breads to illustrate what all bakers know: nothing is more satisfying than a good loaf.

The bread-making process

Yeast is a living organism that causes bread doughs to rise as it grows and ferments. As yeast reproduces in dough, it generates carbon dioxide gas, heat, and some alcohol. These by-products leaven bread and give it texture and flavor.

When you work with yeast, your recipe will almost always include some quantity of wheat flour because of two specific proteins found in wheat, glutenin and gliadin. When wheat flour is moistened and repeatedly stretched—as during the mixing and kneading of bread dough—these proteins turn into strands of gluten, a stretchy, springy web within the dough that captures the gas given off by the yeast and causes the dough to expand like a balloon. The gluten is both flexible enough to stretch and strong enough to keep the balloon from bursting (as long as the baker has balanced the ingredients correctly). All wheat flours contain the building blocks for gluten, although some types of wheat flour have a higher protein content because of the wheat variety and growing conditions. When other types of flour—rye, barley, or corn, for example—are used for bread making, some wheat flour is typically included as well.

The various steps in bread baking are intended to capitalize on yeast's activity and to develop gluten. In the mixing stage, the gluten starts to form and looks like a rough, stringy mass. With continued mixing and kneading, the gluten becomes more uniform, longer, and stretchier. The dough changes from a rough mass into a tight, smooth dough. The first rise (or fermentation) gives the yeast a chance to develop. Folding over the dough redistributes the yeast and lowers the dough's

temperature. A second rise gives the gluten a chance to relax so that you can shape the dough more easily. The final rise after the dough is shaped determines the shape and volume of the finished bread or roll.

Preferments and starters

The longer yeast grows, the more complex a bread's flavor and the finer its texture. Bakers have developed extended mixing methods, called "preferments" by professionals, to increase the yeast's life cycle and make a more flavorful loaf. *Biga*s and sponges are examples of preferments. Some breads, such as sourdoughs, are based on starters, which also keep yeast alive long enough to create an interesting flavor.

*Biga*s and sponges aren't complicated to make, but you do need to plan ahead. A *biga* calls for blending a portion of the yeast, flour, and liquid called for in a recipe; covering the mixture; and leaving it to ferment at room temperature. The *biga* rises and then falls back slightly, a process that typically takes 8 to 10 hours. A sponge is made in the same way, except that it is left to ferment for only 3 or 4 hours before you finish the mixing and kneading process, giving less of a flavor boost than a *biga*.

Sourdough starters, a mixture of flour and water permeated with the wild yeasts present in the air, must be made at least 3 days before you use them, but the flavor and texture of the resulting bread can be sufficient inducement for even home bakers to lovingly manage and feed their sourdough starter, sometimes over the course of years.

You can create a richly flavored bread even without the benefit of preferments, however, simply by extending the time that your dough rises. To keep the yeast from growing so much that it exhausts its food source during a long rise, place it somewhere cool, even in the refrigerator. Although the rising times in our recipes are based upon letting doughs rise at around 75°F, the average temperature in most home kitchens, you can adapt them for a cool rise (see First rise, page 39). For some rich doughs, such as challah, a long rise under refrigeration is essential. This means you can mix a dough in the morning and let it rise during the day to bake for dinner that night, or mix it in the evening and let it rise overnight to bake the next day.

Types of dough

Some breads are made from "lean" doughs and others from "rich" doughs. Lean doughs are those made with little or no added fat. Rosemary Bread (page 47), Ciabatta (page 55), Focaccia (page 57), White Wheat Bread (page 46), and Baguettes (page 54) are all examples of lean breads. These breads have a wonderful resilient texture. The crumb is open and airy and the crust well developed and crisp. This texture comes from the use of hard-wheat (high-protein) flour, the type sold as "bread flour" in most markets.

Rich doughs include ingredients such as eggs, sugar, butter, milk, or cream. Introducing these elements makes breads softer and more cakelike. Challah (page 60) and Brioches à Tête (page 59) are two classic examples.

Any dough, lean or rich, can be embellished in a number of ways. You can introduce flavor and color by brushing the dough with egg wash or milk before it bakes. Folding or kneading in nuts, dried fruits, cheeses, herbs, or vegetables is another option; the classic example of a garnished lean dough is nothing more exotic than pizza.

Shaping breads

Some breads are traditionally shaped into free-form loaves. Others are placed in a mold, pan, or tin to give them shape. Still others are elaborately braided. The shape of a loaf of bread does more than make it look good. The shape affects the texture of the interior of the loaf, as well as the crust.

Free-form breads are those that are rolled or stretched into shape and baked on either a flat baking sheet or a baking stone. Lean doughs are often shaped as free-form loaves; they may be referred to as boules (rounds), bâtardes (oblong loaves), or baguettes (long, slender loaves). Pan loaves can be made from either lean or rich doughs. When the dough, shaped into a cylinder, is placed into the pan it should fill the pan about half full, leaving enough room for the dough to rise before it goes into the oven (a step known as pan proofing), as well as for the bread's final rapid rise as it bakes (something called oven spring). Very rich breads usually require more support as they bake in order to keep their volume. Both braiding (as for challah) and placing the dough in a mold (as for brioche) are common methods for shaping and supporting rich breads.

Baking, cooling, and storing breads

Most breads are baked in a moderate oven, around 350°F. Once breads are baked, they should be allowed to cool completely before being sliced; otherwise, they may collapse. To store bread, keep it wrapped at room temperature for a day or two (the richer the bread, the longer it will keep); for longer storage, wrap it well and freeze it for up to 2 months. Bread that is slightly stale is great for making croutons or bread crumbs for coatings or stuffings. Bread puddings, French toast, and bread salad (panzanella) are also excellent ways to use up stale bread.

Making bread allows you to enjoy baking at a slower pace, and you can even learn to adjust the timing to suit your schedule. If you are new to bread baking, remember that your hand-shaped loaves and rolls really shouldn't look like they came from a machine. As with any new skill, your dexterity will improve with each batch you bake.

Using yeast

Yeast is an organic, or living, leavening agent that requires a food source, moisture, and a moderate temperature in order to grow and reproduce.

1 Creating the proper environment

Yeast feeds on sugar; flour, which contains both complex and simple carbohydrates (that is, both starches and sugars), is typically an adequate food source, although sometimes sugar is added to a dough to enhance the yeast activity. The yeast cannot interact with the food source until it is exposed to water. Yeast thrives when temperatures are moderate (75–80°F is ideal). The liquid you use in a bread recipe should be at room temperature (somewhere between 68 and 76°F) for most breads; it will feel slightly cool but not cold. Warm or hot water is generally not needed unless your kitchen and the ingredients are very cold. Similarly, if the kitchen is very warm, you may want to use slightly cooler water (60–70°F) to prevent the dough from rising too quickly.

Note that many bread recipes ask you to "proof" yeast by combining it with about twice its volume in water and letting it rest until a foam develops on the surface, a sign that the yeast is alive and working. This step is largely unnecessary with today's packaged commercial yeasts, so many of the recipes in this book forgo this step.

For more information on yeast-based starters, see page 36.

Combining ingredients

Although most of the recipes in this chapter call for the use of a stand mixer, almost all can also be mixed by hand. Use the following techniques to ensure a good loaf of bread.

1 Combining the flour and water

When mixing a dough by hand, combine about half of the flour and the yeast in a large bowl, then pour in the room-temperature liquid and add the salt. Stir this mixture until it is very smooth and you can see strands of gluten starting to develop. Continue adding flour, about a cup at a time, until the dough is too stiff to stir, then turn it out onto a floured work surface and continue kneading by hand. If using a stand mixer, put all the flour in the bowl, followed by the yeast. Add the liquid and salt, then mix on low speed with the dough hook until the flour is evenly moistened. You may prefer to hold back about 1 cup of the flour, then add the remaining flour as necessary while the machine kneads. Some recipes call for making a *biga* or sponge, which involves mixing a portion of the yeast, water, and flour in advance of mixing the dough, to give the yeast a head start. A sponge ferments for 3 to 4 hours, and a *biga* 8 to 10 hours. (A sponge is typically soft enough to accept the rest of the flour right away, but you will need to break up a *biga* before adding more flour and liquid to it.)

2 Adding the remaining ingredients

Although the simplest breads contain nothing more than flour, yeast, water, and salt, rich bread doughs used to make challah and rolls contain sugar, butter, eggs, or oil. These ingredients make bread doughs softer and more pliable, as well as a little stickier and harder to handle during kneading and shaping. Breads like brioche call for room-temperature butter to be added to the dough after the flour, yeast, and liquid have been thoroughly combined. To ensure that the enriching ingredients can be blended evenly into the dough, let them come to room temperature and add them at the point recommended in a recipe.

3 Adding flavorings

Flavoring ingredients or preparations, including eggs, herbs, and grated cheeses, are added to the dough after the initial mixing stage. The ingredients should be soft and warm enough not to interfere with the development of the dough or slow the yeast's activity too much. When bakers add a coarse grain or meal to bread dough, they often let it soak in water first—hence the term "soaker." This softens the grain so that it is easier to blend into the dough. If these whole grains or meals were not soaked first, they would steal moisture from the dough, resulting in a tight, dry loaf of bread. Garnishes such as raisins, nuts, or olives can be worked in as the dough is kneaded or shaped.

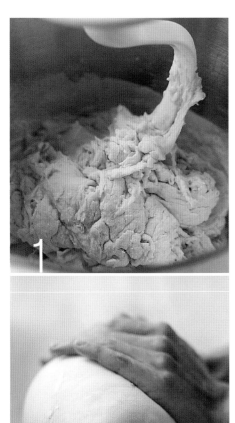

Kneading

Kneading dough stretches the gluten in the flour, making it strong, flexible, and elastic.

1 Gathering into a shaggy mass

Whether you are mixing dough with a stand mixer or by hand, look for the dough to become heavy, stiff, and shaggy in appearance. It is now ready to move from the mixing stage into the kneading stage. To knead by hand, turn the dough out of the bowl onto a floured work surface and follow the steps below. To knead by machine, simply increase the machine's speed. If your machine starts to "walk" as it kneads the dough, you can finish kneading by hand, incorporating the additional flour as needed.

2 Pushing the dough away

To knead by hand, press the heels of your palms into the dough and push the dough away from you.

3 Folding the dough back

Give the ball of dough a quarter turn as you fold the far edge back over onto the dough. As you continue to push and pull the dough, stretching it evenly in all directions, dust the dough, the work surface, and your hands lightly with flour to prevent sticking.

When the dough is smooth and elastic, it is ready for the first rise. This can take 10–15 minutes with a machine or longer if kneading by hand. Check the elasticity of the dough with a "gluten window" made as follows: pinch off a small piece of the dough and stretch it. It should stretch into a thin, translucent sheet without snapping in half.

First rise

Once dough has been kneaded, it can capture the gases released by the yeast and grow in volume.

1 Letting the dough rise

Lightly rub with oil a bowl big enough to hold the dough after it doubles in size. Place the dough in the bowl and turn it to coat with oil. You want it to remain moist and flexible so that it will not form a crust and will expand easily as the yeast goes to work. Observe (or even mark) how large the dough is when you first put it into the bowl so that you have a point of comparison later. Cover the bowl with plastic wrap or a lightly dampened clean towel to prevent the dough from drying out.

Warmer temperatures hasten the dough's first rise. Cooler temperatures slow the rise and allow complex flavors to develop. Doughs can even rise in the refrigerator. To retard a rise for up to 8 hours in the refrigerator, reduce the amount of yeast by half. Let the dough come back to room temperature before you shape it.

2 Dividing the dough

Turn the dough out onto a lightly floured work surface and cut the dough into pieces, as directed. Use a very sharp knife or a bench scraper to cut through the dough rather than sawing at it. If you have a scale, it can be very helpful in cutting the dough into pieces of a uniform size. Equally sized pieces will rise and bake more evenly, for better overall flavor, texture, and color.

3 Rounding the dough

Rounding the divided dough creates a smoother, less sticky outer surface. This means that you can use less flour during the final shaping for a better texture in the finished bread. (Some flat breads, such as ciabatta, are not rounded; see the information about shaping wet doughs on page 42.) Using the outer edges of your palms, pull the outer layer of the dough in a downward motion and gather the dough together at the bottom. Pinch or press it together lightly. To make an even round, cup your hands around the dough and press it lightly against the work surface while moving your hands over its surface to round and shape it.

4 Resting before shaping

Once rounded, the dough is allowed to rest so that it will be easier to make up into its final shape. This resting period allows the gluten activated by handling the dough to relax enough that the dough won't spring back on itself. Set the rounded dough on a lightly floured work surface or baking sheet and cover it loosely. Doughs typically need a 15–20 minute rest at room temperature.

Folding over and dividing dough

Folding over dough after the first rise redistributes the yeast and the yeast's food source. Dividing dough into pieces prepares it for final shaping.

1 Assessing the dough

Most yeast bread recipes suggest a duration for the first rise, but if your kitchen is very cool or warm, you cannot rely upon the clock alone. Dough that is ready to fold over will have nearly doubled in size. In addition, when you press the dough with a fingertip, you should leave behind an indentation that does not fill in again rapidly. Instead of "punching" the dough as some cookbooks recommend— a little too vigorous for most doughs—gently fold the dough over on itself from the edges to the center and gently press down. You should be able to hear and feel the gases release. Once folded, some doughs are given a second rise, whereas some are simply rested briefly before dividing or shaping them.

the rectangle, lift and stretch the dough until it is approximately the length you want in the finished loaf. Fold the dough lengthwise into thirds, sealing the long edges after each fold. Roll the dough back and forth into a cylinder, palms parallel to the work surface and hands moving from the center of the loaf out to the ends. Increase the pressure on the loaf when you reach the last inch or so of the loaf to create tapered ends.

3 Shaping round free-form breads

Turn the rounded ball of dough seam side up. Use your fingertips to gently spread the dough into a square. Fold the top of the square to meet the bottom edge and press the seam closed with your fingertips or the heel of your palm. Give the dough a quarter turn and repeat folding and sealing the dough. Finally, tuck the edges under so the seam ends up on the bottom and round the dough, stretching the outer layer taut.

4 The final rise

Bread dough needs another partial rise after shaping and before baking. For pan loaves, simply lift the dough and transfer the dough to a prepared pan; it will spring back on itself and fit snugly. Free-form breads can be transferred to baking sheets scattered with cornmeal or lined with parchment paper for the final rise. Baguettes or similar long loaves may be settled in the folds of a lightly floured flat-weave cloth. For round loaves, set the dough in a bowl-shaped basket lined with a lightly floured cloth. The basket weave will become part of the loaf's texture. Use a flat-bottomed basket to make a horseshoe shape (page 50).

Shaping yeast doughs

Bakers use various shaping techniques to create a taut outer skin so yeast can work effectively during the final stages of rising and the first part of baking.

1 Shaping pan breads

After resting, turn the ball of dough seam side up. Gently press the dough out into a rectangle approximately the same width as the loaf pan's length. Garnishes may be added now by spreading them in a layer over the dough. Roll the dough into a cylinder, pressing the seams with your fingertips or the heel of your hand to tighten the outer layer. Roll the dough back and forth, keeping your palms parallel to the work surface and moving your hands from the center of the loaf out to the ends, until the cylinder is about 2 inches longer than the pan.

2 Shaping baguettes and bâtardes

Turn the ball of dough seam side up. Use your fingertips to gently press the dough out into a rectangle. Holding the short edges of

Working with wet doughs

Breads like ciabatta and focaccia are made with extra liquid in the doughs. These wet, or slack, doughs demand slightly different handling techniques during kneading and shaping.

1 The first rise

When doughs are mixed with a large amount of water, the dough's gluten develops less readily. Even after the dough is properly mixed and kneaded, it looks loose and feels sticky. After kneading, transfer the dough to a lightly oiled bowl, turn to coat, and cover as you would any other dough during the first rise.

2 Folding carefully

Wet doughs need to be stretched a bit as you fold them so that the gluten has a chance to develop. With the dough still in the bowl, lift the edges of the dough up and over the center of the dough in 3 or 4 places. Folding the dough makes it more elastic and resilient. Letting the dough rest after you fold it develops an open, light crumb in the bread.

3 Shaping

Unlike doughs that require preshaping and bench proofing, ciabatta and similar wet doughs are handled as little as possible once they are folded over. They may be flattened and gently stretched before you divide them to make it easier to give them their final shape, but typically you only need to turn the folded dough out of the bowl and cut it into pieces if necessary. Let the dough rest after you divide it, then stretch the pieces into shape. It receives a final rise before baking. Use a gentle touch to lift the dough onto a baking sheet.

Braiding yeast doughs

Rich, golden loaves made with eggs are often woven into braids to help the delicate dough hold its shape during baking.

1 Rolling the dough into strips

For even loaves, cut pieces of equal size and preshape them into rectangles. After they have relaxed on the work surface for 15 minutes, they will be easy to roll into long strips. Work with one piece at a time and allow yourself plenty of room. Roll from the center to the ends of the strip, gently stretching the dough. Use a little extra pressure on the ends to taper them slightly.

2 Braiding the dough

Lay the dough strips parallel to one another, perpendicular to the edge of the work surface, on a parchment paper–lined baking sheet. Starting in the center of the strips, begin to braid the dough. Work from the center to one end, pinching together the strands when they are too short to braid any more. Pinch the ends of the braid together to seal them in place. To finish the braid, turn the loaf (or the entire baking sheet) around and roll or flip the braid over. Braid the second half of the loaf and pinch the ends together to seal. Tuck both ends neatly under the braid.

3 Sealing the dough

After the dough has been braided, apply a thin coat of egg wash with a pastry brush. Brush the excess away. After the loaf has risen for the final time and is ready to go into the oven, brush it with egg wash once more.

Baking yeast breads

The final steps before bread goes in the oven include applying a wash for a great texture and color on the crust and scoring the crust to get it ready for the yeast's final, dramatic rise to full volume, known to bakers as "oven spring."

1 Applying washes

Keeping the outer surface of the bread moist during the early stages of baking permits the bread to finish rising in the oven for a good final shape and volume. Use a brush to apply a light coating and wipe away any wash that pools in indentations or along the edges of the loaf. The type of wash you apply to a baked good determines the texture and color of the finished crust. Milk provides both sugars and proteins for caramelization, while egg yolks add color and egg whites add gloss. All these washes tend to hold moisture in the crust, making it more tender.

2 Scoring

Breads baked without pans or molds are scored before they go into the oven to keep the bread from bursting open as it bakes. Use a very sharp blade to just cut through the surface. Breads scored with clean cuts not only look better after baking, but taste better too, because they bake evenly. Loaves baked in pans are less likely to burst open as they bake since the pan holds the loaf in place as long as it is positioned with the seam on the bottom of the loaf. However, these breads may be scored for a decorative appearance, if desired.

3 Steaming and finishing

Breads and rolls made from lean doughs (with little or no eggs, sugar, butter, or oil) are treated with steam for a crisp crust. To replicate the effect of a steam-generating oven at home, brush or mist the bread lightly with water before it bakes. This keeps the outer layer of dough moist enough to expand before it settles into a firm crust. For a truly crisp crust, you can use one of the following techniques. During the first 5 minutes of baking time, open the oven door as little as possible and lightly brush or mist the loaves with water once or twice. Or, you can set a shallow pan directly on the floor of the oven while it preheats and add a little cold water or a couple of ice cubes when you put the bread into the oven.

To determine when your bread is done, you should rely upon your eyes, your nose, and your hands. It should have a golden brown crust on the top and the bottom and smell rich and almost toasty. The most common method for checking doneness is to thump the bottom of the loaf and listen for a hollow sound. If you'd like a little more guidance, you can use an instant-read thermometer; almost all bread types are fully baked when their internal temperature is about 200°F. Once the bread is baked, remove it from the pan and let cool completely on a rack. (One important exception is pizza, served very hot straight from the oven.) Resist the temptation to cut into hot breads; they lose their texture and may collapse if they are cut into while too warm.

Honey-Wheat Sandwich Loaves

4 cups bread flour plus extra as needed

1 cup whole wheat flour

2½ tsp active dry yeast

2 cups whole or low-fat milk, boiled and cooled to room temperature

⅓ cup vegetable oil plus extra for greasing

⅓ cup honey

2 tsp salt

Cooking spray for greasing

Egg wash (1 large egg whisked with 2 Tbsp cold milk or water) or milk for brushing

Makes 2 loaves

Combine the flours and yeast in the bowl of a stand mixer fitted with the dough hook. Add the milk, oil, honey, and salt and mix on low speed until the dough forms a shaggy but evenly moistened dough, about 2 minutes. Increase the speed to medium and knead until the dough feels satiny and elastic, about 5 minutes.

Transfer the dough to a lightly oiled bowl, turn to coat, cover with plastic wrap or a damp towel, and let rise in a warm place until nearly doubled in size, about 1 hour. Fold the dough over on itself, pressing gently to release the gas. Turn it out onto a floured work surface and cut into 2 equal pieces. Round each piece into a smooth ball, pulling the outer layer taut and pinching together the excess dough at the base of the ball. Place the dough seam sides down on a lightly floured work surface. Cover the dough and let rest until relaxed, about 20 minutes.

Coat two 9-inch loaf pans lightly with cooking spray. Stretch each dough ball into an 8 x 12–inch rectangle. Fold each short end of the rectangle 1 inch toward the center of the dough to keep the sides straight and the corners square. Fold a long edge into the center and use the heel of your hand to seal the edge to the dough. Fold the dough in half lengthwise and use your fingertips to seal the 2 edges together; keep the seam straight. The dough should be about 10 inches long. Roll the dough into an even cylinder 12 inches long. Push the ends of the cylinder toward the center until it is 10 inches long and place seam side down into the loaf pans. Brush with egg wash or milk.

Let the dough rise in a warm place, uncovered, until the pans are three-quarters full and the dough springs back slowly to the touch, 1 hour. Meanwhile, preheat the oven to 400°F.

Bake until the loaves have a rich golden brown crust and the sides of the bread retain their structure when pressed, 40–50 minutes. Remove the bread from the pans immediately and let cool completely on wire racks before slicing and serving.

You can take advantage of a technique professional bakers swear by, known as "autolyse," to give whole-grain breads such as this one a lighter texture and more even crumb. Blend all the flour and all the liquid (but not the yeast, salt, eggs, butter, or garnishes) just until they are evenly combined. Let this mixture rest for 30–45 minutes before continuing with the recipe. As it rests, the dough changes from rough to smooth as the water hydrates the starch granules and helps the gluten strands relax.

kneading p. 39

folding over and dividing dough p. 40

White Wheat Bread

5 cups bread flour plus extra
as needed

2½ tsp active dry yeast

2 cups room-temperature water
(68–76°F)

2½ tsp salt

Vegetable oil for greasing

Cornmeal for dusting

Makes 2 loaves

Combine the flour and yeast in the bowl of a stand mixer fitted with the dough hook. Add the water and salt and mix on low speed for 2 minutes. Increase the speed to medium and knead until the dough is smooth and elastic, about 3 minutes more.

Transfer the dough to a lightly oiled bowl, turn to coat, cover with plastic wrap or a damp towel, and let rise in a warm place until nearly doubled in size, about 30 minutes. Fold the dough over gently, let rise a second time for 30 minutes, and fold over again. Divide the dough into 2 equal pieces. Round each piece of dough into a smooth ball, pulling the outer layer taut and pinching together the excess dough at the base of the ball. Place the dough seam sides down on a lightly floured work surface. Cover the dough and let rest until relaxed, 15–20 minutes.

Prepare 2 baking sheets by scattering them with cornmeal.

To shape the dough into bâtardes, place each dough round on a work surface with the seam facing up and press lightly with your fingertips to release any air. Stretch each piece into a 10 x 14–inch rectangle. Fold the long top edge to the center, pressing in place with your fingertips. Fold the dough in half lengthwise and use the heel of your hand to seal the 2 edges together; keep the seam straight. With the palms of your hands, roll the dough back and forth in a tapered shape, about 10 inches long, rolling outward from the center and slightly increasing the pressure as you roll toward the ends to gently taper them. Increase the pressure at the ends to seal them.

Transfer the loaves to the prepared baking sheets seam sides down. Let the dough rise in a warm place, covered, until it springs back slowly to the touch but does not collapse, 45 minutes. Meanwhile, preheat the oven to 425°F.

With a thin, sharp blade, score each bâtarde straight down the center of the loaf. Mist or brush each loaf with water. Bake the bâtardes until they have a golden brown crust and sound hollow when thumped on the bottom, 20–25 minutes. For a very crisp crust, mist the loaves 1 or 2 more times during the first 5 minutes of baking time. Let cool completely on wire racks before slicing and serving.

A specialized tool called a *lame* is used to score proofed yeast bread and rolls before they are baked to create patterns and designs on the crust. The very thin, sharp, curved blade is used in swift angled motions to create clean slices without pulling or tearing the dough. If you don't have a lame, a clean razor blade or sharp paring knife will do.

using yeast p. 38

folding over and dividing dough p. 40

shaping yeast doughs p. 41

Rosemary Bread

4 cups bread flour plus extra as needed

1½ tsp active dry yeast

1½ cups room-temperature water (68–76°F)

2 Tbsp coarsely chopped fresh rosemary

2 tsp salt

Extra-virgin olive oil for greasing

Cornmeal for dusting

Coarse sea salt for sprinkling (optional)

Makes 2 loaves

Combine the flour and yeast in the bowl of a stand mixer fitted with the dough hook. Add the water, rosemary, and salt and mix on low speed for 3 minutes. Increase the speed to medium and knead for 4 minutes. The dough should be slightly stiff, smooth, and elastic.

Transfer the dough to a lightly oiled bowl, turn to coat, cover with plastic wrap or a damp towel, and let rise in a warm place until nearly doubled in size, about 40 minutes. Fold the dough over on itself, pressing gently to release the gas. Let the dough rise a second time, about 40 minutes more.

Divide the dough into 2 equal pieces and round into smooth balls, pulling the outer layers taut and pinching the excess dough together at the base of the balls. Place seam sides down on a lightly floured work surface, cover, and let rest until relaxed, 15–20 minutes.

Prepare 2 baking sheets by scattering them with cornmeal. Put your hands under each dough round and stretch and pull it gently into a rough 6 x 8–inch rectangle. It is important to maintain an even thickness. Transfer to the prepared baking sheets.

Brush or mist the surface of the dough lightly with water. Let the dough rise for a third time in a warm place, covered, until the dough springs back slowly to the touch but does not collapse, 30–40 minutes.

Preheat the oven to 425°F. Score the dough 5 times, starting at the same corner each time and tracing a line to each of the other 3 corners with 3 of the 5 scores. The remaining 2 scores will be in between the first 3, radiating out from the same corner. Brush or mist the dough with water once more. Bake until the loaves have a golden brown crust and sound hollow when thumped on the bottom, 25–30 minutes. Let cool completely on wire racks. Brush or drizzle with olive oil and sprinkle with sea salt if desired.

This recipe gives instructions for making a rectangular free-form loaf, scored to create a fanlike effect on the surface. The dough may also be shaped into rounds or bâtardes.

shaping yeast doughs
p. 41

baking yeast breads
p. 43

VARIATION

Thyme and Sun-Dried Tomato Bread

Replace the rosemary with 3 Tbsp fresh thyme leaves. Add ⅓ cup minced sun-dried tomatoes with the thyme. Increase the water by 2 Tbsp. Proceed as directed above.

Rustic Olive Bread

½ cup pitted dry-cured olives, chopped

Cool water as needed

1⅔ cups bread flour plus extra as needed

½ tsp sugar

1½ tsp active dry yeast

¾ cup room-temperature water (68–76°F)

¼ tsp salt

Vegetable oil for greasing

Makes 1 loaf

Soak the olives in cool water to cover for at least 20 minutes and up to 1 hour to remove the excess salt. Drain and blot dry before adding them to the dough.

In a stand mixer fitted with the dough hook, combine the flour and the sugar. Add the yeast, water, and salt and mix on low speed until the dough becomes smooth, elastic, and very springy, 8–10 minutes.

Transfer the dough to a lightly oiled bowl, turn to coat, cover with plastic wrap or a damp towel, and let rise in a warm place until nearly doubled in size, about 30 minutes. Add the olives to the bowl. Fold the dough over on itself, pressing gently to release the gas, and repeat the folding until the olives are evenly distributed. Cover the dough and let rest until relaxed, about 30 minutes.

Turn the dough out onto a lightly floured work surface and round it into a smooth ball, pulling the outer layer taut and pinching the excess dough together at the base of the ball. Leave the dough seam side down on the floured work surface, cover it with a cloth, and let rest for 15 minutes.

To finish shaping the dough, turn it seam side up and stretch it into a square. Fold the square in half from top to bottom, pressing lightly with your fingertips to tighten the outer layer of the dough. Fold the dough in half again, this time from side to side, and seal the 2 edges together. Round the dough, forming a taut outer surface, and place seam side up in a bowl or round basket lined with a floured clean, flat-weave cloth. Cover loosely.

Let the dough rise until it has nearly doubled in size and the dough springs back slowly to the touch but does not collapse, 1 hour.

Preheat the oven to 425°F. Line a baking sheet with parchment paper.

Turn the dough out seam side down onto the prepared baking sheet. Brush or mist the bread lightly with water. Cut a shallow X into the top of the loaf. Bake until the crust is crisp and well browned and the loaf sounds hollow when thumped on the bottom, 25–30 minutes. Let cool completely on a wire rack before slicing and serving.

Select dry-cured olives for the best flavor in this bread. You can identify dry-cured olives, which are prepared using salt, by their slightly wrinkled skin. Some dry-cured varieties are coated in oil or packed with herbs. Be certain to allow time for the olives to soak and then dry before you mix the dough. This bread is best eaten the day it is made.

combining ingredients p. 38

folding over and dividing dough p. 40

Roasted Potato Bread

Biga

2 cups bread flour

1½ cups whole wheat flour

1½ cups room-temperature water (68–76°F)

¼ tsp active dry yeast

Soaker

1 cup cracked wheat

½ cup room-temperature water (68–76°F)

Roasted Potatoes

2 Yukon gold potatoes, thinly sliced

2 Tbsp olive oil

1 tsp kosher salt

¼ tsp freshly ground pepper

2 cups bread flour plus extra as needed

½ cup whole wheat flour

½ cup medium rye flour plus extra as needed

1½ tsp active dry yeast

1½ cups room-temperature water (68–76°F)

2 tsp salt

Extra-virgin olive oil for greasing

Cornmeal for dusting

Makes 1 large loaf

To prepare the *biga,* in a stand mixer fitted with the dough hook, mix the flours, water, and yeast on low speed until combined, 3 minutes. Transfer to a bowl, cover, and let rise in a warm place until it has risen and begun to recede but is still bubbly and airy, 8–10 hours.

To prepare the soaker, combine the cracked wheat and water in a bowl, cover, and soak in the refrigerator for 8–10 hours.

Preheat the oven to 400°F. Toss the potatoes with the olive oil to coat. Season with the salt and pepper, spread on a baking sheet, and roast until soft in the center, 25 minutes. Let cool to room temperature.

To prepare the final dough, combine the flours and yeast in the bowl of a stand mixer fitted with the dough hook. Add the water, *biga,* soaker, and salt. Mix on low speed for 4 minutes. Add all but 1 of the roasted potato slices and knead on medium speed until the dough is slightly stiff and the potatoes evenly distributed, 3 minutes.

Transfer the dough to a lightly oiled bowl, turn to coat, cover with plastic wrap or a damp towel, and let rise until nearly doubled in size, 30 minutes. Fold the dough gently. Let rise for another 30 minutes, then fold again. Cover and let rest for 15–20 minutes.

Turn the dough out onto a work surface dusted with rye flour and stretch into an 8 x 10–inch rectangle. Fold the dough in half lengthwise and seal the seam by pressing firmly with the heel of your palm, keeping the seam straight. Using your palms, roll the dough into an even 12-inch cylinder. Dust a small rolling pin and use it to make a cavity lengthwise in the center of the dough 3 inches wide and deep enough so that the dough on the bottom of the cavity is 1 inch thick. Roll the 2 thicker edges toward each other until they meet in the middle. Place the dough with the seam side down in a couronne basket, forming a horseshoe shape. Let rise in a warm place, covered, until the dough springs back slowly to the touch but does not collapse, 45–60 minutes.

Flip the dough seam side up onto a cornmeal-dusted baking sheet. Score the dough and place the reserved potato slice at the top center of the horseshoe. Brush the dough and the potato slice lightly with olive oil. Bake the loaf on the baking sheet until it has a golden brown crust and sounds hollow when thumped on the bottom, 45–50 minutes. Let cool completely on a wire rack before serving.

To shape this bread, you will need a large, round basket with a flat bottom. A specialized basket in the shape of a crown, called a *couronne,* is ideal, but you can adapt a large circular basket by setting a small bowl in the center to help hold the dough in place as it goes through its final rise before baking. Be sure to use a clean, unvarnished, unpainted basket.

combining ingredients
p. 38

shaping yeast doughs
p. 41

Beer Bread

3⅔ cups bread flour plus extra as needed

½ cup medium rye flour

½ tsp active dry yeast

1½ cups dark beer, at room temperature (68–76°F)

½ cup small-curd cottage cheese

2 tsp salt

Vegetable oil for greasing

Cornmeal for dusting

Makes 2 loaves

Combine the bread and rye flours and the yeast in the bowl of a stand mixer fitted with the dough hook. Add the beer, cottage cheese, and salt and mix on low speed for 3 minutes. Increase the speed to medium and knead for 4–5 minutes. The dough should be sticky but very strong and stretchy.

Transfer the dough to a lightly oiled bowl, turn to coat, cover with plastic wrap or a damp towel, and let rise in a warm place until nearly doubled in size, about 45 minutes. Fold the dough over on itself, pressing gently to release the gas.

Turn the dough out onto a lightly floured work surface and divide into 2 equal pieces. Round the pieces into smooth balls, pulling the outer layer taut and pinching together the excess dough at the base of the ball. Leave the dough seam sides down on the floured work surface, cover, and let rest for 15 minutes.

Prepare 2 baking sheets by scattering them with cornmeal.

To shape the dough into bâtardes, place each dough round on the work surface with the seam facing up and press lightly along its length with your fingertips to release any air. Press into an 8 x 10–inch rectangle. Fold a long edge of the dough to the center of the rectangle, pressing lightly with your fingertips to tighten the outer layer of the dough. Fold the dough in half lengthwise and use the heel of your hand to seal the 2 edges together; keep the seam straight. Roll the dough into a tapered shape, like an elongated football, by rolling the cylinder outward from the center, increasing the pressure slightly as you roll toward the ends, until both ends of the loaf have an even, gentle taper. Increase the pressure at the ends of the loaf to seal the ends.

Transfer the shaped loaves to the prepared baking sheets, seam sides down, cover, and let rise again until nearly doubled in size, about 45 minutes. Meanwhile, preheat the oven to 425°F.

Make a shallow, straight cut down the center of each loaf and mist evenly with water. Bake the bâtardes until they are golden brown and sound hollow when thumped on the bottom, 25–30 minutes. For a very crisp crust, mist the loaves 1 or 2 more times during the first 5 minutes of baking time. Let cool completely on a wire rack before slicing and serving.

Rye flour is made from whole rye berries from which the germ has been removed. You will see rye flour labeled as light, medium, or dark. The darker the flour, the more bran it contains.

The beer in this recipe enhances the flavor of the bread and complements the rye. The yeast used to make the beer doesn't actually make the bread rise, although yeast from beer was once a common leavener for bread.

folding over and dividing dough p. 40

shaping yeast doughs p. 41

Raisin Bread with a Cinnamon Swirl

4½ cups bread flour plus extra as needed

2 tsp active dry yeast

2 cups whole or low-fat milk, boiled and cooled to room temperature

8 Tbsp (1 stick) unsalted butter at room temperature

¼ cup sugar

2 large eggs

2 tsp salt

1 cup dark raisins

1 Tbsp ground cinnamon

Vegetable oil for greasing

Egg wash (1 large egg whisked with 2 Tbsp cold milk or water)

Cinnamon sugar (½ tsp ground cinnamon mixed with ⅓ cup sugar)

Makes 2 loaves

Combine the flour and yeast in the bowl of a stand mixer fitted with the dough hook. Add the milk, butter, sugar, eggs, and salt and mix on low speed for 4 minutes. Increase the speed to medium and knead for 4 minutes. In the last minute of kneading add the raisins. In the last 30 seconds add the cinnamon, kneading just long enough to create a swirl. The dough should be slightly soft.

Transfer the dough to a lightly oiled bowl, turn to coat, cover with plastic wrap or a damp towel, and let rise in a warm place until nearly doubled in size, about 1 hour. Fold the dough over gently. Allow the dough to rest for 15 minutes before transferring it to a lightly floured work surface. Divide into 2 equal pieces and round each into a smooth ball, pulling the outer layer taut and pinching together the excess dough at the base of the ball. Place seam sides down on a lightly floured surface, cover, and let rest until relaxed, 15–20 minutes.

Lightly grease two 9-inch loaf pans.

On a lightly floured work surface, stretch each piece of dough into an even 12 x 8–inch rectangle. Brush the dough lightly with egg wash and sprinkle with cinnamon sugar. Fold each short end of the rectangle in about 1 inch. Roll the long top end of the dough toward the center and press the seam closed with your fingertips. Continue to roll the dough into a cylinder and seal the seam with the palm of your hand. Gently roll the cylinder back and forth until it is about 11 inches long and of even thickness.

Place each cylinder of dough, seam side down, into a prepared loaf pan. Brush the loaf lightly with egg wash. Let the dough rise in a warm place, uncovered, until the dough fills the pan and springs back slowly to the touch but does not collapse, 1½–2 hours. Meanwhile, preheat the oven to 425°F.

Gently brush the dough with egg wash again before baking. Bake until the loaves have a brown crust and the sides retain their structure when pressed, 25–30 minutes. Immediately remove the bread from the pans and let cool completely on wire racks before slicing and serving.

This dough is sprinkled with fragrant cinnamon sugar before rolling up, creating a swirl. Mixing raisins into the dough studs the entire loaf with plump, sweet fruit. Although the recipe calls for dark raisins, you could easily substitute dried currants (Zante grapes) or diced dried apricots or prunes.

combining ingredients
p. 38

shaping yeast doughs
p. 41

Baguettes

1¾ cups room-temperature water (68–76°F)

1 tsp active dry yeast

4½ cups bread flour plus extra as needed

1 tsp salt

Vegetable oil for greasing

Cornmeal for dusting

Makes 2 loaves

Combine the water and yeast in the bowl of a stand mixer fitted with the dough hook and blend with a fork until the yeast is completely dissolved. Add the flour and salt and mix with the dough hook on low speed just to incorporate. Increase the speed to medium and knead until the dough is smooth and elastic, 10–12 minutes.

Transfer the dough to a lightly oiled bowl, turn to coat, cover with plastic wrap or a damp towel, and let rise in a warm place until nearly doubled in size, about 30 minutes. Fold the dough gently, then let rise for another 45 minutes.

Fold the dough over on itself, pressing gently to release the gas. Transfer the dough to a lightly floured work surface, cut into 2 equal pieces, and round each piece into a smooth ball, pinching the seams together at the bottom of the ball. Cover the dough and let rest, seam sides down, until relaxed, about 30 minutes.

Prepare a baking sheet by scattering it with cornmeal.

To shape the baguettes, on a lightly floured surface, press each ball of dough into a rectangle. Holding the short edges of the rectangle, lift and stretch the dough until the rectangle is about 8 inches long. Roll the dough into a cylinder, pressing the seam closed with the edge of your palm. Transfer the dough, seam side down, to the prepared baking sheet. Cover the loaves and let rise until increased in volume by three-quarters, about 1 hour.

Meanwhile, preheat the oven to 425°F. Score each loaf in several places by making diagonal slashes just through the outer layer of dough with a very thin blade.

Just before baking the bread, brush or mist each baguette lightly with water. Brush or mist the bread 1 or 2 more times during the first 5 minutes of baking time. Bake until the loaves are golden and sound hollow when tapped on the bottom, about 30 minutes. Remove the loaves from the oven and let cool on wire racks before serving.

These long, crisp loaves are the quintessential French bread. A great baguette is usually about 3 inches in diameter with a crisp crust that has been slashed on the diagonal before baking and a chewy interior. The name for the loaf comes from the same root word as the French term for the orchestra conductor's baton. Despite these loaves' universal appeal, it was not until the nineteenth century that the baguette shape became popular.

first rise p. 39

baking yeast breads p. 43

Ciabatta

Biga

1½ cups bread flour

½ cup room-temperature water
(68–76°F)

¼ tsp active dry yeast

3½ cups bread flour plus extra
for dusting

½ tsp active dry yeast

1½ cups room-temperature
water (68–76°F)

2 tsp salt

Vegetable oil for greasing

Cornmeal for dusting

Makes 2 loaves

To prepare the *biga,* combine the flour, water, and yeast in the bowl of a stand mixer fitted with the dough hook and mix on low speed until thoroughly combined, 3 minutes. Transfer to a bowl, cover, and let rise in a warm place until it has risen and begun to recede but is still bubbly and airy, 8–10 hours.

To prepare the final dough, combine the flour and yeast in the bowl of a stand mixer fitted with the dough hook. Add the water, *biga,* and salt and mix on low speed for 3 minutes. Increase the speed to medium and knead until the dough is blended but not too elastic, 3 minutes more. The dough should be wet and slack.

Transfer the dough to a lightly oiled bowl, turn to coat, cover with plastic wrap or a damp towel, and let rise until nearly doubled in size, about 30 minutes. When you press the dough with a fingertip, the indentation should not fill in again rapidly. Fold the dough over on itself by lifting the edges up and over the center and pressing gently to release the gas. (The dough should feel like jelly.) Allow the dough to relax in the bowl for another 15 minutes.

Turn the dough out onto a well-floured work surface and dust the top of the dough with additional flour. Using your palms, gently stretch the dough into an 8 x 9–inch rectangle that is an even 1 inch thick. Avoid tearing or puncturing the dough with your fingertips. Using a floured bench scraper, cut the dough into two 8 x 4½–inch rectangles.

Cover the dough and let rest again for 15–20 minutes. Gently free the dough from the table with a bench scraper, trying not to stretch or tear the dough. Carefully flip the dough pieces onto a floured, clean, flat-weave kitchen towel. Gently stretch each piece into a 10 x 4½–inch rectangle. Let the dough rise in a warm place, covered, until the dough springs back slowly to the touch but does not collapse, 30–45 minutes.

Meanwhile, preheat the oven to 425°F. Prepare 2 baking sheets by scattering them with cornmeal. Flour the top of the dough lightly. Carefully flip the dough onto the baking sheets. Bake until each ciabatta has a golden brown crust and sounds hollow when thumped on the bottom, 25–30 minutes. Let cool completely on wire racks.

This recipe makes an Italian ciabatta bread with a deep, complex flavor by using a *biga,* a head start for the yeast. A *biga* requires advance planning, since it takes 8–10 hours for the *biga* to develop. However, you can skip this step if you want to make ciabatta in a single day. Simply stir together all of the water (2 cups) and all of the yeast (¾ tsp) until the yeast is dissolved, then add all of the flour (5 cups) and the salt. Mix and knead as directed for the final dough. Rising and baking times will remain the same.

working with wet doughs
p. 42

baking yeast breads
p. 43

Focaccia

Sponge

1½ cups room-temperature water (68–76°F)

2¼ tsp active dry yeast

1 cup bread flour

2¼ cups bread flour plus extra for dusting

4 tsp extra-virgin olive oil plus extra as needed

2 tsp table salt

Coarse salt or salt flakes for garnishing

Makes 1 loaf

To make the sponge, combine the water and yeast in the bowl of a stand mixer fitted with the dough hook or in a large mixing bowl. Stir until the yeast is dissolved. Stir in the flour to make a soft batter about the consistency of pancake batter. Mix by hand until very smooth. Cover the bowl and let rise in a warm place until the sponge is thick and foamy and nearly doubled in size, about 3 hours.

To make the final dough, add the bread flour, 4 tsp olive oil, and table salt. Mix and knead the dough with the dough hook on medium speed until smooth and elastic, about 10 minutes.

Transfer the dough to a lightly oiled bowl, turn to coat, cover with plastic wrap or a damp towel, and let rise in a warm place until nearly doubled in size, about 40 minutes.

Fold the dough over on itself by lifting the edges up and over the center. Cover and allow to relax for another 15 minutes. Preheat the oven to 400°F. Coat a baking sheet liberally with olive oil.

Turn the dough out onto a well-floured work surface and, using your palms, gently stretch the dough into a rectangle that is an even 1 inch thick and nearly the same dimensions as your baking sheet. Avoid tearing or puncturing the dough with your fingertips. Transfer to the baking sheet, cover, and let rise until the dough springs back slowly to the touch but does not collapse, about 40 minutes.

Use your fingertips to gently dimple the surface of the focaccia and drizzle with additional olive oil. Scatter with the coarse salt or other toppings if desired. Bake until the focaccia has a golden brown crust and sounds hollow when tapped on the bottom, 25–30 minutes. Let cool completely on wire racks.

This flatbread may be brushed lightly with a simple combination of garlic and olive oil, or it may be dressed up with any number of toppings. Goat cheese, feta, pine nuts, caramelized onions, sun-dried tomatoes, pesto, poppy seeds, olives, sesame seeds, fresh herbs, and grilled vegetables are just a few suggestions. Pick a combination of flavors that complements the rest of your menu.

using yeast p. 38

working with wet doughs p. 42

Sourdough Bread

Starter

4 cups bread flour (divided use) plus extra as needed

4 cups room-temperature water (68°–76°F) (divided use) plus extra as needed

½ cup grated raw organic potato

1½ cups room-temperature water

½ tsp active dry yeast

3½ cups bread flour plus extra as needed

1 tsp salt

Vegetable oil for greasing

Makes 2 loaves

To make the starter, combine 1 cup of the flour, 1 cup of the water, and the potato in a plastic or glass bowl; the sides of the bowl should be high enough to permit the mixture to triple in volume. Cover the container and set aside at room temperature. After 24 hours, feed the sourdough starter with 1 cup flour and 1 cup water and stir well. Repeat feeding with 1 cup flour and 1 cup water every 12 hours for a total of at least 3 feedings. (You may remove and discard some of the starter before adding the additional flour and water if the amount of starter becomes excessive for your needs.) The sourdough starter is ready to use after 3 feedings; continued feedings will give the sourdough a more pronounced flavor. (To store unused starter, refrigerate and feed once a day.)

To make the bread, combine 1 cup of the sourdough starter, the water, and the yeast in the bowl of a stand mixer fitted with the dough hook and blend with a fork until the yeast is fully dissolved. Add the flour and salt and mix with the dough hook on low speed just to incorporate. Increase the speed to medium and knead until the dough is smooth and elastic, 10–12 minutes. Add more flour as necessary while kneading if the dough seems sticky.

Transfer the dough to a lightly oiled bowl, turn to coat, cover with plastic wrap or a damp towel, and let rise in a warm place until doubled in size, about 75 minutes. Fold the dough over on itself, pressing gently to release the gas. Turn the dough out onto a lightly floured work surface.

Cut the dough into 2 equal pieces and round each piece into a smooth ball, pinching the seams together at the bottom of the ball. Place each round, seam side up, in a bowl or round basket lined with a floured flat-weave towel. Let the dough rise until it has increased in volume by three-quarters, 20–30 minutes. Meanwhile, preheat the oven to 375°F.

Tip the proofed rounds out of the bowl or basket onto a parchment paper–lined baking sheet, seam sides down. Score the top of each loaf. Bake until the crust is crisp and well browned and the loaves sound hollow when thumped on the bottom, 25–30 minutes. Let cool on wire racks before slicing and serving.

Organic potatoes are important to the success of your sourdough starter for two reasons. Organically raised potatoes have a number of yeast cells already present on their surface to help get the sourdough starter growing. They will also be free from pesticides and chemical fertilizers, which tend to concentrate in the skins— an important consideration when you will be using a potato unpeeled.

shaping yeast doughs p. 41

folding over and dividing dough p. 40

Brioches à Tête

5 cups bread flour plus extra as needed

2½ tsp active dry yeast

4 large eggs, plus 1 beaten egg for brushing

½ cup whole milk

¼ cup sugar

2 tsp salt

1½ cups (3 sticks) unsalted butter, diced, at room temperature

Cooking spray for greasing

Makes 24 individual brioches

Combine the flour and yeast in the bowl of a stand mixer fitted with the dough hook. Add the eggs, milk, sugar, and salt and mix on low speed until evenly blended, scraping down the bowl with a rubber spatula as needed, about 4 minutes.

Gradually add the butter with the mixer running on low speed, scraping down the bowl with a rubber spatula as needed, 2 minutes. After the butter has been fully incorporated, increase the speed to medium and knead until the dough begins to pull away from the sides of the bowl and is quite elastic, about 15 minutes.

Remove the dough from the bowl, shape into a brick, wrap well in plastic wrap, and refrigerate for at least 8 hours.

Coat individual brioche tins or muffin pans with cooking spray.

To shape brioches *à tête,* remove the dough from the refrigerator and cut into 24 equal pieces, about 2 ounces each. Preshape each piece by rolling it into a 3-inch-long cylinder. Coat the edge of your palm with flour, then roll the dough back and forth about 1 inch from one end of the cylinder to create a head *(tête)* that is still attached to the cylinder; it should look like a bowling pin. Transfer the brioche, *tête* up, to a prepared mold. Hold the *tête* with the fingertips of one hand and push it down against the larger portion of the dough so that the *tête* sits up on the surface of the brioche. Brush lightly with egg wash. Repeat until all the brioches are shaped. (If the dough starts to get warm and sticky as you work, return it to the refrigerator until it is cool and easy to handle again.) Cover the shaped brioches with a clean, damp towel and let rise until they are nearly doubled in size, 1½–2 hours. Meanwhile, preheat the oven to 375°F.

Brush the brioches with beaten egg once more before putting them in the oven. Bake until they are a rich golden brown, about 15 minutes. Let cool in the tins or muffin pans for 10 minutes, then unmold and finish cooling on a wire rack before serving.

A classically shaped brioche has a topknot of dough, known as the *tête,* French for "head." This rich dough includes a large quantity of butter—so much, in fact, that it can affect the texture of the dough. To fully develop the gluten, you must mix and knead the dough for a long time. Note that brioche dough must be chilled in the refrigerator for at least 8 hours before you shape it. It holds for up to a week in the refrigerator, however, and can be frozen for up to 2 months.

kneading p. 39

combining ingredients p. 38

Challah

3½ cups bread flour plus extra as needed

2 tsp active dry yeast

1 cup room-temperature water (68–76°F)

3 large eggs

2 large egg yolks

¼ cup vegetable oil plus extra for greasing

¼ cup sugar

2½ tsp salt

Egg wash (1 large egg whisked with 2 Tbsp cold milk or water)

Makes 1 large or 2 small loaves

Combine the flour and yeast in the bowl of a stand mixer fitted with the dough hook. Add the water, eggs and egg yolks, oil, sugar, and salt and mix on low speed for 4 minutes. Increase the speed to medium and knead for 4 minutes. The dough should be soft but not sticky.

Transfer the dough to a lightly oiled bowl, turn to coat, cover with plastic wrap or a damp towel, and let rise in a warm place until nearly doubled in size, about 1 hour.

Fold the dough gently, cover, and let rest until relaxed, 20 minutes. Divide the dough into 3 equal pieces. Cover and let rest until relaxed, 15–20 minutes. Working with 1 piece at a time, place the dough on a lightly floured work surface and press lightly with your fingertips to stretch into a 6 x 10–inch rectangle, using only as much flour as needed to keep the dough from sticking. Fold the long top edge of the dough to the center of the rectangle, pressing lightly with your fingertips to tighten the outer surface of the dough. Fold the dough in half lengthwise so the top edge meets the bottom and use the heel of your palm to seal the edges together; keep the seam straight.

Roll each piece of dough into a tapered cylinder 12 inches long, increasing the pressure of your hands as you work outward from the center. Lay the 3 ropes of dough parallel to one another. Begin braiding in the center of the strands. Place the left strand over the center strand, and then the right strand over the center strand. Continue until you have reached one end, and pinch the ends together tightly. Turn the braid around so that the unbraided strands are facing you. Flip the braid over and repeat the braiding until you have again reached the end of the dough. Pinch the ends together tightly, tuck them under, and place the dough on a parchment paper–lined baking sheet.

Brush the dough lightly with egg wash and let rise a second time until it springs back slowly to the touch but does not collapse, 1 hour. Do not cover the dough; the egg wash will make it sticky.

Preheat the oven to 350°F. Very gently brush the dough with egg wash again before baking. (If the first layer of egg wash is dry before you apply a second coat, the challah will be shinier after it is baked.) Bake until the challah is a dark golden brown, shiny, and lightweight, 25–30 minutes. Let cool completely on a wire rack before serving.

Challah is a special kind of bread, enriched with whole eggs, used for the Jewish Shabbat and holidays. The term "challah" once referred to the portion of the dough that was separated from the bread dough and ritually burned. This portion represents the first, or best, portion of the dough. Although challah is generally formed into a braid, other shapes are also traditional, such as a round loaf for Rosh Hashanah.

first rise p. 39

braiding yeast doughs p. 42

Parker House Rolls

½ cup room-temperature water
(68–76°F)

2 tsp active dry yeast

2 Tbsp sugar

¾ cup whole or low-fat milk,
boiled and cooled to room
temperature

3 Tbsp unsalted butter, at
room temperature, plus 8 Tbsp
(1 stick) unsalted butter,
melted, or as needed

2 large eggs, lightly beaten

2½–3 cups bread flour (divided
use) plus extra as needed

1 tsp salt

Vegetable oil for greasing

Egg wash (1 large egg whisked
with 2 Tbsp cold milk or water)

Sesame seeds or poppy seeds
for garnish (optional)

Makes 24 rolls

Combine the water, yeast, and sugar in a large bowl. Let sit until frothy, 2–3 minutes. Add the cooled milk, the 3 Tbsp butter, the eggs, 1½ cups of the flour, and the salt. Stir until the dough begins to form long elastic strands, 5–6 minutes. Gradually add more flour until the dough is too heavy to stir.

Turn the dough out onto a floured work surface and knead for about 10 minutes, adding flour only to prevent the dough from sticking. The dough should be moist, smooth, and springy when it is properly kneaded. Transfer to a lightly oiled bowl, turn to coat, cover with a clean, damp cloth, and let rise in a warm place until doubled in size, 1–2 hours. Fold the dough over and let rest for 10 minutes.

Lightly grease two 9 x 11–inch baking pans with oil. Turn the dough out onto a lightly floured surface. Cut the dough into 24 equal pieces. Cover and let rest until relaxed, 15–20 minutes. Use a rolling pin to roll each piece into a 2 x 5–inch oval. Press the dull edge of a table knife in the center of each oval lengthwise to make a crease. Brush each roll with a thin coat of melted butter, and fold each in half so that the butter is on the inside. Place the rolls in the prepared pans seam sides up. They should be close, but not touching one another. Cover the rolls with a damp cloth and let rise until nearly doubled in size. Preheat the oven to 350°F.

Brush the rolls lightly with egg wash. If desired, scatter with sesame seeds or poppy seeds. Bake until golden brown, 15–20 minutes. Let the rolls cool slightly before serving.

These buttery rolls are best served warm. Instead of eating them only with a special-occasion dinner, try them in place of Danish or croissants with big cups of frothy cappuccino or hot chocolate for breakfast. The dough can be prepared the night before and allowed to rise very slowly in a cool spot, even for 12 hours in the refrigerator if the quantity of yeast is reduced. Let the dough come back to room temperature before the final shaping and baking.

preparing pans p. 70

kneading p. 39

VARIATIONS

Knot or Cloverleaf Shapes

For knots, after cutting the dough into pieces, roll each into a 6-inch-long cylinder. Wrap it around the index and middle fingers of 1 hand to make a circle, bring 1 end up and through the circle to make the knot, and pinch the ends together. Set in the prepared baking pans. Brush lightly with the egg wash and let rise until nearly doubled before baking as directed. For cloverleafs, after cutting the dough into pieces, cut each piece into thirds. Gently roll into rounds and place 3 rounds in each cup of a greased muffin pan. Brush lightly with egg wash and let rise until nearly doubled before baking as directed.

Cheddar and Onion Rye Rolls

2⅔ cups bread flour plus extra as needed

¾ cup medium rye flour

2 tsp active dry yeast

1½ cups room-temperature water (68–76°F)

2 tsp salt

2 tsp sugar

1 Tbsp molasses

1 Tbsp vegetable oil plus extra for greasing

1 cup coarsely diced Cheddar cheese

1 cup coarsely diced onion

Cornmeal for dusting

Makes 24 rolls

Combine the flours and yeast in the bowl of a stand mixer fitted with the dough hook. Add the water, salt, sugar, molasses, and oil and mix on low speed for 4 minutes. Increase the speed to medium and knead for 2 minutes. Add the cheese and onion and knead on medium speed for 1 minute more. The dough should be tight and very springy.

Transfer the dough to a lightly oiled bowl, turn to coat, cover with plastic wrap or a damp towel, and let rise in a warm place until nearly doubled in size, about 75 minutes. Fold the dough over gently. Cover the dough and let rest until relaxed, 15–20 minutes.

Prepare 2 baking sheets by scattering them with cornmeal. Turn the dough out onto a lightly floured work surface, press into a rectangle, and divide into 24 equal pieces, about 2 ounces each. Cover and let rest until relaxed, 10 minutes. Press each piece of dough lightly with your fingertips to make a square shape. Fold the top edge of the dough to the center of the dough, pressing lightly with your fingertips to tighten the outer layer. Rotate the dough 90 degrees; fold the dough in half from top to bottom and use the heel of your hand to seal the 2 edges together to make a round, pinching the seams together at the bottom of the ball.

Transfer the rolls seam sides down to the prepared baking sheets. Mist or brush them with water. Cover loosely with plastic wrap or a clean, damp towel and let rise until nearly doubled in size and the dough springs back slowly to the touch but does not collapse, about 40 minutes.

Make a shallow, straight cut down the center of each roll and mist evenly with water.

Bake the rolls until they have a golden brown crust and sound hollow when tapped on the bottom, 15–20 minutes. For a very crisp crust, mist the rolls 1 or 2 more times during the first 5 minutes of baking time. Let cool slightly before serving.

Rye doughs can be heavy and difficult to knead, even in a machine. Some bakers recommend adding most, but not all, of the flour to the mixer when you begin to mix. If you hold back about 1 cup of the flour, a 5-quart mixer can readily mix and knead the dough. Then, turn the dough out onto a floured work surface and knead the remaining flour in by hand.

using yeast p. 38

baking yeast breads p. 43

Semolina Pizza with Fresh Herbs and Goat Cheese

Pizza Dough

3½ cups bread flour plus extra as needed

½ cup semolina or durum flour

1½ tsp active dry yeast

1½ cups room-temperature water (68–76°F)

3 Tbsp olive oil plus extra for greasing

2 tsp salt

Cornmeal for dusting

Topping

4 Tbsp extra-virgin olive oil

1 red onion, cut into matchsticks or thin slices

1 Tbsp chopped fresh basil leaves

1 tsp chopped fresh oregano leaves

1 clove garlic, minced

Freshly ground pepper

5 oz fresh goat cheese, crumbled

4 Tbsp freshly grated Parmesan cheese

Makes two 12-inch pizzas

To prepare the dough, combine the flours and yeast in the bowl of a stand mixer fitted with the dough hook. Add the water, olive oil, and salt and mix on low speed for 2 minutes. Increase the speed to medium and knead until the dough is quite elastic but still a little sticky, 4 minutes.

Transfer the dough to a lightly oiled bowl, turn to coat, cover with plastic wrap or a damp towel, and let rise in a warm place until nearly doubled in size, about 30 minutes. Fold the dough gently, cover, and let rest until relaxed, 15–20 minutes, before cutting it into 2 equal pieces and rounding into smooth balls. Cover the dough and let rest another 15–20 minutes.

Preheat the oven to 450°F. Prepare 2 baking sheets by scattering them with cornmeal.

To shape the pizza dough, turn the dough out onto a lightly floured work surface and, working with one piece at a time, press the dough into a disk of even thickness, ⅛–¼ inch, stretching and turning the dough as you work or using a rolling pin. You may finish stretching the dough by flipping it: With the dough resting on the backs of your hands, simultaneously spin the dough and toss it into the air. As it falls back down, catch it on the backs of your hands once more. Continue until the dough is an evenly thick 12-inch round.

Transfer the dough rounds to the cornmeal-scattered baking sheets. Drizzle each pizza with 1 Tbsp of the olive oil, then scatter with the remaining topping ingredients, leaving a ½-inch-wide margin around the edge. Drizzle an additional 1 Tbsp of oil over each pizza and bake until golden brown around the edges, 10–12 minutes. Serve at once.

Using a baking stone or tiles will help approximate the intense heat of a wood-fired pizza oven, resulting in a better pizza crust. Use a baker's peel to transfer the prepared pizza to the stone. If you don't have a peel, you can substitute a baking sheet with no edge on one or more sides. Scatter the peel or baking sheet with cornmeal, place the dough round on it, layer on the toppings, and then use a quick, jerking motion to slide the bread from the peel or pan onto the hot stone.

kneading p. 39

shaping yeast doughs p. 41

2 Quick Breads

Making a batch of banana bread or a few dozen biscuits can lead you quite naturally along the path from being a beginning baker to an accomplished one. The recipes in this chapter introduce the basic mixing and baking methods you'll use again and again as you make not only quick breads, but also cookies, pies, and cakes. Seasoned bakers often return to these recipes, too, since they are easy to change according to the season or the menu: blueberries can take the place of cranberries in a scone, while different spices and seeds can flavor a muffin.

How quick breads differ from yeast breads

Most batters and doughs contain one or more leaveners that determine the texture of the finished baked good. Traditional breads are leavened by yeast, an organism that needs time to reproduce in order to leaven a dough. Quick breads, on the other hand, don't require time to rise because they rely upon other means for leavening. Ingredients like baking soda and baking powder, as well as a variety of mixing techniques, are used to develop their textures.

Chemical leaveners

Both baking soda and baking powder, referred to as chemical leaveners, give breads and cakes a light texture by introducing carbon dioxide gas into the batter. The gas expands the bubbles that are already present in the batter due to the action of mixing or creaming. Once the baked good goes into the oven, the heat causes the gas to expand so that the bread rises even higher. Eventually, the other ingredients of the batter settle into a firm structure. These little pockets of empty space cause the baked item to crumble or break apart easily when we eat it.

Baking soda is about four times as powerful as baking powder, but requires the presence of an acid (buttermilk or citrus juice, for example) to react and produce carbon dioxide. Bakers used to add cream of tartar to react with the baking soda if the recipe didn't use acidic ingredients, a trick that is reflected in older recipes. Baking soda reacts immediately when it is moistened in the presence of an acid, so recipes that include it always instruct you to bake the batter right after mixing.

Baking powder is a mixture of an alkali and an acid, plus cornstarch to keep the powder dry until use. Double-acting baking powder contains two acids that react at different times, one when the powder is moistened and the other when it is heated, so the batter gets a second boost of leavening when it goes into the oven. Widely introduced to home bakers in the 1850s, double-acting baking powder made it much easier to bake consistent quick breads. The fact that there are two reactions also gives the baker a little extra time to work. A batter may even be stored overnight, as for the Cream Scones on page 85; letting the mixed and shaped scones freeze overnight before baking results in a delicate, crisp, flaky scone.

Chemical leaveners are not the only way that quick breads are raised. You might use a physical leavener such as foam, usually made of beaten egg whites. As you beat egg whites, air is trapped in the protein network, adding volume to a batter. The air pockets expand in the heat of the oven, contributing still more volume to the finished baked good. Another physical leavener is air trapped as you cream butter.

Quick-bread mixing methods

Quick breads rely upon a variety of mixing methods seen in other baked goods: the straight mixing method (page 30), also used for some cakes and cookies; the creaming mixing method (page 31), also used for other cakes and cookies; and the rubbing mixing method (page 32), used to make biscuits, pie crusts, and some pastry doughs such as puff pastry.

Choosing ingredients

All-purpose flour works beautifully in the recipes in this chapter. It has enough protein to maintain a quick bread's shape and volume as the batter bakes, but not so much that it becomes tough or rubbery. There are also recipes here that call for whole wheat flour, cornmeal, and even oat flour in addition to all-purpose flour.

Most quick breads include at least a little sweetener for flavor and color, as well as an appealing texture. White and brown sugars are the most common sweeteners, but molasses and honey are sometimes used, too.

The garnishes you choose for a quick bread can change its character from a sweet treat to something savory or spicy. Cornbread, for example, may be lightly sweetened, or it can take on a fiery character if you add some chiles. Most add-ins or garnishes are blended or folded into a batter just before you put it in the pan to bake. Among the many options you will find in this chapter are cheeses, herbs, chiles, fresh and dried fruits, and nuts. A common problem for bakers is finding that the add-in has sunk to the bottom of the muffin or bread. To prevent this, be sure to prepare the add-ins according to the recipe directions. Some should be dusted with a bit of flour, and others need to be cut or grated to the right size.

Storing and reheating

For many home bakers, one of the best things about quick breads is their simplicity. You can easily double the recipes in this book, making some to enjoy right away and some to store for later. Most muffins and quick breads can be stored in resealable plastic bags or rigid plastic containers and will last in the freezer for up to 2 months. To defrost them, simply take them out of the freezer and let them rest at room temperature for an hour or so; a frozen muffin tucked into a bagged lunch in the morning will be perfect by lunchtime.

Using chemical leaveners

Baking soda and baking powder are the chemical leaveners most commonly used in the kitchen. In contrast to yeast, their leavening action occurs rapidly.

1 Using baking soda and powder

Baking soda, also known as bicarbonate of soda, needs to come into contact with both a liquid and an acid in order to work. Batters that include buttermilk, yogurt, sour cream, or fruits often call for baking soda. Recipes leavened by baking soda alone should be baked soon after mixing to take full advantage of the leavening power.

Baking soda keeps for up to 2 years if it is stored in a cool, dry place, but it does gradually lose its effectiveness. To test it, mix about ¼ teaspoon with 2 teaspoons of vinegar. It should foam up immediately.

Double-acting baking powder begins working when it comes into contact with a liquid, and it receives another boost when it goes into the heat of the oven.

Baking powder lasts about 6 months. Check it by mixing 1 teaspoon baking powder with 1 cup hot water. If it bubbles immediately, it is still potent enough to leaven a batter.

When chemical leaveners aren't fully blended into the batter, they clump together. Biting into a pocket of baking powder leaves a bitter or soapy taste in your mouth. Combine the baking soda or powder completely with the flour by sifting, stirring, or whisking together the dry ingredients before mixing in the remaining ingredients.

Zesting and juicing citrus

The peels of lemons, limes, and oranges are rich in aromatic oils, while their juices add bright flavor to both sweet and savory dishes.

1 Choosing citrus

When selecting citrus fruits for their zest, choose those with firm skins rather than very soft or withered peels. If possible, choose organic fruit for zesting, since pesticides accumulate in the peel. Thoroughly scrub the fruit under hot water with a stiff brush.

2 Zesting citrus

Depending on how the zest will be used in a recipe, remove it in wide pieces, thin strips, or fine gratings. Use a vegetable peeler for thick strips that can infuse a liquid with flavor and easily be removed later. You can also cut these pieces crosswise for thin strips. Specially designed zesters create thin, delicate strips of zest for sauces or garnish. For finely grated zest, use a grater with very small holes and rotate the fruit frequently as you grate. Whichever method you use, avoid cutting into the white pith. If you need both citrus zest and juice for a dish, note that it is easier to zest before juicing.

3 Juicing citrus

A citrus fruit at room temperature gives more juice than chilled fruit. Before cutting and juicing it, roll the fruit firmly against a hard surface to crush its pulp; this will help it release even more juice. Slice the fruit in half crosswise, then use a fluted reamer or mechanical juicer to extract as much juice as possible.

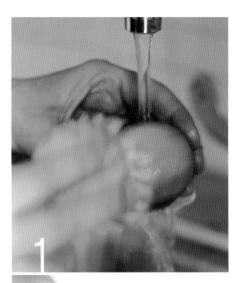

These pans or irons should be coated with flourless cooking spray and preheated before you add any batter.

2 Flouring

The more sugar and eggs in a batter, the more delicate it is and the likelier to stick to a pan. For these batters, recipes sometimes recommend a dusting of flour after the pan is greased. Scatter a tablespoon or two of flour into the pan. Turn the pan, tilting and shaking it, so that the flour rolls over every part of the pan. Tap the pan firmly against a flat surface and pour out any flour that shakes free.

3 Lining baking sheets with parchment paper

Line baking sheets for biscuits, scones, and cookies with sheets of parchment. The paper keeps even the most delicate of baked goods and any stray egg wash from sticking and burning on the pan.

4 Lining round baking pans with parchment paper

If you are using a round baking pan, such as a cake pan, cut a round by repeatedly folding a square of parchment paper in half diagonally, until it is a narrow triangle. Hold the tip of the triangle over the center of the pan and trim away the paper that extends beyond the rim of the pan.

For muffin pans, use muffin liners. These paper liners are pleated so that they can expand when filled with batter. They are sold in sizes to fit miniature, regular, and large muffin pans.

Preparing pans

Quick bread and cake batters often contain sugar and eggs, which tend to make them stick to untreated surfaces. Greasing and flouring your baking pans or using liners prevents sticking.

1 Greasing

The fastest way to apply a light, even coating of oil to a baking pan, whether the sides are straight, fluted, or scalloped, is with a cooking spray. Sprays made from canola oil have a neutral flavor. Some sprays include flour; while these are fine for coating pans and tins, don't use them on griddles, skillets, sauté pans, or waffle irons, where the flour might burn. You can also brush or rub the pan with oil, softened butter, or shortening. Be sure to brush it evenly into the corners of the pan.

Certain quick breads, including crêpes and pancakes, are cooked over direct heat. Waffles are cooked on special waffle irons.

Sifting

Sifting dry ingredients aerates them by breaking apart any tightly packed pockets, and also distributes ingredients evenly.

1 Sifting dry ingredients

The recipes in this book call for the flour and other dry ingredients to be measured out first, then sifted. When you use recipes from other books, check the ingredients list to determine whether the author intended you to sift the ingredients and then measure, or to measure first and then sift. This can make a difference in the amount measured. To sift more than one ingredient together, add the properly measured ingredients to a sieve or sifter. Shake or tap the sieve to sift the dry ingredients into a bowl or directly onto a piece of parchment or waxed paper. If you use paper, you can simply lift the paper, fold it to create a cone, and pour the dry ingredients directly into the mixing bowl.

Filling pans

When baking pans or muffin pans are filled correctly, baked goods rise properly for a wonderful texture and a nicely browned crust.

1 Filling baking pans

Batters leavened with baking powder or baking soda continue to rise during the first stage of baking. When you fill pans two-thirds to three-quarters full, the batter expands to fill the pan and rises slightly over the top, forming a dome-shaped crust as it bakes. If pans are filled too high, the batter can run over the edges before rising is complete. If they are not filled enough, the batter may rise too rapidly and too high in the center during the initial stages of baking. Eventually, the center, which is not supported by the sides of the pan, may fall from its own weight, and the entire item can turn out dense and chewy rather than light and airy.

If your recipe makes enough batter for 2 or more loaves or you are making muffins, divide the batter evenly between the pans or among the muffin cups so they bake in the same amount of time. Use ice cream scoops or measuring cups to fills pans evenly. You can substitute one baking pan size for another using the tips and the chart in the back of this book (pages 293–95). Be certain to adjust the baking time to match the new pan size.

Determining doneness

As muffins, quick breads, scones, and biscuits bake, they increase in volume, puffing up as the chemical leaveners do their work. When fully baked they have a golden brown color.

1 Testing for doneness

Use the suggested time range in recipes as a general guideline, but also use as many of the following tests as possible to test baked items for doneness.

Quick breads and cakes prepared in a skillet or on a griddle, like crêpes or pancakes, are cooked on the first side until the edges just start to set and small bubbles break through the upper surface. When fully cooked, the cakes are browned on both sides and the sides appear set and no longer wet. Test thick pancakes by pressing them lightly with your fingertip. You should feel relatively little give.

Test simple cakes and loaf-style quick breads for doneness by gently pressing them near the center with the pad of your index finger. When fully baked, the cake springs back, leaving no indentation. Another common test calls for inserting a wooden skewer or toothpick near the center of the cake; the skewer should come out of the cake clean or with only a few moist crumbs clinging to it. Test biscuits and scones by tapping them on the bottom with your fingertips and listening for a hollow sound.

Blueberry Muffins

Flourless cooking spray for greasing

2 cups plus 2 Tbsp all-purpose flour (divided use)

1½ tsp baking powder

½ tsp salt

¼ tsp freshly grated nutmeg

¾ cup whole or low-fat milk

1 large egg

½ tsp vanilla extract

8 Tbsp (1 stick) unsalted butter, at room temperature

1 cup sugar

1½ cups fresh blueberries, washed and patted dry, or unthawed frozen blueberries

Makes 12 muffins

Preheat the oven to 400°F. Spray muffin pans lightly with cooking spray or use paper liners to line them. Sift the 2 cups flour, the baking powder, salt, and nutmeg into a bowl and set aside.

In a separate bowl, blend the milk, egg, and vanilla extract.

In a stand mixer fitted with the paddle, cream together the butter and sugar until light and smooth in texture, 3–4 minutes. Add the flour mixture in 3 additions, alternating with the wet ingredients, mixing on low speed and scraping down the bowl with a rubber spatula as needed to blend the batter evenly. Increase the speed to medium and mix until the batter is very smooth, 2 minutes.

In a bowl, scatter the 2 Tbsp flour over the berries and toss to coat them evenly. Working by hand with a wooden spoon or rubber spatula, fold the blueberries into the batter, working gently and just long enough to distribute the berries evenly.

Divide the batter evenly among 12 muffin cups. Bake until the top of a muffin springs back when lightly pressed, 18–20 minutes.

Let the muffins cool in the pans on wire racks for 5 minutes. Remove them from the pans to finish cooling.

Blueberries can turn a peculiar green color as they bake. This is the result of acids in a batter, such as buttermilk, interacting with the berries. In this recipe, whole milk and baking powder are used in place of the more traditional buttermilk and baking soda to make a tender, golden muffin dotted with rich, purple berries.

sifting p. 71

the creaming mixing method p. 31

VARIATIONS

Blueberry Bran Muffins

Replace ½ cup of the flour with wheat or oat bran. If you like, you can also replace ½ cup of the sugar with ⅓ cup honey. These muffins will be denser and less cakelike than the original version.

Streusel-Topped Blueberry Muffins

In a bowl, blend ¼ cup quick-cooking oats, ¼ cup chopped walnuts, ¼ cup tightly packed light brown sugar, ¼ cup all-purpose flour, and ⅛ teaspoon salt. With your fingertips or a pastry knife, or with short pulses in a food processor, cut 4 Tbsp (½ stick) cold unsalted butter into the dry ingredients until the streusel is crumbly. Scatter a generous tablespoon of the streusel over each muffin before baking.

Smoked Provolone and Thyme Muffins

Flourless cooking spray
for greasing

2 cups all-purpose flour

2 Tbsp powdered mustard

1 Tbsp baking powder

1 tsp kosher salt

¼ tsp freshly ground black
pepper, or to taste

1 pinch cayenne pepper

1 cup grated smoked provolone
cheese

1 Tbsp chopped fresh thyme
leaves, or 2 tsp dried thyme

1 large egg

1½ cups whole or low-fat milk

4 Tbsp (½ stick) unsalted butter,
melted and cooled

1 dash Tabasco sauce,
or to taste

Makes 12 muffins

Preheat the oven to 350°F. Spray muffin pans lightly with cooking spray or use paper liners to line them.

Stir together the flour, mustard, baking powder, salt, black pepper, and cayenne in a large bowl. Add the cheese and thyme; toss with a fork to distribute the cheese evenly. Make a well in the center of these dry ingredients.

In a separate bowl, blend the egg, milk, butter, and Tabasco sauce. Pour the wet ingredients into the well in the dry ingredients. Stir together the wet and dry ingredients, mixing just until all ingredients are combined. Do not overmix.

Fill each muffin cup two-thirds full with batter. Bake until the top of a muffin springs back when lightly pressed with your fingertip, 20–25 minutes.

Let the muffins cool in the pans on wire racks for 10 minutes, then turn them out of the pans. Serve while still warm.

The flavor of these muffins may be varied with ease. Substitute other cheeses as desired for the smoked provolone: smoked Gouda, smoked mozzarella, aged Cheddar, or Monterey jack. Replace the thyme with other herbs, such as chives, basil, oregano, or marjoram.

the straight mixing method p. 30

filling pans p. 71

Irish Soda Bread

Cornmeal for dusting

4 cups cake flour plus extra for
dusting

⅓ cup sugar

2 Tbsp baking soda

1 pinch salt

¼ cup vegetable shortening

1 cup plus 2 Tbsp cold whole
or low-fat milk

3 Tbsp dark raisins

1 Tbsp caraway seeds

Makes 2 loaves

Preheat the oven to 400°F. Scatter a baking sheet with cornmeal.

Sift the flour, sugar, baking soda, and salt into a large bowl. Using a pastry cutter or 2 knives, cut the shortening into the dry ingredients until it resembles a coarse meal. Add the milk, raisins, and caraway seeds. Mix the dough until it forms a shaggy mass. Turn out onto a lightly floured work surface and knead for 20 seconds.

Divide the dough into 2 equal pieces. Form each piece into a ball, pressing the seams together on the bottom. Dust the rounds with flour and lightly score a cross into the top of each with a sharp knife. Place them on the prepared baking sheet.

Bake the loaves until they are lightly browned and sound hollow when tapped on the bottom, 30 minutes. Let cool on wire racks.

Soda bread is among the simplest of breads to make. It is especially delectable when split horizontally, toasted, and stuffed with chewy, thick-cut bacon.

cutting fat into flour p. 112

determining doneness p. 71

Buttermilk Pancakes

1½ cups all-purpose flour

2 Tbsp sugar

½ tsp baking powder

¼ tsp baking soda

¼ tsp salt

1¾ cups buttermilk

2 large eggs

3 Tbsp unsalted butter, melted and cooled slightly

Vegetable oil for greasing

Makes 24 pancakes

Sift the flour, sugar, baking powder, baking soda, and salt into a bowl and set aside.

In a separate bowl, blend the buttermilk, eggs, and butter. Add the buttermilk mixture to the flour mixture and stir by hand just until the batter is evenly moistened.

Heat a large nonstick skillet or griddle over medium-high heat. Grease it lightly by brushing with oil. Drop the pancake batter onto the hot skillet by large spoonfuls (2–3 Tbsp). Leave about 2 inches between the pancakes to allow them to spread and to make turning them easier.

Cook on the first side until small bubbles appear and then break on the upper surface of the pancakes and the edges are set, about 1 minute. Use an offset spatula or a palette knife to turn the pancakes and finish cooking on the second side, 1–2 minutes more. Adjust the heat as needed to produce a golden brown color.

Serve the pancakes immediately.

When a recipe calls for both baking powder and baking soda, the baking soda is used mainly to neutralize an acid in the batter (in this case, buttermilk), while the baking powder is the element responsible for the majority of the leavening action.

using chemical leaveners p. 69

sifting p. 71

Four-Grain Waffles

1½ cups buttermilk

2 large eggs

¼ cup vegetable oil plus extra for greasing

¾ cup all-purpose flour

½ cup whole wheat flour

½ cup oat flour

¼ cup cornmeal

2 Tbsp sugar

1 Tbsp baking powder

Makes 6 waffles

Preheat a waffle iron to medium heat.

Combine the buttermilk, eggs, and oil in a large bowl.

In a separate bowl, combine the flours, cornmeal, sugar, and baking powder. Add the liquid ingredients to the dry ingredients and mix by hand with a wooden spoon just until the batter is evenly moistened.

Lightly brush the preheated waffle iron with vegetable oil. Ladle about ⅓ cup of batter (check the waffle iron manufacturer's instructions, since sizes may vary) into the waffle iron and cook until the waffles are golden brown and the iron opens easily without tearing the waffles, about 3 minutes. If necessary, keep warm in a 200°F oven while you finish cooking the remaining batter.

Oat flour is available in health food stores or in the natural foods section of some larger supermarkets. However, if you can't find it, you can make your own by grinding rolled oats in a blender or food processor until you have a relatively fine flour.

the straight mixing method p. 30

using chemical leaveners p. 69

Dutch Baby with Spiced Peaches

½ cup all-purpose flour

½ tsp salt

2 large eggs

½ cup whole or low-fat milk

2 Tbsp unsalted butter, melted, plus extra for greasing

Spiced Peaches

2 Tbsp unsalted butter

3 peaches, peeled (p. 127) and sliced

2 tsp ground cinnamon

2 Tbsp tightly packed light brown sugar

1 Tbsp fresh lemon juice

Confectioners' sugar for dusting

Makes 6 servings

Place a 10-inch cast-iron skillet or ovenproof sauté pan in the oven and preheat to 450°F. Sift the flour and salt into a bowl and set aside.

While the pan heats, put the eggs in a blender and blend at low speed. Add the flour mixture and the milk alternately, in 3 additions. Scrape down the sides of the blender and continue to blend until smooth, 15–20 seconds. Blend in the melted butter. Brush the hot skillet with additional melted butter and pour in the batter. Bake for 10 minutes without opening the oven. Reduce the heat to 350°F and bake until the Dutch baby is very puffy and the edges are starting to pull away from the edges of the pan, 15–20 minutes more.

Meanwhile, prepare the spiced peaches: Melt the butter in a medium sauté pan over high heat. Add the peaches, cinnamon, and brown sugar. Reduce the heat to medium and stir until the fruit is just heated through, about 5 minutes.

Remove the Dutch baby from the oven. Drizzle with the lemon juice and dust with the confectioners' sugar. Fill the center of the Dutch baby with the hot fruit mixture. Serve immediately.

According to one culinary legend, these light, fluffy baked pancakes were served as a small version of a traditional German-style pancake at Victor Manka's restaurant in Seattle. His children called them Dutch babies, and, eventually, the name spread to all puffy baked pancakes, small or large.

The Dutch baby may be topped with whipped cream, sour cream, or yogurt instead of sugar. The peaches can be replaced with another fruit or combination of fruits such as bananas, raspberries, apples, or strawberries.

sifting p. 71

Pumpkin Bread

½ cup dark raisins

1½ cups all-purpose flour plus extra for dusting

1¼ cups whole wheat flour

1 tsp baking powder

¾ tsp baking soda

½ tsp *each* salt and cinnamon

¼ tsp freshly grated nutmeg

⅛ tsp ground cloves

1 cup canned pumpkin purée

¾ cup sugar

2 large eggs

½ cup vegetable oil plus extra for greasing

Makes 2 loaves

Preheat the oven to 375°F. Grease and flour two 8½-inch loaf pans. Pour ½ cup warm water over the raisins and let plump for 10 minutes.

Sift together the flours, baking powder, baking soda, salt, cinnamon, nutmeg, and cloves and set aside. Combine the raisins and soaking liquid, pumpkin, sugar, eggs, and oil in a large bowl and mix well.

Pour the dry ingredients into the pumpkin mixture and stir just until all the ingredients are combined. Pour the batter into the prepared loaf pans and bake until a toothpick inserted into the bread comes out with a few moist crumbs and the top and sides are light golden brown, 50–55 minutes. Let the loaves cool in the pans on wire racks for 10–15 minutes. Turn them out of the pans and continue cooling on the racks before serving.

This recipe produces a dense, moist bread that delivers the same heady aroma and flavor as a pumpkin pie. If desired, fold a small handful of chopped walnuts into the batter just before baking. Serve with a main-course salad, or spread with cream cheese at breakfast.

sifting p. 71

filling pans p. 71

Cornbread

Unsalted butter for greasing

1 cup yellow cornmeal plus extra for dusting

¾ cup all-purpose flour

½ cup sugar

1½ tsp baking powder

1 tsp salt

2 large eggs

½ cup buttermilk

¼ cup vegetable oil

Makes 16 pieces

Preheat the oven to 350°F. Lightly grease an 8-inch square pan and lightly dust with cornmeal.

Mix together the cornmeal, flour, sugar, baking powder, and salt.

In a separate bowl, whisk together the eggs, buttermilk, and oil until blended. Add the wet ingredients to the dry ingredients and combine until just mixed.

Pour the batter into the prepared pan and bake until the surface is golden brown and springs back when lightly pressed with your fingertip, 25–30 minutes.

Let the bread cool in the pan for about 10 minutes before cutting it into 2-inch-square pieces.

Conventional wisdom about the "correct" way to make cornbread varies from one region of the country to another. Southerners tend to use little if any sugar in their cornbread, and they often make it with white cornmeal. In other parts of the country, yellow cornmeal is preferred, and the amount of sugar is noticeably increased.

Serve this bread quite warm. It does not keep well, but any leftovers can be made into bread crumbs and frozen for later use.

preparing pans p. 70

determining doneness p. 71

VARIATIONS

Country-Style Cornbread

For a delicious, crisp bottom crust, bake the bread in a cast-iron skillet. Place a 9-inch skillet in the oven as it preheats. When the batter is ready, remove the skillet from the oven and brush the inside lightly with vegetable oil (or rendered bacon fat, if available). Pour the batter into the skillet and bake as directed.

Chipotle Cheddar Corn Diamonds

Reduce the sugar to ¼ cup. Substitute ¾ cup whole or low-fat milk for the buttermilk and add ¾ cup grated sharp Cheddar cheese, ½ cup corn kernels (fresh or thawed frozen), and 2 Tbsp chopped chipotle chiles (if using canned chipotles en adobo, add a bit of the sauce). Increase the baking time to about 40 minutes. Proceed as directed.

Allow the cornbread to cool slightly before cutting it into diamond shapes. Serve while still warm.

The addition of chipotle chiles to this cornbread batter results in an excellent accompaniment to hearty soups or chili. Canned chipotles en adobo may be found in the ethnic foods aisle of many well-stocked supermarkets.

Boston Brown Bread

Flourless cooking spray for greasing

½ cup boiling water plus extra for hot water bath

½ cup dark raisins

½ cup all-purpose flour

½ cup whole wheat flour

½ cup rye flour

½ cup cornmeal

¾ tsp baking soda

½ tsp salt

1½ cups buttermilk

½ cup dark molasses

1 large egg

Makes 1 loaf

Preheat the oven to 375°F. Generously coat an 8½-inch loaf pan or a 1-pound coffee can with cooking spray.

Pour the boiling water over the raisins and let plump for 10 minutes. Sift the flours, cornmeal, baking soda, and salt into a bowl. Make a well in the center of these dry ingredients and set aside.

In a separate bowl, beat together the buttermilk, molasses, and egg. Drain and stir in the raisins, discarding the plumping liquid.

Pour the wet ingredients into the well in the dry ingredients and mix just until the batter is smooth. Pour the batter into the prepared pan or coffee can.

Cover the loaf pan tightly with aluminum foil, then place it in a larger pan or casserole (the sides of the larger pan should be taller than the loaf pan). Pour enough boiling water into the large pan to come halfway up the sides of the loaf pan. (To make the bread in a coffee can, place the filled can in a stock pot or similar large pot with ovenproof handles. Add enough boiling water to cover about two-thirds of the coffee can.) Tightly cover the larger pan with foil and place in the preheated oven. Bake undisturbed for 2½ hours. Insert a skewer into the center of the bread. If it comes out clean, the bread is done; otherwise, continue to bake another 15–20 minutes. Do not open the oven door while the bread is cooking, to keep the temperature consistent.

When the bread is done, remove the loaf pan from the larger pan and remove the foil. Let the bread cool in the loaf pan for 10 minutes, then loosen the edges, turn the loaf out onto a wire rack, and cool slightly. Serve while still warm.

Dried fruits like the raisins in this recipe are often "plumped" in a warm liquid such as water, wine, juice, or spirits before use in baking. This step makes them moist enough that they will not draw the moisture out of a batter or finished dish.

This bread is steamed, like a steamed pudding. With its molasses tang, its moist, dense texture, and nutty cornmeal flavor, it makes a fine accompaniment to hearty dishes like baked beans, pot roast, and stews.

making steamed puddings p. 170

sifting p. 71

Zucchini Bread

Flourless cooking spray
for greasing

3½ cups all-purpose flour
plus extra for dusting

2 tsp baking powder

½ tsp baking soda

1 tsp salt

1 tsp ground cinnamon

½ tsp freshly grated nutmeg

¼ tsp ground cloves

2½ cups grated unpeeled
zucchini

1 cup sugar

4 large eggs, lightly beaten

½ cup vegetable oil

2 Tbsp grated orange zest

1 cup coarsely chopped toasted
walnuts or pecans

Makes 2 loaves

Preheat the oven to 350°F. Grease and flour two 8½-inch loaf pans.

Sift the flour, baking powder, baking soda, salt, cinnamon, nutmeg, and cloves into a bowl and set aside.

Combine the zucchini, sugar, eggs, oil, and orange zest in a large bowl and mix by hand until evenly blended.

Add the sifted dry ingredients to the zucchini mixture. Stir by hand just until the batter is evenly moistened and blended. Fold in the nuts. Divide the batter between the prepared loaf pans.

Bake until the edges are browned and starting to pull away from the pan and the bread springs back when lightly pressed with your fingertip, 50–55 minutes. Remove the loaves from the pans and let cool on wire racks before serving.

If you grow zucchini in your garden, you'll be glad to have this recipe come late summer. Note that the larger a zucchini grows, the tougher its skin, the drier its flesh, and the more bitter its seeds. If you are using large zucchini for this recipe, cut them in half and scoop out the seeds and fibrous flesh surrounding them. Grate the remaining zucchini.

toasting nuts p. 138

zesting and juicing citrus p. 69

Banana Nut Bread

3 cups all-purpose flour plus extra for dusting

1 tsp salt

½ tsp baking powder

8 Tbsp (1 stick) unsalted butter, at room temperature, plus extra for greasing

½ cup sugar

⅓ cup honey

1 Tbsp grated orange zest

2 tsp vanilla extract

3 very ripe medium bananas, peeled and lightly mashed

2 large eggs, at room temperature

1 cup coarsely chopped toasted walnuts or pecans

Makes 2 loaves

Preheat the oven to 350°F. Grease and flour two 8½-inch loaf pans.

Sift the flour, salt, and baking powder into a bowl and set aside.

In a stand mixer fitted with the paddle attachment, cream together the butter and sugar on medium speed until light in texture, about 3 minutes. Add the honey, orange zest, vanilla extract, and bananas and mix until well combined, another 2 minutes. Scrape the bowl down as needed to mix evenly. Add the eggs to the banana mixture one at a time, beating well after each addition.

Remove the bowl from the mixer. Add the dry ingredients to the banana mixture all at once. Stir by hand just until the batter is evenly moistened. Fold the nuts into the batter, then divide the batter evenly between the prepared loaf pans.

Bake until the bread begins to pull away from the edges of the pans and the center of the loaves spring back when lightly pressed with your fingertip, about 1 hour.

Remove the loaves from the oven and let rest for 10–15 minutes before turning them out of the pans. Continue cooling on a wire rack before serving.

As bananas ripen, their yellow color deepens and brown freckles develop. If you have bananas that are in danger of becoming overripe and black, it is time to make banana nut bread. Serve this bread as part of a basket of bread at a brunch or lunch. Or, serve it lightly toasted and topped with cream cheese or peanut butter as an open-faced breakfast sandwich.

the creaming mixing method p. 31

filling pans p. 71

toasting nuts p. 138

Buttermilk Biscuits

3 cups all-purpose flour plus extra for dusting

2½ Tbsp sugar

1½ Tbsp baking powder

1 tsp salt

8 Tbsp (1 stick) cold unsalted butter, diced

⅔ cup buttermilk

½ cup whole or low-fat milk plus extra for brushing

Makes 12 biscuits

Preheat the oven to 425°F.

Blend or sift together the flour, sugar, baking powder, and salt. Cut the butter into the flour until it forms pea-sized pieces. Add the buttermilk and the milk. Mix just to combine the ingredients.

Roll the dough out to a 1-inch thickness on a lightly floured work surface, fold in half, turn, and repeat 3 or 4 times for a final thickness of 1 inch. Cut the dough into rounds using a 3-inch cutter, rerolling and cutting the scraps until you have 12 rounds.

Place the biscuits on an ungreased baking sheet. Brush the tops with a little milk to make the tops shiny, if desired. Bake until golden brown, 10–15 minutes. Let cool on wire racks.

This dough is rolled and folded repeatedly before it is cut into biscuits, a technique referred to as lamination. Laminating a dough in this manner creates layers that add extra flakiness and height to the finished biscuit. Try to make as few scraps as possible. After cutting, you can reroll the dough scraps and cut out more biscuits, but the biscuits made from the trimmings are usually a little less tender than the first ones.

the rubbing mixing method p. 32

VARIATIONS

Cheddar Biscuits

Stir 1½ cups grated Cheddar cheese into the buttermilk and milk before adding them to the dough.

A sharp, farm-style aged Cheddar cheese is best for this recipe.

Fennel, Caraway, or Dill Seed Biscuits

Soften 2 tsp fennel, caraway, or dill seeds by soaking them in warm water for 15 minutes, then drain and dry on paper towels. Stir the seeds into the buttermilk and milk before adding them to the dough.

Home-Style Strawberry Shortcake

Slice hulled strawberries and sprinkle with sugar, ¼–⅓ cup of sugar for every 1½ cups berries, depending on how sweet they are. Let rest at room temperature until a syrup forms, about 20 minutes. Split freshly baked biscuits in half, add a dollop of unsalted butter, then cover with generous spoonfuls of berries and their juice. Top with Chantilly Cream (p. 281).

Cream Scones

½ cup sugar

3¾ cups bread flour

2 Tbsp baking powder

2 tsp salt

2 Tbsp grated orange zest

1 cup dried sweetened cranberries

2½ cups heavy cream, chilled

Cooking spray for greasing

Egg wash (1 large egg whisked with 2 Tbsp heavy cream)

Makes 12 scones

Combine the sugar, flour, baking powder, and salt in a stand mixer fitted with the paddle attachment on medium speed until well blended, about 1 minute. Blend the orange zest and cranberries into the flour mixture. Add the cream and mix on medium speed until just combined.

Remove the dough from the mixer, pat into a 10-inch-diameter round ¼ inch thick, and divide into 12 equal wedges. Wrap in plastic and freeze until solid, at least 4 hours and up to 4 weeks.

Preheat the oven to 350°F. Lightly grease a baking sheet. Arrange the frozen scones on the baking sheet, brush with egg wash, and bake until golden brown, 35–40 minutes.

Let the scones cool on the baking sheet for a few minutes before transferring to a wire rack. Let cool completely before serving.

These scones develop a wonderful texture if the dough is frozen overnight. Freeze individual scones, and then bake as many as needed straight from the freezer to accompany breakfast, brunch, or dinner.

zesting and juicing citrus p. 69

preparing pans p. 70

Gingercake

1½ cups all-purpose flour plus extra for dusting

2 tsp ground ginger

1 tsp baking powder

½ tsp baking soda

1 tsp salt

8 Tbsp (1 stick) unsalted butter, at room temperature, plus extra for greasing

1 cup sugar

½ cup molasses

½ cup buttermilk

2 large eggs

Confectioners' sugar for dusting (optional)

Makes one 9-inch cake

Preheat the oven to 350°F. Grease and flour a 9-inch square baking pan. Sift the flour, ginger, baking powder, baking soda, and salt into a bowl and set aside.

Cream together the butter and sugar in a stand mixer fitted with the paddle attachment on low speed until light in texture, about 3 minutes. Add the molasses and buttermilk and continue beating until the mixture is evenly blended, 1 minute. Increase the speed to medium and cream until smooth and light, about 2 minutes.

Add the eggs one at a time, mixing on medium speed, beating well after each addition and scraping down the bowl with a rubber spatula as needed. Add the sifted dry ingredients and mix on low speed until the batter is evenly blended and smooth.

Spread the batter evenly in the prepared pan and bake until the edges shrink away from the pan and the center springs back when lightly pressed with a fingertip, about 45 minutes.

Let cool completely in the pan on a wire rack. Slice and serve, dusted with confectioners' sugar if desired.

Sweet, fragrant, and spicy, this cake is delicious for breakfast, during an afternoon coffee break, or as the conclusion to a simple family meal. It freezes well, and it can be warmed just before serving to bring out its distinctive spiced aroma.

The batter is a very light taffy color, but the finished cake will be quite dark.

preparing pans p. 70

the creaming mixing method p. 31

3 Cookies

From chocolate chunk cookies you have to break in half to fit into your glass of milk to delicately glazed and filled petits fours served with coffee, cookies are a universal favorite. While some cookies in this book are quite homey, containing just a few simple ingredients, others are elaborate affairs that come close to being confections.

Types of cookies

When the terms *drop, icebox, cutout, pressed, piped, bar, twice-baked,* and *stenciled* are used to describe cookies, they refer to the way the cookies got from the bowl onto the baking sheet. Drop cookies are shaped by simply dropping the dough from a spoon onto a baking sheet, while icebox cookies are shaped into a log and chilled, then sliced and baked (this was going on long before you could buy prepared sleeves of dough in the dairy case). The dough for cutout cookies is rolled out into a thin sheet, then cut with cookie cutters or a knife; sugar cookies, gingerbread, and some shortbread cookies are made this way.

If a cookie batter is soft enough, you can press it through a cookie press or pipe it through a pastry bag to give it a special shape; this is the method used for macaroons, madeleines, and spritz cookies. Bar cookies are made from soft batters that are spread in a pan before baking, then cut into individual cookies once baked. Twice-baked cookies are first shaped into a single, large log-shaped cookie, then baked and sliced. Once the cookies are cut into slices, you bake them a second time for a wonderful crisp texture, perfect for enjoying with coffee or tea, or, as the Italians traditionally enjoy their biscotti, with a dessert wine.

Very delicate cookies known as tuiles are made by spreading a batter in a thin layer in a stencil on a baking sheet. They bake quickly, and when they are removed from the oven, they can be rolled, curled, curved, or draped to make edible containers or elegant garnishes.

Cookie-mixing methods

Cookies can be made using a number of different mixing techniques. Many cookies, like certain quick breads and cakes, are made with the creaming mixing method (page 31). The technique, however, varies slightly when applied to oatmeal raisin cookies, for example, rather than muffins. The creaming step is purposely shortened in cookie recipes to minimize the amount they will rise in the oven. Even though cookies are essentially little cakes, most cookies should have a crisper exterior and a denser interior than cake. The shorter creaming time also means that the butter or shortening stays cooler longer. If the dough becomes too warm as you mix and shape it, the cookies may spread too much and run into each other. When the batter remains cool until it goes into the oven, cookies spread out at the correct rate, producing a thin, crispy edge and a softer, higher center. (Dough or batter for cookies that are intended to spread will contain a significant amount of butter to encourage this.)

The foam mixing method (page 33), used to make sponge and angel food cakes, is also used to make some cookies. Whipping eggs and sugar into a thick foam allows you to make a delicate cookie with very little flour. These cookies crumble less than those made by the creaming mixing method and have a delightful resilient texture; the Fudge Brownies in this book (page 97) and Anise Biscotti (page 104) are two examples from this chapter made using this technique.

Keeping cookies on hand

Dedicated cookie bakers know how to store the treats so that a fresh cookie is always available. The most important step in storing cookies is to let them cool completely on racks before you put them away. A good cookie jar or tin with a tight-fitting lid that makes the container airtight keeps plump cakelike treats like Chocolate Chunk Cookies (page 93) from becoming stale. If they start to dry out, you can put an apple slice, skin side down, in the cookie jar; take it out after a day or two. Because cookies contain a significant amount of sugar, which attracts moisture from the air, they can turn soggy or stick together. If cookies turn soft, carefully separate them and put them on an ungreased cookie sheet in a warm (300°F) oven for about 5 minutes. Very delicate cookies, such as tuiles, may need to be stored with a cushion of waxed or parchment paper between layers, both to prevent them from drying and to keep them from jostling around in the tin and breaking under their own weight. Once bar cookies are cut into pieces, they keep best if they are individually wrapped; exposing the cut edges to the air dries them out. If you prefer, leave them uncut until you are ready to serve them. Most cookies freeze well for up to 2 or 3 months, wrapped well in plastic or stored in freezer bags or containers with tight lids. Remember to label the cookies and include the date they went into the freezer.

You can store unbaked cookies in the refrigerator or freezer as well, as long as they are made using the creaming mixing method. Form the dough into a log as you would for an icebox cookie, then wrap the log well. Cookie dough shaped and wrapped this way stays fresh in the refrigerator for up to 2 weeks. For longer storage, place the log in the freezer; because the dough has so much butter and sugar, the batter won't freeze into a solid block and you can slice the dough when it is still frozen and transfer it straight to the oven. Well-wrapped dough will last in the freezer for up to 4 months.

For many of us, eating cookies still warm from the oven is one of our fondest childhood taste memories. Having homemade cookies on hand can be a great source of culinary comfort.

Baking cookies

The way you prepare cookie sheets for baking can help ensure even cooking and browning and better texture overall.

1 Preparing cookie sheets

Not all cookie recipes require you to grease the pan, so be sure to read your recipe carefully before you start. Cooking sprays make it simple to apply a very even but light coating of oil that permits the cookies to spread slightly as they bake. You can also use a paper towel to rub the surface lightly with oil, softened butter, or shortening. Or, you can substitute parchment paper or heat-resistant and reusable silicone mats, sold under the name Silpat or Exopat. You'll also find these mats useful for making candy.

2 Baking in batches

Cookie sheets and baking pans should be at room temperature when you grease and fill them; otherwise, the cookie dough might start to bake even before it goes into the oven. This results in cookies' overspreading and overcooking.

If you are baking several batches of cookies and don't want to wait while the baking sheets cool down between each batch, portion out the remainder of the cookie batter on additional sheets of parchment paper. Then, you can quickly slide the baked cookies off the baking sheet and slide the parchment filled with unbaked cookies onto the sheet and put it right into the oven.

Check cookies for uneven doneness as they bake. Switch the pans from the bottom to the top rack and rotate them if necessary.

Making drop cookies

One of the keys to beautiful, evenly baked cookies is making sure that all the cookies on the sheet are approximately the same size.

1 Portioning evenly

To ensure that your cookies are all the same size, shape drop cookies by scooping up some batter with a spoon or an ice cream scoop. To use spoons, scoop up a portion of dough with one spoon, then use a second spoon of the same size (turned upside down) to push the dough off the first spoon and onto the cookie sheet. Fill the spoon with the same amount of dough each time. Ice cream scoops with thumb levers are great for portioning medium or large cookies. It's easiest to overfill the scoop and then scrape off the excess on the rim of the bowl. Leave plenty of room between the cookies to permit them to spread as they bake. A margin of 1–2 inches is generally suggested for soft, buttery drop cookies.

Making bar cookies

Evenly spreading batter for bar cookies improves the cookies' texture and appearance.

1 Filling pans and cutting carefully

Batters for bar cookies are softer than other cookie doughs, so they are baked in a pan with sides to give them a shape as they bake. Line the pan with parchment paper and leave an overhang on 2 sides of the pan to make it easy to remove the entire bar from the pan without breaking it. The batter should be spread to an even thickness; if the corners and edges aren't as thick as the center, they can overbake and dry out. Before you put the pan into the oven, use a rubber or offset spatula to spread the batter into an even layer, holding it nearly parallel to the surface of the batter as you work. For neat cookies, allow the bar to cool completely before you make any cuts. Use a knife with a thin blade to make square or rectangular pieces. You may need to wipe the blade clean between cuts for straight, clean sides.

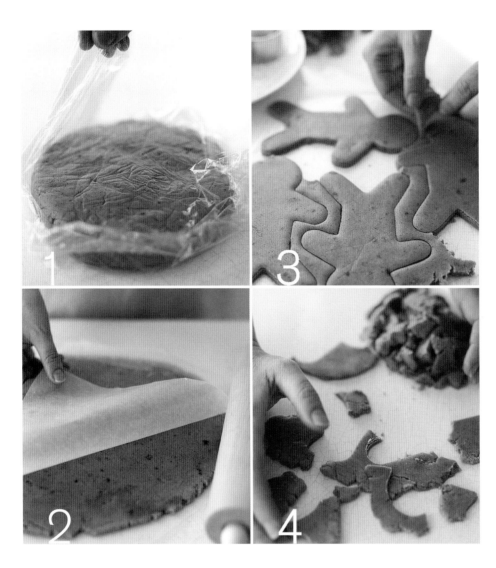

the dough for a smooth surface with no wrinkles. If the dough is warm or sticky after rolling it out, refrigerate it before you cut out the cookies. When you are ready to cut out the cookies, peel the paper from one side, then replace it lightly. Flip the dough over gently, then remove and discard the second sheet of paper. This makes it easy to lift the cutout cookies away from the paper without stretching and distorting them.

3 Cutting the cookies

Cut out cookie shapes freehand or use cookie cutters. To keep the dough from sticking to the cutters, keep a small dish nearby with flour, confectioners' sugar, or (for chocolate doughs) cocoa powder. Dip the cutting edge of the cutter and tap off any excess. Make clean cuts through the dough by pressing the cutter firmly into the dough and then lifting it away. Twisting the cutter will twist the dough and can cause the cookies to shrink or lose their shape.

4 Rerolling the scraps

The first rolling of any cookie dough generally makes the most tender cookies. To get the most cookies from the first rolling, cut out cookies as close together as you can so that you have as few scraps as possible. Gather up the scraps and gently knead them together just until they are blended evenly. Chill the dough before you roll it out again. You can reroll the scraps a third time, but usually the cookies become noticeably tougher after that.

Making cutout cookies

Sugar cookies and gingerbread cookies are made from stiff doughs. Follow these basic handling guidelines to turn out tender, delicate cookies.

1 Chilling the dough

To avoid overmixing the dough for rolled and cutout cookies, follow the mixing instructions in the recipe carefully. Some cookie doughs appear sandy or crumbly just after mixing, and others may look or feel sticky. Resist the temptation to continue mixing until the dough is very smooth, or the resulting cookies may be tough. Chill the dough for 10 minutes to firm it up before you start to roll it.

2 Rolling out the dough evenly

Some doughs are sturdy enough to roll out easily on a lightly floured work surface. Others are easiest to handle when you put them between 2 sheets of parchment or waxed paper. Turn the dough as you roll it to ensure that there are no thin or thick areas. Pull off the paper and reposition it as you roll

Making icebox cookies

Many drop cookies may also be rolled into a log and sliced before baking.

1 Rolling dough into a log

Chill soft doughs for icebox, or roll-and-slice, cookies for 10 minutes after mixing. Cut a large sheet of parchment or waxed paper and mound the dough evenly along the long side, leaving 2–3 inches at each end. Roll the paper around the dough, smoothing it into an even cylinder as you work.

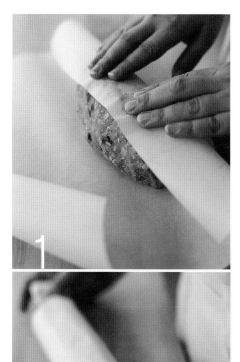

2 Compacting the dough log

When the paper is wrapped tightly around the dough, gather the ends and twist to compact the dough into a log. If the roll becomes flattened on one side, round it by gently rolling it again.

3 Slicing into cookies

Once the dough is rolled into a cylinder, chill it until it is very firm, about 30 minutes. It is easy to keep this dough on hand to make a fresh batch of cookies whenever you want them. You can store the dough in the refrigerator for up to 1 week. For longer storage, wrap the log in freezer-weight plastic wrap and secure it with tape so that the wrap won't come loose. Most frozen dough stays soft enough to slice directly from the freezer. Use a sharp knife to make crosswise slices ½–¾ inch thick. Refer to the instructions in your recipe for preparing the baking sheets and spacing the cookies on the sheets.

Making stenciled cookies

Stenciled cookies are among the most time-consuming to shape and bake, but the results are dramatic and rewarding.

1 Making stencils

If you don't have stencils at hand, trace a design onto a piece of cardboard or posterboard and cut it out with scissors or a craft knife. Line your baking sheet with parchment paper and set the stencil on the paper. Spoon a bit of chilled batter into the center of the design and use a small knife or offset spatula to spread it in an even layer to the edges of the stencil. Lift the stencil up and away from the sheet, scrape off any excess batter, and repeat. As soon as the cookies come out of the oven, you can drape them over rolling pins, dowels, or inverted cups. As they cool, they will set into that shape. Store the cookies in airtight containers layered with waxed paper to keep them from softening or shattering.

Finishing and decorating cookies

There are a number of ways to dress up a cookie with an elegant touch.

1 Finishing and shaping techniques

Cookies bake most evenly if they have neat, uniform shapes. Some drop cookies need to be flattened slightly before baking so that the centers and edges finish cooking at the same time. One simple technique is to use the back of a fork to gently press the dough into an even disk; dip the fork in sugar to prevent sticking. Or, use a flat-bottomed glass to slightly flatten cookies. Sometimes, cookies have peaks or tails that might turn too brown before the rest of the cookie finishes baking. To remove stray bits of dough, use a lightly moistened fingertip to press the dough back into place.

2 Brushing and garnishing

Some recipes specify brushing cookies lightly with egg wash, milk, or water before baking. This will add color and shine to the surface. The moisture on the surface also helps toppings like coarse or colored sugar, dried fruit, and nuts stay in place during baking. Use only enough egg wash for a light, even coating. When you add a garnish such as a glacé cherry or pecan half, gently press the garnish into the surface of the cookie with the most attractive side up.

3 Glazing

There are several ways to apply icings and glazes to cookies after baking. You can arrange the cookies on wire racks set over baking sheets and pipe icing or glaze over the surface to create a design (page 266), or simply drizzle the icing or glaze randomly. You can spread icing or ganache with a small palette knife to coat the cookie smoothly. Or, dip the cookie into melted chocolate or warm ganache and let the excess drain back into the bowl. Scrape the excess from the bottom and set the coated cookies on wire racks. Let the coating set until it is firm.

4 Sandwiching

Linzer Cookies (page 101) are a type of sandwich cookie made by gluing 2 cookies together with a thin layer of jam. Shape the cookies as uniformly as possible before baking, especially in thickness. Let the cookies cool completely before applying a layer of jam or other filling that is just thick enough to hold the cookies together, but not so thick it oozes out the sides. Spread the filling so that it doesn't quite reach to the edge of the cookies; the filling will spread when you press the cookies together.

Oatmeal-Raisin Cookies

Flourless cooking spray
for greasing

2¾ cups all-purpose flour

1½ tsp baking soda

1 tsp ground cinnamon

1 tsp salt

2 cups (4 sticks) unsalted
butter, at room temperature

2 cups tightly packed light
brown sugar

1 cup granulated sugar

2 tsp vanilla extract

3 large eggs

5 cups rolled oats

1¼ cups dark raisins

Makes 48 cookies

Preheat the oven to 375°F. Lightly spray cookie sheets with cooking spray or line them with parchment paper. Sift the flour, baking soda, cinnamon, and salt into a bowl and set aside.

In a stand mixer fitted with the paddle attachment, cream together the butter, sugars, and vanilla extract on medium speed until smooth and light in texture, 2 minutes. Add the eggs one at a time, beating well after each addition. On low speed, mix in the dry ingredients, oats, and raisins until just combined. Scrape down the bowl as needed to blend evenly. Chill the dough for 10 minutes.

Divide the dough into 4 equal pieces and roll each piece in waxed or parchment paper to make a 12-inch-long log about 2 inches in diameter. Refrigerate until firm enough to cut, about 30 minutes. Slice each log into 12 pieces and place the slices on cookie sheets in even rows, spacing the cookies about 2 inches apart. In batches, bake until the cookies are cracked on top but still slightly moist, rotating the pans as necessary to bake evenly, 14–15 minutes. Transfer to wire racks and let cool completely.

Rolled oats, or old-fashioned oats, are made from oats that are steamed slightly to soften them, then flattened between rollers. Quick-cooking oats are also steamed and rolled, but are cut into three or four pieces before they are flattened. Both old-fashioned and quick-cooking rolled oats can be used in cookie recipes with no significant change to texture. Steel-cut oats are not steamed; they are not used in cookies or similar preparations, since they require a relatively long time and large amount of water to soften properly.

baking cookies p. 89

making icebox cookies
p. 91

Chocolate Chunk Cookies

Flourless cooking spray
for greasing

2½ cups all-purpose flour

1 tsp baking soda

1 tsp salt

1 cup (2 sticks) unsalted butter,
at room temperature

1 cup granulated sugar

¾ cup tightly packed light
brown sugar

2 large eggs, at room
temperature

1 tsp vanilla extract

2 cups bittersweet chocolate
chunks or chips

Makes 48 cookies

Preheat the oven to 375°F. Lightly spray cookie sheets with cooking spray or line them with parchment paper. Sift the flour, baking soda, and salt into a bowl and set aside.

In a stand mixer fitted with the paddle attachment, cream together the butter and sugars on medium speed until light in texture and smooth, about 2 minutes. Add the eggs one at a time and the vanilla extract and blend until incorporated. On low speed or by hand with a wooden spoon, mix in the sifted dry ingredients and the chocolate chunks. Scrape down the bowl as needed to blend evenly.

Use 2 serving spoons to drop the dough onto the prepared baking sheets, spacing them about 2 inches apart. If desired, slightly flatten the cookies before baking. In batches, bake until the cookies are cracked on top but still slightly moist, rotating the pans as necessary to bake evenly, 14 minutes. Transfer the cookies to wire racks and let cool completely.

Sweetened dried cherries, chopped nuts (pecans, walnuts, macadamias, or hazelnuts), toffee bits, or different types of chocolate (white chocolate, milk chocolate) can all be added to this simple cookie recipe.

making drop cookies
p. 89

Mudslide Cookies

Flourless cooking spray
for greasing

¾ cup plus 2 Tbsp cake flour

1 Tbsp baking powder

⅛ tsp salt

1 Tbsp powdered instant coffee

1 Tbsp boiling water

1 tsp vanilla extract

7 oz unsweetened chocolate,
coarsely chopped

6 oz bittersweet chocolate,
coarsely chopped

8 Tbsp (1 stick) unsalted butter

7 large eggs

2¾ cups sugar

2 cups chopped walnuts

1½ cups bittersweet chocolate
chips

Makes 24 large cookies

Preheat the oven to 350°F. Lightly spray cookie sheets with cooking spray or line them with parchment paper.

Sift the flour, baking powder, and salt into a bowl and set aside.

Combine the instant coffee and boiling water to make a paste. Blend in the vanilla extract.

Melt the unsweetened chocolate, chopped bittersweet chocolate, and the butter in a saucepan over low heat or in a bowl in the microwave in 15- to 20-second intervals. Gently stir to blend.

In a stand mixer fitted with the whisk attachment, beat together the eggs, sugar, and coffee paste mixture on high speed until light in texture and thick, 6–8 minutes. Add the chocolate mixture with the machine running on medium speed. On low speed, mix in the dry ingredients until just blended. Mix in the walnuts and chocolate chips until blended. Scrape down the bowl as needed during mixing to blend evenly.

Using a ¼-cup measure as a scoop, fill it with dough, level it, and drop the dough onto a prepared cookie sheet, leaving 3–4 inches between the cookies.

In batches, bake the cookies until they are cracked on top but still slightly moist, rotating the pans as necessary to bake the cookies evenly, 14 minutes. Allow the cookies to cool slightly on the baking sheet before transferring them to wire racks to cool completely.

Mudslide cookies get their name because the batter is very soft, almost pourable. They get their rich coffee flavor from a coffee paste made by blending instant coffee with a little hot water. Instant coffee is made by either dehydrating or freeze-drying freshly brewed coffee. Instant espresso has a deeper and slightly more bitter taste than coffee. It may also be used in this recipe.

melting chocolate p. 242

baking cookies p. 89

Citus Shortbread

Flourless cooking spray
for greasing

2 cups all-purpose flour plus
extra for dusting

1 cup cornstarch

1 tsp salt

1½ cups (3 sticks) unsalted
butter, at room temperature

1¼ cups confectioners' sugar

2 Tbsp grated orange zest

1 Tbsp grated lemon zest

Makes about 30 cookies

Preheat the oven to 350°F. Lightly spray cookie sheets with cooking spray or line them with parchment paper. Or, spray a shortbread mold or stamp evenly with cooking spray and dust very lightly with flour.

Sift the flour, cornstarch, and salt into a bowl and set aside.

In a stand mixer fitted with the paddle attachment, cream the butter on medium speed until light in texture and smooth, 2 minutes. Add the confectioners' sugar and orange and lemon zests; cream until light and smooth, scraping down the bowl with a rubber spatula as needed, about 2 minutes. On low speed, mix in the sifted dry ingredients until just blended. Scrape down the bowl as needed during creaming and mixing to blend evenly.

To make molded shortbread: Pack the dough into the prepared mold and run a rolling pin over the surface a few times to fill the mold completely. Prick the surface with the tines of a fork. Cover and chill for 30 minutes before baking.

To make cutout or stamped shortbread: Roll out the dough on a lightly floured work surface to ¼-inch thickness, sprinkling with flour as needed to prevent sticking. (Alternatively, roll out the dough between sheets of parchment or waxed paper.) Cut into 3 x 2–inch rectangles and place on the prepared cookie sheets about 1 inch apart. If desired, prick the cookies with the tines of a folk to create a decorative pattern. To make stamped cookies, press the prepared stamp into each cookie and remove quickly. Use a paring knife to trim the edges. Cover and chill for 30 minutes before baking.

Bake until the edges of the shortbread are a very light gold, rotating the pans as necessary to bake evenly, 20 minutes for cutouts or 30 minutes if baked in a mold. Transfer to wire racks and let cool completely before serving.

Shortbread cookies originated in Scotland in the sixteenth century. The "short" in the cookies' name refers to the rich and crumbly texture that butter produces in a dough by literally shortening the gluten strands in flour. While these cookies were originally made with oatmeal, today they are more often made with only wheat flour. The classic round shape and crimping around the edges of the cookie are meant to represent the sun and its rays. The cookie was traditionally served at New Year's festivals.

zesting and juicing citrus
p. 69

making cutout cookies
p. 90

Fudge Brownies

Flourless cooking spray
for greasing

¾ cup (1½ sticks) unsalted
butter

4 oz unsweetened chocolate,
chopped

2 large eggs

1⅓ cups sugar

2 tsp vanilla extract

¼ tsp salt

¼ cup cake flour, sifted

¾ cup coarsely chopped
toasted walnuts

Makes 9 brownies

Preheat the oven to 350°F. Lightly spray a 9-inch square baking pan with cooking spray or line it with parchment paper, leaving an overhang on 2 sides to help remove the brownies from the pan.

Melt the butter and chocolate in a saucepan over low heat or in a bowl in the microwave in 15- to 20-second intervals, stirring and blending gently with a spoon.

In a stand mixer fitted with the whisk attachment, whip the eggs, sugar, vanilla extract, and salt together on high speed, scraping down the bowl with a rubber spatula as needed, until thick and light in color, 4–5 minutes.

While stirring, pour some of the egg mixture into the melted chocolate mixture to lighten it, then pour the chocolate mixture into the remaining egg mixture and blend on medium speed, scraping down the bowl as needed. Mix in the flour and nuts on low speed until just blended. The batter will be very wet. Pour the batter into the prepared pan and spread evenly.

Bake until a skewer inserted into the center of the brownies comes out with a few moist crumbs still clinging to it, rotating the pan as necessary to bake evenly, 30–40 minutes. Allow the brownies to cool completely in the pan on a wire rack. Use the parchment overhang to help unmold the brownie bar, then cut into 3-inch-square pieces.

Brownies are often distinguished as either "cake" or "fudge" style, a reference to the texture of the baked brownie. This recipe makes a rich, moist, fudgy brownie, soft from edge to edge.

Determining when these brownies are done is a little tricky. To get the correct fudgy texture, you have to ignore the usual visual cues and remove them from the oven when the center still appears slightly wet.

melting chocolate p. 242

making bar cookies
p. 89

toasting nuts p. 138

VARIATION

Glazed Brownies

Brownies may be glazed with Chocolate Glaze (page 284) after removing from the pan, but before they are cut into squares (opt to line the pan with parchment paper to facilitate removing them uncut). The brownies should be refrigerated after glazing for approximately 30 minutes to allow the glaze to set before cutting them into individual bars.

Rugelach

2 cups all-purpose flour plus extra for dusting

¼ tsp salt

1 cup (2 sticks) unsalted butter, at room temperature

8 oz cream cheese, at room temperature

1½ cups pecans, toasted (p. 138)

⅓ cup chopped semisweet chocolate (optional)

1 cup raspberry jam

Flourless cooking spray for greasing

⅓ cup cinnamon sugar (½ tsp ground cinnamon mixed with ⅓ cup sugar)

Egg wash (1 large egg whisked with 2 Tbsp cold milk or water)

Makes 64 cookies

Sift the flour and salt into a bowl and set aside.

In a stand mixer fitted with the paddle attachment, cream together the butter and cream cheese on medium speed, about 2 minutes. On low speed, mix in the sifted dry ingredients until just combined. Scrape down the bowl as needed to blend evenly. Wrap the dough tightly and chill until firm, 15–20 minutes.

On a lightly floured surface, roll the dough to an even thickness of 1 inch and fold in thirds, like a letter. Wrap the dough and let it rest for at least 1 hour and up to overnight in the refrigerator.

To make the filling, combine the pecans and chocolate, if using, in a food processor and chop, pulsing the machine on and off, until an even, coarse paste forms. Transfer to a bowl and blend in the jam.

Preheat the oven to 375°F. Lightly spray cookie sheets with cooking spray or line them with parchment paper.

Divide the dough into 4 equal pieces and roll each into a 10-inch round. Spread one-fourth of the filling over each round, sprinkle with 1 Tbsp of the cinnamon sugar, then cut each into 16 wedges. Roll the wedges up starting with the wide end.

Brush each wedge lightly with egg wash and sprinkle with some of the remaining cinnamon sugar.

In batches, bake until the cookies are a light golden brown, rotating the pans as necessary to bake evenly, 25–30 minutes. Transfer to wire racks and cool completely before serving.

Rugelach is one of several shaped cookies popular throughout central Europe, particularly in Russia and Austria. The pecans may be replaced with walnuts. Both nuts are commonly used in baking; if possible, purchase unsalted raw (unroasted) nuts and keep them in the freezer, where they will last for up to 1 year. The oils in nuts cause them to turn rancid over time, and they have a shorter shelf life if stored in a cupboard.

making cutout cookies p. 90

sifting p. 71

Almond Spritz Cookies

Cooking spray for greasing

⅓ cup packed almond paste

2 large egg whites (divided use)

¾ cup (1½ sticks) unsalted butter, at room temperature

⅔ cup sugar

1 Tbsp light rum

1 Tbsp grated lemon zest

½ tsp vanilla extract

1¾ cups cake flour, sifted

¼ cup raspberry jam

Makes about 24 cookies

Preheat the oven to 375°F. Lightly spray cookie sheets with cooking spray or line them with parchment paper. In a stand mixer fitted with the paddle attachment, blend the almond paste with 1 egg white on low speed until smooth, 2 minutes. Add the butter and sugar and cream together on high speed until smooth and light in texture, 2 minutes. Add the remaining egg white, rum, lemon zest, and vanilla extract; mix on medium speed until completely blended. On low speed, mix in the flour until just blended. Scrape down the bowl as needed to blend evenly.

Press the batter onto the prepared cookie sheets with a cookie press, making 1½-inch diameter cookies spaced about 1 inch apart. Use your thumb to indent the center of each cookie. Using a parchment paper cone (page 268), pipe a small amount of raspberry jam into each indentation.

In batches, bake the cookies until light golden brown, 10 minutes. Transfer to wire racks and cool completely before serving.

Doughs for spritz cookies are firm enough to hold their shape but soft enough to force through a cookie press. Assemble the cookie press (also called a cookie gun) according to the manufacturer's instructions and then fill the cylinder with dough. Using the tamper, press the dough through the opening directly onto the prepared baking sheet. Use even pressure to make cookies of uniform size. Alternatively, the dough can be piped with a pastry bag.

baking cookies p. 89

piping p. 266

Gingerbread Cookies

3¾ cups all-purpose flour plus extra for dusting

2 tsp baking soda

1½ tsp ground ginger

1½ tsp ground allspice

1 tsp salt

8 Tbsp (1 stick) unsalted butter, at room temperature

¾ cup tightly packed dark brown sugar

½ cup honey

2 large eggs

Flourless cooking spray

1 recipe Royal Icing (p. 281) (optional)

Makes about 24 cookies

Preheat the oven to 375°F. Lightly spray cookie sheets with cooking spray or line them with parchment paper. Sift together the flour, baking soda, ginger, allspice, and salt and set aside.

In a stand mixer fitted with the paddle attachment, cream together the butter, brown sugar, and honey on medium speed until smooth, about 2 minutes. Add the eggs and mix until smooth and light, another 2–3 minutes. Add the sifted dry ingredients and mix on low speed just until the dough is evenly mixed.

Turn the dough out onto a lightly floured work surface, pat into an even disk, and chill for 10 minutes. Roll out the dough to a ¼-inch thickness. Use 5½-inch cookie cutters to cut out cookies. Transfer to the prepared cookie sheets, spacing them about 1 inch apart.

Bake the cookies until they are firm, 12–14 minutes. Transfer to wire racks and let cool completely before decorating, if desired. Bake the remaining dough in batches as directed.

For information on decorating gingerbread cookies with Royal Icing, see page 281. These cookies are also candidates for being pressed with cookie stamps to create relief designs; see page 96.

making cutout cookies p. 90

finishing and decorating cookies p. 92

Linzer Cookies

3¾ cups cake flour plus extra for dusting

2 tsp baking powder

1 tsp ground cinnamon

1½ cups (3 sticks) unsalted butter, at room temperature

1½ cups granulated sugar

1 Tbsp vanilla extract

3 large eggs

½ cup finely ground ladyfinger crumbs (p. 127)

2 cups (6 oz) finely ground toasted hazelnuts

Flourless cooking spray for greasing

Confectioners' sugar for dusting

1¼ cups raspberry jam

Makes about 30 cookies

Sift the flour, baking powder, and cinnamon into a bowl and set aside.

In a stand mixer fitted with the paddle, cream together the butter, granulated sugar, and vanilla extract on medium speed, scraping down the bowl as needed, until smooth and light in color, about 2 minutes. Add the eggs one at a time and mix on medium speed, beating well after each addition and scraping down the bowl with a rubber spatula as needed. Add the flour mixture, ladyfinger crumbs, and hazelnuts all at once, mixing on low speed until just blended.

Turn the dough out onto a floured work surface. Divide the dough into 4 equal pieces, wrap tightly, and refrigerate for at least 1 hour before rolling.

Preheat the oven to 375°F. Lightly spray cookie sheets with cooking spray or line them with parchment paper.

Working with one piece of dough at a time, on a lightly floured board or between 2 sheets of parchment paper, roll out the dough into an even rectangle ¼ inch thick. Cut as many circles as possible from the piece using a 3-inch fluted cutter. Transfer the circles of dough to a prepared baking sheet, placing them about 1 inch apart, and return them to the refrigerator while you roll and cut out the remaining dough.

Remove the chilled circles from the refrigerator and cut a hole from the center of half of them with a plain 1½-inch round cutter to make rings. Gather together the 1½-inch rounds and the other remaining scraps and roll out and cut again, chilling as necessary to keep the dough cool enough to work with.

In batches, bake until the cookies are light golden brown, rotating the pans as necessary to bake evenly, 12 minutes. Transfer to wire racks and cool completely.

Sift confectioners' sugar over the cool rings. Spread 1 tsp jam on each whole cookie circle. Carefully center a sugar-dusted ring on top of each jam-filled bottom and press gently to secure.

These eye-catching, rich-tasting cookies are made from a nut-enriched dough, similar to pastry dough. You can make them any size you like, from the 3-inch cookies we suggest here to miniature cookies, perfect for an assortment to give or serve at the holidays. Replace the raspberry jam with red currant, blackberry, apricot, or damson plum jam, if you prefer, or make them with an assortment of jam flavors and colors.

toasting nuts p. 138

finishing and decorating cookies p. 92

Coconut Macaroons

1 cup sugar (divided use)

2 Tbsp all-purpose flour

3½ cups shredded unsweetened coconut

6 large egg whites

2 tsp grated orange zest

2 tsp vanilla extract

Makes about 32 macaroons

Preheat the oven to 350°F. Line cookie sheets with parchment paper.

Combine ⅓ cup of the sugar with the flour and set aside.

Combine the remaining ⅔ cup sugar, the coconut, and egg whites in the top of a double boiler. Heat over simmering water, stirring constantly, until the mixture thickens and holds together, about 3 minutes. Remove from the heat. Fold in the flour mixture, orange zest, and vanilla extract.

Drop tablespoonfuls of batter onto the prepared cookie sheets, spacing them 2 inches apart and shaping into neat mounds as needed.

In batches, bake until the macaroons are a light golden brown on the outside but still soft enough to give slightly when you press them lightly with your fingertip, 20–25 minutes. Transfer the macaroons, still on the parchment paper, to a wire rack to cool completely. When cool, they will lift off easily.

Macaroons, whether coconut- or almond-based, are moist, tender cookies held together and lightened with egg whites. Since the cookie's name can be traced to an Italian word for paste (which also gave us the term "macaroni"), it seems likely that they come from an Italian baking tradition. However, some have speculated that they were first made in a French monastery in the 1700s.

using a double boiler p. 167

zesting and juicing citrus p. 69

Madeleines

Flourless cooking spray for greasing

⅔ cup all-purpose flour plus extra for dusting

½ tsp baking powder

4 Tbsp (½ stick) unsalted butter, at room temperature

⅓ cup sugar

½ tsp finely grated lemon zest

1 large egg

2 Tbsp cold whole or low-fat milk

¼ tsp vanilla extract

Makes 48 madeleines

Preheat the oven to 375°F. Coat madeleine pans lightly with cooking spray and dust with flour.

Sift the flour and baking powder together and set aside.

In a stand mixer fitted with the paddle attachment, cream together the butter, sugar, and lemon zest on medium speed until smooth and light in texture, 5 minutes. In a separate bowl, combine the egg, milk, and vanilla extract. Add the egg mixture to the butter mixture in 2 or 3 additions, beating well after each addition. On low speed, mix in the sifted dry ingredients. Scrape down the bowl as needed during creaming and mixing to blend evenly.

Fill a pastry bag fitted with a ½-inch wide plain pastry tip with the batter. Pipe into the prepared madeleine pans, filling the molds to the top. In batches, bake until the edges of the madeleines turn a medium golden brown, rotating the pans as necessary to bake evenly, 12 minutes. Turn the madeleines out onto a wire rack while they are still warm, and let cool before serving.

Madeleine pans are tinned steel sheets with scalloped impressions for molding madeleines. They are available with or without a nonstick coating and have 12 to 40 cavities. The impressions may be large or small.

piping p. 266

preparing pans p. 70

Anise Biscotti

Flourless cooking spray for greasing

2 cups all-purpose flour

1 tsp baking soda

3 large eggs

¾ cup sugar

1 tsp salt

1 tsp anise extract

1¼ cups whole almonds

2 Tbsp aniseed

Makes 32 biscotti

Preheat the oven to 300°F. Lightly spray a cookie sheet with cooking spray or line with parchment paper.

Sift the flour and baking soda into a bowl and set aside.

In a stand mixer fitted with the whisk attachment, whip the eggs, sugar, salt, and anise extract on high speed until thick and light in texture, about 4 minutes. On low speed, mix in the dry ingredients until just incorporated. Add the almonds and aniseed and blend until evenly combined, scraping down the bowl with a rubber spatula as needed.

Form the dough into a 4 x 16–inch log and place on the prepared cookie sheet. Bake until light golden brown, 30 minutes. Remove the pan from the oven and let cool for 10 minutes.

Lower the oven temperature to 275°F. Using a serrated knife, cut the log crosswise at a 45-degree angle into ½-inch-thick slices. Place the sliced cookies on 2 unlined cookie sheets and bake until golden brown and crisp, 40 minutes. Transfer the cookies to wire racks and let cool completely.

Biscotti are crisp, dry cookies that can trace their lineage back to the hardtack that sailors and other adventurers ate on long journeys. Christopher Columbus included hardtack in his ships' stores when he sailed west across the Atlantic. The sweet, dry cookies we know today as biscotti are thought to have originated in the town of Prato in the Italian region of Tuscany. They are often served with coffee or cappuccino, or with a glass of Vin Santo, one of Tuscany's famous sweet dessert wines. Their crisp texture makes biscotti perfect for dunking without disintegrating.

baking cookies p. 89

VARIATIONS

Orange Biscotti

Replace the anise extract with 1 Tbsp orange juice concentrate and 2 Tbsp finely grated orange zest and omit the aniseed.

Chocolate Espresso Biscotti

Replace ½ cup of the flour with cocoa powder, replace the anise extract with 1 Tbsp powdered instant espresso dissolved in 1 Tbsp hot water, and replace the aniseed with ½ cup chocolate chips or chopped bittersweet chocolate.

Petits Fours

Flourless cooking spray for greasing

¾ cup packed almond paste

14 Tbsp (1¾ sticks) unsalted butter, at room temperature

¾ cup granulated sugar

5 large eggs, lightly beaten

¾ cup cake flour, sifted

⅓ cup seedless raspberry jam

Confectioners' sugar for dusting

¾ cup packed marzipan

Chocolate Glaze (p. 284)

1 cup (3 oz) finely ground toasted almonds (optional)

Makes about 50 petits fours

Preheat the oven to 375°F. Lightly spray a 15 x 10–inch jelly roll pan with cooking spray or line with parchment paper.

In a stand mixer fitted with the paddle attachment, cream together the almond paste, butter, and granulated sugar on medium speed until light in texture and smooth, 5 minutes. Add the eggs in 2 or 3 additions, beating well after each addition. On low speed, mix in the flour until just blended. Scrape down the bowl as needed during creaming and mixing to blend evenly.

Spread the mixture evenly in the prepared jelly roll pan and bake until golden brown, about 20 minutes. Let cool completely on a wire rack, then turn the cake out of the pan.

Trim the edges from the cake. Cut the cake crosswise into 3 equal strips (you will have 3 approximately 5 x 10–inch strips). Place one of the strips on an inverted baking sheet and spread with one-third of the jam. Place a second strip on top, gently press to adhere, and spread with half of the remaining jam. Place the third and final layer on top, gently press to adhere, and spread with the remaining jam.

Lightly dust a work surface with confectioners' sugar and roll out the marzipan to ¹⁄₁₆-inch thickness. Place the marzipan on top of the final layer of jam, smooth to adhere, and trim the excess marzipan from the edges using a very sharp knife.

Wrap tightly and refrigerate until firm, about 20 minutes. Cut the chilled cake into 1-inch squares. Place the petits fours on a wire rack set over a cookie sheet. Ladle the glaze on top, using a small offset spatula to make sure the sides are completely coated. If using, press the ground toasted almonds onto the sides of each glazed petit four.

What is the difference between almond paste and marzipan? Both are made from the same basic ingredients: blanched almonds, egg whites, and sugar. However, marzipan usually contains more almonds for a stiffer consistency. The greater quantity of almonds gives marzipan a stronger flavor and aroma than almond paste. It also makes marzipan well suited to rolling and shaping, as needed for these small cookie-like cakes, whose name means "little ovens" in French.

toasting nuts p. 138

glazing a cake p. 264

Lace Nut Tuiles

4 Tbsp (½ stick) unsalted butter, at room temperature

⅓ cup sugar

1 Tbsp finely grated orange zest

¼ cup light corn syrup

3 Tbsp all-purpose flour, sifted

¾ cup coarsely ground pecans, walnuts, or almonds

Makes about 24 tuiles

Preheat the oven to 350°F. Line cookie sheets with parchment paper or silicone baking mats. Prepare a stencil by cutting a 3-inch round, oval, or other shape out of a piece of stiff cardboard or thin plastic. Have an offset spatula as well as shaping implements such as a rolling pin, dowel, or teacups ready to use once the batter is mixed.

In a stand mixer fitted with the paddle attachment, cream together the butter, sugar, and orange zest on medium speed until light in texture and smooth, 5 minutes. Gradually add the corn syrup, mixing until smooth. Reduce the speed to low and mix in the flour and nuts. Scrape down the bowl as needed during creaming and mixing to blend evenly. Chill the batter for a few minutes.

Place your stencil on the lined baking sheet. Drop a small amount of batter into the cutout using a spoon. Spread the batter with an offset spatula to evenly fill in the stencil. Pick the stencil up and move it to an empty part of the cookie sheet, repeating as necessary. (It is easiest to shape and bake only a few tuiles at a time. Keep the batter chilled.)

In small batches, bake until the tuiles are an even light brown color, rotating the pans as necessary to bake evenly, 7 minutes. Remove from the oven and allow to set until the tuiles are firm enough to lift but still pliable and warm, about 1 minute. Drape the tuiles over the rolling pin, dowel, inverted teacups, or other implement to shape, or let them cool flat on a wire rack. Once they are completely cooled, they can be served or stored in an airtight container between layers of waxed paper.

The name for these delicate stenciled cookies means "tiles" in French. They are traditionally shaped to look like the terra-cotta tiles used on roofs throughout the Mediterranean. The batter is soft enough to spread in a thin layer. You can spread the batter into simple circles freehand, or create special shapes by using a stencil. While you may be able to find stencils in shops or through catalogs that specialize in baking equipment, you can easily make your own by tracing a shape onto a thin but stiff piece of plastic (such as the lid from a yogurt container) or cardboard to produce stars, ovals, hearts, even Christmas trees.

making stenciled cookies p. 91

baking cookies p. 89

4 Pies and Tarts

Pies and tarts are enjoyed around the world, but in the United States, we've adopted pie—a sweet dish cut into wedges and sometimes served with ice cream—as a national favorite. In other parts of the world, especially Europe, tarts are more common than pies and can be sweet or savory.

While pies are commonly baked in plates or pans with sloping sides and may have a top crust or lattice topping, tarts are made in molds, often with removable bottoms, that have relatively short and straight sides compared to the typical pie pan. Free-form tarts and galettes, like the Rustic Peach Galette in this chapter (page 127), are baked without a tart pan, directly on a baking sheet. A single layer of crust forms the bottom of the tart, and the sides are gently rolled or folded back on the fruit. A quiche is often baked in a tart pan, although it can also be baked in a pie pan. Tarte Tatin, a simple dessert from France, is a cross between a deep-dish pie and an upside-down cake; a fruit filling (originally apple) is piled into a pan already used to make a rich caramel, then is topped with a crust and baked until tender and golden. Another category of baked goods we've included here is cobblers and crisps, popular fruit desserts made with topping layers rather than crusts.

Making the crust

The notion of making pastry dough from scratch can induce instant panic in some, but it doesn't have to be that way. If you are a novice baker, ease into the process by making pies that don't require a flaky pie dough. Try a recipe that calls for a simple crumb crust, like Key Lime Pie (page 122). And although we tend to think of tarts as more elegant than pies, making a short tart dough (page 117) may be a good stepping-stone toward making flaky pie dough (page 116) if you already have experience making creamed cookies. Short dough crusts are more forgiving, both in mixing and in shaping.

Principles of pastry making

Pastry doughs turn the rules of making yeast doughs upside down. Here, you want ingredients to be cold or cool, not warm. Instead of working the dough until it is springy and resilient, the baker strives for as little agitation as possible in order to produce a tender crust.

Different types of pastry dough call for different ratios of ingredients and different mixing techniques. The rubbing mixing method (page 32) results in a flaky pastry that practically shatters at the touch of a fork and contrasts delightfully with rich, juicy fruits. Keeping the dough cold is the most important step in making flaky pastry. If it gets too warm, the fat in the dough starts to melt and blend with the flour, much like a batter. If the dough remains properly cold, the fat and flour will remain in many separate little layers, resulting in a desirable flaky texture. In order to keep the dough cold, chill the ingredients, the equipment, and the finished dough. Work quickly when you cut the fat into small pieces and distribute it throughout the flour before adding the water. Using ice-cold water is another critical factor in making a good flaky pie dough. The cold water keeps the starch granules in the flour from starting to swell and turn gummy.

The creaming mixing method (page 31) creates a cookie-like pastry that holds creamy fillings and custards without turning soggy. The more sugar and butter you add to the dough, the more like a cookie it becomes, since the butter and sugar are creamed together before the flour is added. These doughs rich in butter and sugar are known to French pastry chefs as *pâte sucrée* and *pâte sablée* ("sugary" and "sandy" pastry), but we know them as short dough, or tart dough.

For a good texture, work pie or tart dough as little as possible as you mix it, especially once the liquid is added. To avoid overdeveloping the gluten in the flour, good pie dough recipes keep water to a minimum and instruct you to add it a little at a time. The amount of water as well as the amount the dough is worked both play a role in keeping the dough tender. Rather than stirring, use a pushing and smearing motion against the side of the bowl to mix the water into the flour. This "rubbing" motion is what gives the technique its name. When the ingredients are combined properly, pie and tart doughs develop just enough gluten to bake into a crust that holds its shape during slicing and serving, but not so much that it feels tough. Letting the dough rest in the refrigerator after mixing also allows the gluten to relax so that you can roll out the dough without having to stretch it as much. A dough that has rested properly won't tend to shrink as it bakes.

Fat for doughs

Each type of fat that may used in making pie crust offers different advantages. Butter gives crusts a rich flavor and a deep gold color because of the milk solids it contains, but it also slightly increases the overall moisture content of the recipe; adding more liquid can result in a slightly tougher crust. Butter tends to warm up easily at room temperature, so it can be a bit trickier to work with, too; you may need to add a few extra teaspoons of flour to a recipe. Vegetable shortening doesn't add much flavor but contributes great flakiness; many bakers like to combine equal amounts of shortening and butter to get the best of both worlds. Lard has a distinctive aroma and also contributes extra flakiness to doughs. It is often used in doughs for savory pastries, like quiche. However, lard's flavor may be too intense for some palates.

Pie and tart fillings

Almost any fruit can be used to fill a pie, but you need to prepare the fruit according to its type or the season for a successful outcome. Peaches, pears, and apples can simply be sliced and tossed with sugar, spices, and a bit of a thickener to make a great filling. Very moist fruits such as berries tend to bake into a very loose, liquid filling—even when mixed with thickeners like cornstarch—but the filling sets up slightly as it cools. Some fruits are best cooked before they are used in a filling; cherries, for example, make a good pie when they are simmered until tender and the cooking liquid is properly thickened with a bit of cornstarch and tapioca. To capitalize on the naturally rich taste of ripe bananas, fold them together with a cooled pastry cream filling. Citrus juice and zest are excellent flavors for a custard or curd filling, and they provide a zesty counterpoint of flavor in a wide range of pies and tarts.

Custard fillings, including those used to make quiche or nut fillings, are blended and then baked in a crust that has already been partially baked. This seals the crust so that it does not become soggy. Puddings, cream fillings, and curds are prepared and cooled, and then added to a fully baked crust.

Baking pies and tarts

Preheat your oven to the temperature a recipe recommends and position the baking rack in the center of the oven. Some pies need a hot oven, whereas others are best baked at a moderate temperature. The recommended temperature should produce a pie with a perfectly cooked filling, a crisp and appealing bottom crust, and a top crust or edge that turns a delicate golden brown.

Fill the pan to just below the rim if you are using a custard so that it won't slosh out on the way to the oven. Fruit fillings are generally mounded high in the center of the pan and sealed with a top crust. They will settle as they bake. To keep the filling from bursting through the crust, a few vents are cut into the top crust. To make it easy to get the pie in and out of the oven, as well as to prevent any drips from spilling on the oven's floor, set the pie pan directly on a baking sheet.

Warm pies are wonderful, but be sure to allow pies and cobblers with juicy fruit fillings (especially berry fillings) to rest for 15 minutes after being removed from the oven so that the juices will thicken enough to let you cut the pie into slices. Custard and nut pies also need to set so that they can be cut into slices. Keep pies well wrapped in the refrigerator once they are baked, especially if they have a cream- or egg-based filling. The pastry may lose some of its texture in the refrigerator, so rewarm pies in a low oven until the crust is dry and crisp again before serving them the second day.

The edge of a pie or tart crust can start to brown before the rest of the crust or filling is fully baked. Check the pie frequently and if the crust is browning around the edges too quickly, use thin strips of aluminum foil to cover the edge of the crust.

The oven temperatures and times in the recipes that follow are based upon a 9-inch aluminum pie pan with 1½-inch sides. Pies in glass pie plates tend to brown more quickly, so you should lower the oven temperature by 25 degrees. Pie pans with dark surfaces also cause quicker browning; keep an eye on the pie as it bakes and lower the oven temperature if necessary.

Cutting pies and tarts into neat, even wedges can be a challenge. To set yourself up for success on the hardest piece to remove—the first piece—be sure that your pie pans are very clean before filling them, and that the oven is properly preheated. Once pies and tarts are baked, allow them to rest for the recommended length of time. The dessert plates should be positioned right next to the pan. Using a sharp serrated knife, cut gently through every layer of the crust and the filling to completely separate that piece from the rest of the pie. Gently insert a wedge-shaped pie server or an offset spatula to completely release the crust from the pan and keep the server level as you lift the piece up and onto the plate.

Making pie dough

The way you combine the ingredients for pie dough affects the results.

1 Cutting fat into flour

Recipes for pie dough and certain other dishes call for using the rubbing mixing method (page 32) to combine fat into dry ingredients. Whether you use a food processor, a pastry blender, or two table knives, the goal is to cut the chilled fat into small bits and disperse it throughout the flour, rather than blending the fat and flour into a smooth mixture.

2 Adding cold water

The water for pie dough should be ice cold, so fill a glass with ice and water before you start making the pastry. Add the water to the dough gradually, just a tablespoon or so at a time, and stop when the dough is just moist enough to hold together when a handful is squeezed. Instead of stirring the dough, use a table fork to push and smear the dough, rubbing it against the side of the bowl, to keep the pastry tender.

3 Gathering the dough

Turn the pie dough out onto a lightly floured work surface and gently gather and press it into a ball. Flatten the dough into a disk (or 2 disks for a double-crust pie), wrap with plastic, and refrigerate the dough long enough for the fat to firm up slightly and the gluten to relax, at least 20 minutes.

Making tart dough

Tart crust has a more cookie-like texture than pie crust, and is a little more prone to crumbling as you work with it.

1 Making tender dough

The butter for short dough should be just warm enough to cream without becoming too soft and melting. Cream the butter with the sugar just until it is smooth; overmixing the butter and sugar will make the butter too soft. If you are adding eggs or other liquid ingredients, let them sit at room temperature 10–12 minutes before you start mixing. Very cold ingredients could harden the butter into small flecks. Stir in dry ingredients by hand using a folding motion or with the paddle attachment; mix only long enough to make an evenly moistened but still very rough-looking dough. Turn the short dough out onto a lightly floured work surface and gently gather and press it into a disk. Wrap it with plastic, and refrigerate the dough long enough for the fat to firm up enough to roll and shape easily, at least 20 minutes.

Rolling out dough

Keep dough cool and avoid overworking it as you roll it out.

1 Rolling out chilled dough
Chilling dough makes it easier to roll out and prevents sticking. If the dough is very cold, however, let it rest at room temperature for 5–10 minutes to make rolling easier. Dust the work surface, rolling pin, and top of the dough very lightly with flour. Roll in all directions with even, steady pressure to make a large circle. For a bottom crust, roll the dough into a round 4 inches wider in diameter than the top of your pan. For a top crust, the round need be only 2 inches wider than the pan. To keep the round of dough even and to prevent sticking, periodically give the dough a quarter turn.

2 Transferring dough to the pan
When transferring rolled-out dough to a pie pan, avoid stretching or tearing it. One way to do this is to fold the dough round loosely in half. Lift the folded dough with both hands, position it over one side of the pan, then carefully unfold the dough. An alternative method is to roll the dough loosely around the rolling pin. Position the loose edge at the edge of the pan and unroll the dough directly into the pan.

3 Easing the dough into the pan
Avoid stretching the dough as you fit it into the pan so that it doesn't shrink as it bakes. Gently lift the edges of the dough just enough to ease it into the corners of the pan. Adjust the position of the dough if you need to so that the overhang extends evenly all around the rim. Use the pads of your fingertips or a small ball of scrap dough to gently push the dough into position. If you are using a fluted tart pan, press the dough against the sides to fill in the fluting for the best appearance after unmolding.

4 Patching and trimming
The richer and more tender your dough, the more likely it is to tear. To patch a hole, take a small piece from the outer edge, moisten it lightly with water, and position it over the hole. Roll or press the patch gently into place. To repair a tear, lightly moisten the edges and use your fingertips to gently press the dough back together, stretching as little of the surrounding dough as possible.

Finishing pies

The following techniques develop the best possible flavor, texture, and color in a finished pie.

1 Fluting

Pinching or pressing a decorative border into the rim of a single-crust pie keeps the pastry from slipping down into the pan as the pie bakes. After the dough is fitted into the pan, trim away any excess dough, leaving a 1-inch overhang all around the pie. To make an even rim, tuck the overhang back under the crust.

A classic way to flute is to press the dough between the index finger and thumb of one hand on the inside edge of the rim and the index finger of the other hand on the outer edge to make a scalloped edge. You can also press with the back of a fork to make a decorative effect on a single-crust pie edge.

2 Cutting vents

Cutting vents in a top crust before baking allows steam to escape and keeps fruit juices from bursting out around the edges. To cut vents, make short cuts in a neat arrangement around the pie; these cuts can mark the cutting line for slices, or they can be given a special decorative shape. You can use round, scalloped, or specialty cutters to remove small shapes from the top crust before you transfer the dough to the filled pie. Vents should be evenly spaced. If you cut just one vent, position it in the center of the pie.

3 Crimping

Sealing the edge of a double-crust pie keeps the top and bottom crusts from separating as the pie bakes. Brush the edge of the bottom crust with water, milk, or egg wash before setting the top crust in place. Press the top crust down lightly onto the bottom crust to make a firm seal. Trim the excess dough from both the top and bottom layers so that the edges of the dough are almost even with the edges of the pan. You can press with the tines of a fork to seal the crusts together, or use your fingertips to pinch the edges together (and then flute if desired).

4 Finishing the pie crust

Brushing your pie crust with egg wash gives it a deep golden color and shine. You can also sprinkle a washed crust with sugar before baking. The sugar will caramelize as the pie bakes, making the crust shiny and crunchy. Always check the dough's temperature before you put it into the oven. If the dough doesn't feel cool to the touch, refrigerate the pie for 10–15 minutes.

Making a lattice top

A lattice top is a nice alternative to a full top crust. If you'd rather not weave the strips as described below, simply brush them with egg wash or milk and lay them on top of the pie in a grid pattern.

1 Placing the vertical strips

Roll a round of dough about 2 inches larger in diameter than the top of your pie pan so that the strips will be the right length. Using a pastry cutter or a knife, cut an even number of strips from the rolled-out dough. Fourteen to sixteen strips, each about ½ inch wide, will make a generous lattice top for a 9-inch pie. Transfer every other strip to the pie top, arranging them vertically about ½ inch apart.

2 Placing the horizontal strips

Fold every other strip on the pie top in half, back on itself. Now lay another strip on the pie perpendicularly, so that it crosses every other strip still laid across the top. Lay the folded strips flat again; the horizontal strip is under every other strip now, and the weave is started. Continue to fold back alternate vertical strips, laying the horizontal strips ½ inch apart, to complete the lattice.

3 Continuing the weave

As you lay down the horizontal strips, it is easiest to work from the center of the pie to the edge closest to you, then turn the pie around and weave from the center to the opposite edge. Brush all of the strips evenly and lightly with egg wash, trim the overhang, and crimp the edges to finish the crust.

Blind baking

Baking an unfilled pastry shell, called blind baking or prebaking, sets its shape and texture so that the filling won't make the crust soggy.

1 Lining and weighting the dough

Once the dough is in the pan and the edges are fluted, use a dough docker or table fork to poke holes in the bottom and sides of the pastry. This will help keep the pastry from puffing up as it bakes. Line the pastry with parchment paper or aluminum foil and add enough pie weights to fill the pan from one-third to one-half full. If you don't have pie weights, dry beans or rice work just as well.

2 Partial blind baking

Bake the pastry in a preheated 400°F oven until the dough is just set and the edges look dry, 10–12 minutes. When the weights and paper or foil are removed, the center of the dough may still appear moist, which is fine. After cooling, the crust is ready to fill with a custard mixture or other liquid filling and return to the oven to finish baking.

3 Full blind baking

If you are filling a pie with a precooked filling such as a mousse or cream, finish blind baking the pastry crust by returning it to the oven after you have removed the weights and paper. For added protection against wet fillings, brush the crust lightly on the bottom and sides with a whisked egg white. Bake until the dough appears evenly dry and the edges are just starting to brown, another 6–8 minutes, or a total of 16–20 minutes' baking time. Let the crust cool completely before adding chilled fillings and serving.

Pie Dough

Single-Crust Pie

1⅓ cups all-purpose flour plus
extra for dusting

½ tsp salt

½ cup (1 stick) cold unsalted
butter, lard, or vegetable
shortening, diced (or a
combination of butter and
shortening equal to ½ cup)

¼ cup ice water, or as needed

Double-Crust Pie

2⅔ cups all-purpose flour plus
extra for dusting

1 tsp salt

1 cup (2 sticks) cold unsalted
butter, lard, or vegetable
shortening, diced (or a
combination of butter and
shortening equal to 1 cup)

½ cup ice water, or as needed

Makes enough for one 9-inch pie

Stir together the flour and salt with a fork to blend. Cut the fat into the flour using a food processor, pastry blender, or 2 knives. (For pies with liquid fillings like custard or cooked fruit fillings that are thickened with cornstarch or tapioca, the bits of fat should be evenly small, and the mixture should resemble a coarse meal. This will result in a mealy pie crust, which is less likely to become soggy as the pie bakes. For pies to be filled with fruit or another nonliquid filling, leave some bits of fat in larger pieces, about the size of a small pea, for a crisp and flaky texture in the baked crust.)

Drizzle a few tablespoons of the ice water over the surface of the flour mixture and quickly rub the water into the flour. Continue to add the water, a tablespoon or so at a time, just until it holds together when you press a handful of it into a ball. The dough should be evenly moist, not wet, and shaggy or rough in appearance.

Turn the dough out onto a lightly floured work surface. Gather and press the dough into a ball. For a double-crust pie, divide the dough into 2 roughly equal pieces. Pat each ball into an even disk, wrap well, and let chill in the refrigerator for 20 minutes.

Working with one disk at a time, unwrap the dough, place it on a lightly floured work surface, and scatter a little flour over the top. Alternatively, place the dough between sheets of parchment or waxed paper. Roll out the dough for the bottom crust of a pie into an even round about 13 inches in diameter (for a 9-inch pie pan). It should be about ⅛ inch thick.

Fold the dough in half or roll it loosely around the rolling pin, and gently lift and position it over the pan. Unfold or unroll and ease the dough into the pan without stretching, making sure that the pan sides and the rim are evenly covered. Press the dough gently against the sides and bottom. Trim the overhang to 1 inch.

For a single-crust pie, tuck the dough overhang under itself and flute the edges. Fill and bake the pie according to recipe directions.

For a double-crust pie, roll out the second piece of dough into an 11-inch round (for a 9-inch pie pan), then cut vents in it. Fill and finish the pie according to recipe directions.

Pie doughs may be soft and difficult to roll either because they are too warm, a little too much water has been added to the dough, or the weather is humid. Using marble pastry boards and rolling pins, which stay cooler than the surrounding air, helps to keep pastry dough cool and easy to handle. Another trick to working with pie dough is to roll out the dough between two pieces of parchment or waxed paper. This technique can be a big help to the novice baker.

making pie dough p. 112

rolling out dough p. 113

Tart Dough

8 Tbsp (1 stick) unsalted butter, at room temperature

¼ cup sugar

½ tsp vanilla extract

1 large egg yolk

1½ cups cake flour, sifted, plus extra for dusting

Makes enough for eight 3-inch tartlets or one 8-inch tart

In a stand mixer fitted with the paddle attachment, cream together the butter, sugar, and vanilla extract on medium speed, scraping down the bowl with a rubber spatula as needed, until smooth and light in color, about 2 minutes. Add the egg yolk and blend until smooth, 1–2 minutes more. Add the flour all at once, mixing on low speed or by hand with a wooden spoon until just blended, about 30 seconds. The dough will be very crumbly when you remove it from the mixer. Use a gentle touch to press the dough into a disk, being careful not to work it so much that the pastry becomes tough.

Wrap the dough tightly and refrigerate for 20 minutes before rolling.

When you are ready to roll out the dough, place it on a lightly floured work surface or between sheets of parchment or waxed paper. Scatter a little flour over the top of the dough and roll it out into an even round about 2 inches larger in diameter than your tart pan. To transfer the dough to the tart pan, fold the dough in half or roll it loosely around the rolling pin, and gently lift and position it over the pan. Unfold or unroll and ease the dough into the pan. Trim the overhang cleanly by rolling over the edge with a rolling pin. Gently use your fingertips to press the dough against the sides and bottom of the pan. Fill and finish the tart according to recipe directions.

When a fat is combined with flour to make a dough, it produces the effect of surrounding (in effect, greasing) the proteins in the flour and keeping them from joining into long, stretchy strands of gluten. The shorter the strands, the more tender the baked good. Baking fats' ability to do this explains why they are sometimes referred to as "shorteners." The doughs produced this way are often called "short doughs."

making tart dough p. 112

rolling out dough p. 113

VARIATIONS

Chocolate Short Dough

Reduce the amount of flour to 1⅓ cups and stir together with 3 Tbsp cocoa powder.

Almond Short Dough

Reduce the amount of butter to 6 Tbsp and add 3 Tbsp almond paste along with the butter. Reduce the amount of sugar to 3 Tbsp. If desired, replace half of the vanilla extract with almond extract.

Cherry Pie

1 recipe double-crust Pie Dough
(p. 116)

Cherry Filling

2 Tbsp tapioca pearls

2 Tbsp cornstarch

1 cup sugar

½ tsp ground cinnamon

¼ tsp freshly grated nutmeg

¼ tsp salt

1¼ lb pitted fresh, thawed
frozen, jarred, or canned sour
cherries (about 3 cups), juice
reserved if using jarred or
canned

1 tsp freshly squeezed lemon
juice

2 Tbsp unsalted butter

Egg wash (1 large egg whisked
with 2 Tbsp milk or water) for
brushing

Makes one double-crust 9-inch pie

Roll out the pie dough rounds and use one round to line a 9-inch pie pan as directed on page 113. Keep the dough-lined pan and other round chilled while you prepare the filling.

To make the cherry filling, blend the tapioca and cornstarch with about ¼ cup water. (Add just enough water for a thick, soupy consistency.) Set aside.

Stir together the sugar, cinnamon, nutmeg, and salt in a saucepan. Add 1 cup reserved cherry juice or water and the lemon juice and bring to a boil over high heat. Gradually add the tapioca mixture while whisking constantly, and return to a boil. Add the cherries and simmer for another minute. Remove the pan from the heat and stir in the butter. Transfer the filling to a shallow bowl or pan and cool in the refrigerator until completely chilled, about 30 minutes; stir the filling occasionally to cool more quickly.

Preheat the oven to 425°F. Pour the cherry filling into the dough-lined pan, mounding it slightly. Cut the other dough round into 14–16 strips about ½ inch wide using a paring knife or pastry wheel. Brush the rim of the pie shell with egg wash. Lay half of the strips over the filling, parallel to each other and spaced about ½ inch apart. Fold every other strip in half, back on itself. Lay down another strip perpendicular to the first set, so that it crosses every other strip already on the pie, then unfold the folded strips. Fold back the alternate strips and add another perpendicular strip, then unfold the strips. Continue folding back alternate strips and weaving a lattice. Work from the center to the edge of the pie, then rotate the pie 180 degrees and repeat the process on the second side. Trim the excess dough so that the edges of the dough are almost even with the edges of the pan and crimp the edges to seal. Brush the lattice evenly and lightly with egg wash.

Place the pie on a baking sheet and transfer to the oven. Bake just until the crust is lightly browned and the filling is heated through, 30–40 minutes. Let the pie rest for at least 20 minutes before cutting in pieces. Serve warm or at room temperature.

Cherries fall into two major categories: sour (also called "tart" or "pie" cherries) and sweet. Two of the more familiar varieties of sour cherry are Montmorency and Morello. These cherries are smaller and rounder than sweet ones, with a brighter red color. Sour cherries have a short season and don't keep well once picked. When sour cherries are at the peak of ripeness, most of them are picked and pitted, then immediately frozen, canned, or dried. Sometimes, processed sour cherries have already been sweetened, so be sure to check the label. Sweet cherries can be used to replace some or all of the sour cherries, as long as you cut back a little on the amount of sugar.

using a starch slurry
p. 263

making a lattice top
p. 115

Apple Pie

1 recipe double-crust Pie Dough
(p. 116)

¾ cup tightly packed light
brown sugar

¼ cup all-purpose flour

¾ tsp ground cinnamon

¼ tsp freshly grated nutmeg

6–7 medium apples, peeled,
cored, and thinly sliced (about
7 cups)

2 Tbsp freshly squeezed
lemon juice

3 Tbsp unsalted butter, diced

Egg wash (1 large egg whisked
with 2 Tbsp milk or water) or
milk for brushing

Makes one double-crust 9-inch pie

Roll out the pie dough and use one round to line a 9-inch pie pan
as directed on page 113. Keep the dough-lined pan and other round
chilled while you prepare the filling. Preheat the oven to 425°F.

Stir together the brown sugar, flour, cinnamon, and nutmeg in a small
bowl. In a large bowl, sprinkle the apples with the lemon juice. Scatter
the sugar mixture evenly over the apples, and toss to evenly coat all
the slices.

Mound the apples in the dough-lined pan, making the center higher
than the sides. Dot the top evenly with the pieces of butter. Brush the
rim of the pie shell with egg wash. Cut vents in the other dough
round and place the round over the filling. Press together the top
and bottom edges to seal, trim the excess dough so that the edges of
the dough are almost even with the edges of the pan, and then crimp
or flute the edges. Brush the top lightly with egg wash.

Place the pie on a baking sheet and transfer to the oven. Bake the
pie for 15 minutes. Lower the oven temperature to 350°F and bake,
rotating the pan as necessary for even browning, until the top crust
is golden brown and the apples feel tender when pierced through the
steam vents with a knife, 40–45 minutes. Remove the pie from the
oven and cool on a wire rack. Let the pie rest for 20 minutes before
slicing. Serve warm or at room temperature.

*Note: For a decorative effect, use the second half of the dough to create
lattice strips (page 115) instead of a top crust, or roll out the pastry
scraps, cut out leaf shapes, and place them on top of a vented crust.*

Brimming with fragrant
fruit, this irresistible pie
is the perfect example of
the American classic. For
baking, select an apple
that holds its shape well.
Northern Spy, Rome Beauty,
and Golden Delicious are
good choices, but ask your
greengrocer for some
suggestions for other apple
types that may be available
in your part of the country.
This recipe also works well
with pears, peaches, plums,
and apricots. If desired, add
nuts or plumped raisins or
currants for added texture
and flavor. Serve warm
with a scoop of vanilla ice
cream, or with slices of
Cheddar cheese.

finishing pies p. 114

making pie dough p. 112

VARIATION

Deep-Dish Apple Pie

Pour the filling into a lightly greased 9-inch pie pan with sides 2½ inches
deep. You may need an additional apple or two; if so, add another
2 tablespoons of brown sugar and an additional tablespoon of flour, plus
more ground spice to taste. Top with a single pie dough round with
vents cut into it. Seal the crust to the edge of the pan with egg wash and
bake as directed. To serve, spoon the pie directly from the pie pan.

Deep dish pies generally
have no bottom crust. The
lack of a liquid-absorbing
bottom crust will make the
pie soupier.

Mincemeat Pie

1 recipe double-crust Pie Dough
(p. 116)

3 medium apples, peeled, cored,
and cut into eighths

¼ cup apple cider

1 cup dark raisins

1 cup currants

⅔ cup tightly packed light
brown sugar

3 Tbsp diced candied lemon
peel (p. 245)

5 Tbsp diced candied orange
peel (p. 245)

¼ tsp ground cinnamon

¼ tsp freshly grated nutmeg

¼ tsp ground allspice

⅛ tsp ground ginger

3 Tbsp unsalted butter

2 Tbsp bourbon

⅔ cup chopped toasted walnuts
or pecans

Egg wash (1 large egg whisked
with 2 Tbsp milk or water) or
milk for brushing

Makes one double-crust 9-inch pie

Roll out the pie dough and use one round to line a 9-inch pie pan as directed on page 113. Keep the dough-lined pan and other round chilled while you prepare the filling.

Place the apples and the apple cider in a large pot over medium heat and warm. Add the raisins, currants, brown sugar, and candied lemon and orange peels and bring to a boil. Reduce the heat and simmer, stirring occasionally, for 1 hour. Add the spices to the mixture and return to a boil. Remove the pot from the heat and stir in the butter and bourbon. Let cool completely.

Preheat the oven to 425°F. Add the nuts to the apple mixture and stir to incorporate thoroughly. Pour the mincemeat filling into the dough-lined pie pan, mounding the center slightly higher than the sides. Brush the rim of the pie shell with egg wash. Cut vents in the other dough round and place the round over the filling. Press together the top and bottom edges to seal, trim the excess dough so that the edges of the dough are almost even with the edges of the pan, and then crimp or flute the edges. Brush the top lightly with egg wash.

Place the pie on a baking sheet and transfer to the oven. Bake for 10 minutes. Lower the oven temperature to 350°F and bake until the top crust is golden brown, rotating the pan as necessary for even browning, 40–45 minutes.

Remove the pie from the oven and cool on a wire rack. Let rest for at least 20 minutes before slicing. Serve warm or at room temperature.

Sweet and savory mincemeat pies (also called mince pies or shred pies) have been part of English and American winter holiday traditions for centuries. The original mincemeat pies of the seventeenth century featured finely minced or shredded lean beef cooked together with suet (beef fat), nuts, sugar, spices, and fresh and dried fruits. Making pie was a common practice for extending the life span of meats and making them more palatable. By the middle of the nineteenth century, however, the lean meat had been eliminated from mincemeat pie or replaced by nut meats, often walnuts or pecans.

toasting nuts p. 138

Key Lime Pie

Graham Cracker Crust

Cooking spray for greasing

10–12 graham crackers

2 Tbsp sugar

4 Tbsp (½ stick) unsalted butter, melted

Key Lime Filling

4 large eggs

One 14-oz can sweetened condensed milk

½ cup freshly squeezed lime juice, preferably from Key limes

½ cup sugar

Makes one 9-inch pie

Preheat the oven to 350°F. Lightly spray a 9-inch pie pan with cooking spray.

Crumble the crackers into a food processor or blender and grind to the consistency of a fine, even crumb. Or, place the crackers in a resealable plastic bag, pressing out as much air as possible before sealing the bag. Pulverize by rolling with a rolling pin. Measure out 1½ cups crumbs. Stir together the crumbs, the sugar, and the butter in a small bowl. Use the bottom of a glass or a similar flat surface to press the crumbs down into a compact layer in the prepared pan, covering the bottom and sides of the pan.

Bake the crust for 5 minutes. Remove the pie pan from the oven and allow the crust to cool while preparing the filling.

Separate the eggs (page 138). Set aside.

Combine the condensed milk, the lime juice, and the egg yolks and blend. Pour the filling into the prepared crust and bake until the filling is set, about 15 minutes. Prepare the meringue while the filling bakes.

Beat the egg whites and the sugar in a mixing bowl just until blended. Heat this mixture over simmering water (or in the top of a double boiler; see page 167) until the sugar is completely dissolved and the mixture reaches about 110°F on a candy thermometer. Remove from the heat. Whip the warmed egg white mixture until stiff, glossy peaks form.

Remove the baked pie from the oven and increase the oven temperature to 450°F. Spread the meringue over the lime filling while the filling is still hot, making certain to cover the crust with the meringue to help keep the meringue from shrinking. Make decorative peaks and swirls over the surface.

Return the pie to the oven just long enough to lightly brown the meringue, about 5 minutes.

Chill for at least 2 hours before slicing and serving. Serve chilled.

Key limes grow in Florida and throughout the Caribbean. They are smaller and have a mellower flavor and more juice than the more commonly available Persian lime. You'll need about 4 Key limes to yield ½ cup juice. If you cannot find fresh Key limes, make the pie with juice from Persian limes (the limes commonly found in supermarkets). When you use Persian limes, you may want to add an additional tablespoon of sugar to the filling mixture to balance the tartness. A meringue topping is traditional, but if you prefer, you can replace the meringue with a layer of Chantilly Cream (p. 281).

making meringue p. 219

zesting and juicing citrus p. 69

Banana Cream Pie

1 recipe single-crust Pie Dough (p. 116)

2 cups Pastry Cream (p. 282), chilled

2 medium-ripe bananas

½ cup heavy cream

Chocolate shavings for garnish (p. 269)

Makes one single-crust 9-inch pie

Preheat the oven to 400°F. Roll out the pie dough and use it to line a 9-inch pie pan as directed on page 113. Fully blind bake the crust. Let cool to room temperature in the pan on a rack.

Stir the pastry cream until it is light and smooth. Thinly slice the bananas into the pastry cream. Fold the bananas and pastry cream together and spread in an even layer in the cooled pie shell.

Whip the cream in a chilled bowl until it holds a medium peak when the whisk is turned upright. Spread or pipe the whipped cream on top of the pie and garnish with chocolate shavings. Chill for at least 2 hours before slicing and serving.

Bananas for a cream pie should be completely ripe but still firm enough to hold their shape when sliced. If you make sure the sliced bananas are completely covered with pastry cream as you mix and fill the pie, they won't turn brown.

whipping cream p. 263

blind baking p. 115

Sweet Potato Pie

1 medium sweet potato

1 recipe single-crust Pie Dough (p. 116)

1 cup whole or low-fat milk

1 large egg

2 large egg yolks

6 Tbsp sugar

1 tsp ground cinnamon

¼ tsp ground allspice

¼ tsp ground mace

¼ tsp salt

2 Tbsp unsalted butter, melted

Makes one single-crust 9-inch pie

Preheat the oven to 400°F. Bake the sweet potato until it is very tender, about 50 minutes. While it is still very hot, peel the sweet potato and push the flesh through a food mill or sieve. Set aside.

Meanwhile, roll out the pie dough and use it to line a 9-inch pie pan as directed on page 113. Partially blind bake the crust. Cool to room temperature in the pan on a rack. Lower the oven temperature to 350°F.

Blend the milk, egg, and egg yolks until evenly combined. Add the sweet potato, sugar, spices, salt, and butter and whisk until smooth. Place the cooled partially baked pie crust on a baking sheet and pour in the filling. Bake until set, 35–40 minutes.

Remove the pie from the oven and let cool on a wire rack. Let the pie rest for at least 20 minutes before slicing. Serve warm or at room temperature.

The sweet potato, a member of the morning glory family, is noted for its moist flesh and high sugar content. Sweet potatoes and true yams are not related; yams may grow to be much larger than sweet potatoes, and are starchier than sweet potatoes and less sweet. However, many supermarkets in this country use the term "yam" to label what are actually orange-fleshed sweet potatoes.

rolling out dough p. 113

blind baking p. 115

Pecan Pie

1 recipe single-crust Pie Dough (p. 116)

1½ cups toasted pecan halves

½ cup tightly packed light brown sugar

2 Tbsp all-purpose flour

¾ cup light corn syrup

3 large eggs, lightly beaten

4 Tbsp (½ stick) unsalted butter, melted and cooled

2 tsp vanilla extract

¼ tsp salt

Makes one single-crust 9-inch pie

Preheat the oven to 400°F. Roll out the pie dough and use it to line a 9-inch pie pan as directed on page 113. Partially blind bake the crust. Let cool to room temperature in the pan on a rack before filling. Keep the oven temperature at 400°F.

Spread the nuts in an even layer over the bottom of the partially baked pie shell. Stir the brown sugar and flour together in a mixing bowl until well blended. Add the corn syrup, eggs, butter, vanilla extract, and salt and blend well. Pour the mixture over the nuts, disturbing the nuts as little as possible.

Place the pie on a baking sheet and bake until the center is softly set, 30–35 minutes. Let the pie rest for at least 20 minutes before slicing. Serve warm or at room temperature.

Leaving the pecan halves whole gives the pie a wonderful appearance, but may make it more difficult to slice the pie neatly. You can also chop them coarsely. Bakers in the South, where pecan pies are a holiday tradition, often seek out pure "golden" cane syrup, made from mature sugar cane, to replace the more widely available corn syrup used in our recipe.

toasting nuts p. 138

blind baking p. 115

Almond and Pine Nut Tart

1 recipe Almond Short Dough (p. 117)

1 cup packed almond paste

½ cup granulated sugar

1 tsp vanilla extract

3 large eggs

⅓ cup all-purpose flour

½ cup pine nuts

2 Tbsp confectioners' sugar

Makes one 8-inch tart

Preheat the oven to 400°F. Roll out the dough and use it to line an 8-inch tart pan with a removable bottom as directed on page 113. Partially blind bake the crust. Cool to room temperature in the pan on a rack.

In a stand mixer fitted with the paddle, mix the almond paste, the granulated sugar, the vanilla extract, and 1 egg on medium speed until smooth, 2 minutes. Add the remaining eggs one at a time, beating well after each addition. Add the flour and mix until incorporated, scraping down the bowl to blend evenly.

Spread the filling evenly in the tart shell and sprinkle with the pine nuts. Bake until the top of the tart is golden brown, 35 minutes. Cool completely on a wire rack. Unmold the tart before slicing. Serve at room temperature, lightly dusted with confectioners' sugar.

Pine nuts are the edible seeds of various species of pine trees, commonly known as piñons or pinyons. The exact species of tree varies. In North America, pine nuts were an important food for some early Native Americans. They were picked from the ground, taken from squirrel caches, or extracted by hand from the cones. Throughout southern Europe, *pignoli* nuts are now cultivated. They may be salted or used in confections. The terms *pignoli,* piñon, pinyon, and pine nut may be used in the market interchangeably.

making tart dough p. 112

blind baking p. 115

Rustic Peach Galette

1 recipe single-crust Pie Dough (p. 116)

4 medium peaches

2 Tbsp freshly squeezed lemon juice

2 Tbsp granulated sugar

1 tsp ground cinnamon

¼ tsp freshly grated nutmeg

½ cup crumbled ladyfingers

Egg wash (1 large egg whisked with 2 Tbsp cold milk or water)

2 Tbsp coarse sugar

Makes one 8-inch tart

Roll the pie dough as directed on page 113 into a 10-inch round. Keep it chilled while you prepare the peaches.

Preheat the oven to 400°F. Use a paring knife to cut and pull away the skin from the peaches; if the skin is very firmly attached, score the skin in an X on the blossom (or bottom) end of the fruit, lower the peaches into rapidly boiling water for 30 seconds, then transfer to a bowl of ice water to stop the cooking. The skin will pull away easily. Remove the pits. Cut into slices ¼ inch thick and toss with the lemon juice, granulated sugar, cinnamon, and nutmeg.

Transfer the dough round to a parchment paper–lined baking sheet. Sprinkle with the ladyfinger crumbs, leaving a 2-inch border free of crumbs. Pile the peaches on top of the cake crumbs, in the center of the dough round, leaving the border unfilled. Brush a 1-inch perimeter of the dough round lightly with egg wash. Fold the dough edges in toward the center, over the fruit, pinching and folding it to seal the edge and create a pleated border.

Brush the pleated edge of the pastry lightly with egg wash and sprinkle with coarse sugar. Bake until the pastry is golden brown and the peaches hot and juicy, about 25 minutes. Remove the tart from the oven and cool on the pan on a wire rack for at least 20 minutes before slicing. Serve warm or at room temperature.

Note: You can substitute apples, sour cherries, apricots, or pears for the peaches.

While not essential, a layer of cake crumbs in a galette absorbs some of the juices from the fruit during baking so that the crust stays crisp. Cake crumbs are readily available in the bakeshop but a little harder to come by at home, so we call for ladyfinger crumbs in this recipe. You'll need about half of a 3- or 4-oz package. Look for ladyfingers in the cookie aisle, in the frozen foods section, or, especially in the summer, on display near the fresh fruit. Open the package to let them stale slightly before crumbling them with your hands or grinding them in a food processor.

making pie dough p. 112

finishing pies p. 114

Spinach and Goat Cheese Quiche

1 recipe single-crust Pie Dough (p. 116), made with lard if desired, rolled into an 11-inch round

2 Tbsp vegetable oil

½ cup finely diced onions

4 cups spinach leaves, stems and heavy ribs removed

½ tsp salt (divided use)

¼ tsp freshly ground pepper (divided use)

¾ cup heavy cream

2 large eggs

⅓ cup fresh goat cheese, crumbled

¼ cup grated Parmesan cheese

2 Tbsp chopped sun-dried tomatoes (about 4)

Makes one 9-inch quiche

Preheat the oven to 400°F. Roll out the dough and use it to line a 9-inch tart pan as directed on page 113. Partially blind bake the shell. Cool to room temperature in the pan on a rack before filling.

Lower the oven temperature to 350°F. Heat the oil in a large skillet over medium heat. Add the onions and sauté, stirring frequently, until translucent, 3–4 minutes. Add the spinach and toss until the the spinach wilts and turns a deep green, about 4 minutes. Remove from the heat. Season with ¼ tsp of the salt and ⅛ tsp of the pepper.

Whisk together the cream and eggs. Stir in the goat cheese, Parmesan, and sun-dried tomatoes. Season with the remaining ¼ tsp salt and ⅛ tsp pepper.

Spread the spinach mixture evenly over the crust. Add the custard mixture gradually, stirring it with a fork to distribute the filling ingredients evenly. Set the tart pan on a baking sheet and bake until a knife blade inserted in the center comes out clean, 40–45 minutes.

Remove the quiche from the oven and let cool on a wire rack for at least 20 minutes before slicing. Serve warm or at room temperature.

Goat cheese is one food that appears to have made the transition from trend to part of everyday cooking and dining. Although this recipe calls for soft fresh goat cheese, you can feel free to experiment with flavored or aged varieties of goat cheese. If you want an even greater goat cheese presence in this quiche, break up some additional cheese and dot it over the surface of the quiche before it goes into the oven to bake.

making pie dough p. 112

blind baking p. 115

Pineapple Tarte Tatin

1½ cups sugar

2 Tbsp light corn syrup

4 Tbsp (½ stick) unsalted butter

1 medium pineapple, peeled, cored, and cut into small dice (about 4 cups)

1 recipe single-crust Pie Dough (p. 116), rolled out to 10-inch round

Makes one 9-inch tart

Preheat the oven to 400°F. Combine the sugar and corn syrup in a 10-inch ovenproof skillet. Bring to a boil over high heat, stirring constantly, until all the sugar has dissolved. Cover and continue to boil for 1 minute. Remove the cover, reduce the heat to medium, and cook until the mixture is a rich golden brown, about 4 minutes. Add the butter and 2 Tbsp warm water (watch out for spattering). Stir until thoroughly blended and remove from the heat.

Scatter the pineapple in an even layer on top of the caramel mixture.

Place the dough round over the pan, tucking the edges down into the pan around the pineapple.

Bake until the crust is golden brown, 18–20 minutes. Remove from the oven and let rest for about 10 minutes before inverting onto a serving plate and slicing. Serve warm or at room temperature.

The Tatin sisters, who operated an inn in the Sologne region of France, made this dessert famous in the late nineteenth century. Pineapple, although less traditional than apples, responds beautifully to this treatment.

caramelizing sugar p. 171

rolling out dough p. 113

Passion Fruit Tart

1 recipe Tart Dough (p. 117)

2 oz bittersweet chocolate, melted (p. 242)

½ cup passion fruit juice

1 cup Pastry Cream (p. 282)

2 large egg whites

½ cup granulated sugar

Confectioners' sugar for dusting

Makes one 8-inch tart

Preheat the oven to 400°F. Roll out the dough and use it to line an 8-inch tart pan with a removable bottom as directed on page 113. Partially blind bake the crust. Cool to room temperature on a rack before filling. Brush the baked tart shell with the melted chocolate.

Stir the passion fruit juice into the pastry cream. Set aside.

Preheat the broiler. In a stand mixer fitted with the whisk, whip the egg whites on low speed until foamy, 2 minutes. Increase the speed to medium and gradually add the granulated sugar. Continue to whip on high speed until the meringue is glossy and holds medium peaks. Fold half of the meringue into the passion fruit mixture and pour into the prepared tart shell. Spread or pipe (page 266) the remaining meringue over the surface. Dust with confectioners' sugar.

Broil the tart just until the meringue browns slightly, about 4 minutes. Remove from the oven and let cool completely on a rack, about 2 hours, before slicing and serving. Serve the tart chilled or at room temperature.

Use a serrated knife or a cake-decorating comb to give the meringue a decorative finish. To vary the tart's flavor, replace the passion fruit juice with fresh lemon, lime, red currant, or other tart fruit juice.

making meringue p. 219

blind baking p. 115

Strawberry Cream Tart

1 recipe Tart Dough (p. 117)

½ cup strawberry jam

¼ cup melted chocolate (p. 242)
(optional)

2 cups Pastry Cream (p. 282)

2 pints fresh strawberries,
hulled, sliced if large

Makes one 8-inch tart

Preheat the oven to 400°F. Roll out the dough and use it to line an 8-inch tart pan as directed on page 113. Fully blind bake the crust. Cool to room temperature in the pan on a rack.

Heat the jam in a small saucepan over low heat until it is warm enough to strain through a fine-mesh sieve. Strain the jam into a small dish and keep warm (or rewarm in the microwave for a few seconds before using).

Brush the tart shell with the melted chocolate, if using. Spread the pastry cream in the tart shell in an even layer. Arrange the strawberries over the surface of the pastry cream; they should fill the entire tart shell so that no cream is visible.

Use a pastry brush to coat the strawberries very lightly with the warm jam. Let the glaze set for about 10 minutes in the refrigerator. If you are not serving the tart immediately, keep it covered and refrigerated for up to 12 hours.

If you have all the components prepared ahead of time—the pastry shell, the pastry cream, and the strawberries—you can put this tart together in a few minutes and serve it right away. Brushing the crust with chocolate keeps the crust from turning soggy, but even with the chocolate layer, this tart loses its wonderful texture contrast if it sits for more than 12 hours before you serve it.

making tart dough p. 112

blind baking p. 115

Raspberry Mascarpone Tart

1 recipe Chocolate Short Dough
(p. 117)

½ cup mascarpone cheese

¼ cup honey

¼ cup freshly squeezed lemon
juice

½ tsp vanilla extract

1 cup heavy cream

3 cups fresh raspberries

½ cup apple jelly

Makes one 8-inch tart

Preheat the oven to 400°F. Roll out the dough and use it to line an 8-inch tart pan with a removable bottom as directed on page 113. Partially blind bake the crust. Cool to room temperature in the pan on a rack.

Mix the mascarpone cheese with the honey, lemon juice, and vanilla.

Whip the cream in a chilled bowl until it holds a medium peak when the whisk is turned upright (page 263).

Fold the whipped cream into the mascarpone cheese mixture. Spread the filling in the cooled tart shell and spread into an even layer. Cover the filling with fresh raspberries.

Place the apple jelly in a saucepan and warm over low heat, stirring until completely melted. Brush the raspberries and the edge of the crust with the warm jelly. Chill for at least 2 hours before unmolding, slicing, and serving. Serve chilled.

Mascarpone is a rich triple-cream cheese, a specialty of the Lombardy region of Italy, where it is featured in both sweet and savory dishes. Although it is increasingly available in supermarkets and specialty food shops, you can produce a reasonable substitute by blending 4 oz of softened cream cheese with 2 Tbsp heavy cream.

making tart dough p. 112

blind baking p. 115

Lemon Shaker Tart

3–4 organic lemons

2 cups sugar

1 recipe double-crust Pie Dough (p. 116)

5 large eggs

Egg wash (1 large egg yolk whisked with 1 tsp milk or water) for brushing

Makes one double-crust 10-inch tart

Use a mandoline or a Japanese-style slicer to very thinly slice the lemons crosswise into rounds. As you slice the lemon, you'll expose the seeds. Use the tip of a paring knife to remove them. Measure out 2¾ cups thin lemon slices.

Combine the lemon slices with the sugar and toss to combine evenly. Cover the bowl and allow the mixture to rest at room temperature for at least 24 hours and up to 36 hours.

Preheat the oven to 450°F.

Roll out half of the dough into a 13-inch round and ease it without stretching into a 10-inch tart pan with a removable bottom, covering the sides and rim of the pan evenly and making an even overhang on all sides. Trim the overhang to ½ inch.

Using a slotted spoon, transfer the lemon slices to the tart pan, allowing as much of the syrup to drain back into the bowl as possible. Lightly beat the eggs and add them to the syrup left in the bowl and beat well. Pour this custard over the lemons.

Brush the rim of the dough lightly with the egg wash. Do not allow it to form pools in any depressions in the crust.

Roll out the second half of the dough into an 11-inch round. Cut vents in the dough and center it over the filling. Press the top and bottom crusts together around the edges to seal, trim the overhang to ½ inch, and then crimp or flute the edges decoratively. Brush the top lightly with the egg wash.

Bake the tart for 15 minutes. Lower the oven temperature to 350°F and continue to bake until a knife inserted through one of the vents comes out clean, another 30 minutes.

Chill for at least 2 hours before unmolding, slicing, and serving. Serve chilled or at room temperature.

This unusually shaped pie—more like a tart than a pie, but made with two crusts—was a favorite recipe among the Ohio Shakers, a religious sect renowned for their baked goods and pastries. Using organically grown lemons is important here because you eat the rinds, where pesticides concentrate. For the best results, be sure to slice the lemons very thinly and allow them plenty of time to mellow once sprinkled with the sugar. It takes 1 to 2 days from the time you start macerating the lemon slices until the tart is ready to serve.

making pie dough p. 112

finishing pies p. 114

Mixed Berry Cobbler

1½ cups all-purpose flour

2 tsp baking soda

1 tsp cream of tartar

1 tsp salt

8 Tbsp (1 stick) unsalted butter, at room temperature, plus extra for greasing

1 cup sugar (divided use)

1 large egg, lightly beaten

½ cup buttermilk

3 pints raspberries, blackberries, or blueberries, or a mixture

Makes 12 servings

Preheat the oven to 350°F. Butter a 9 x 13–inch baking dish. Sift the flour, baking soda, cream of tartar, and salt into a bowl; set aside.

In a stand mixer fitted with the paddle attachment, cream together the butter and ¾ cup of the sugar on low speed until light in texture, about 2 minutes, or mix by hand in a large mixing bowl. Beat in the egg, mixing until smooth, about 2 minutes. Incorporate the flour mixture into the butter by adding the flour alternately with the buttermilk, beginning and ending with the flour mixture.

Arrange the berries in the baking dish. Add the remaining ¼ cup sugar and mix lightly. Spoon the batter over the berries. Bake until the crust is golden brown and a toothpick inserted into the crust comes out clean, 40–50 minutes. Remove the cobbler from the oven and let cool on a wire rack for 10 minutes before slicing. Serve warm.

Cobblers are part of a robust repertoire of fruit-based desserts enjoyed throughout the United States. Different parts of the country prefer their own interpretations of the dish. Some cobblers feature a cake-like batter, as we have here, while others include either a pastry crust topping or a biscuit topping. Serve cobblers with ice cream, whipped cream, or a pool of heavy cream.

the creaming mixing method p. 31

Spiced Pear Crisp

8 Bartlett or Comice pears

½ cup tightly packed light brown sugar

1 Tbsp fresh lemon juice

1 tsp grated lemon zest

¾ tsp ground cinnamon (divided use)

¼ tsp *each* freshly grated nutmeg and ground ginger

½ cup all-purpose flour

½ cup quick-cooking oats

½ cup chopped toasted almonds, walnuts, or pecans

½ cup granulated sugar

½ tsp salt

4 Tbsp (½ stick) cold unsalted butter, diced, plus extra for greasing

Makes 8 servings

Preheat the oven to 375°F. Lightly butter an 8-inch square baking dish.

Peel, core, and thickly slice the pears. Combine the pears, brown sugar, lemon juice, lemon zest, ¼ tsp of the cinnamon, the nutmeg, and ginger in the baking dish. Spread into an even layer. (This mixture may be held for up to 3 hours at room temperature before topping and baking.)

Combine the flour, the oats, the nuts, the granulated sugar, the salt, and the remaining ½ tsp cinnamon in a food processor. Pulse the machine on and off a few times to combine. Add the butter and process just until the mixture looks crumbly.

Spread the oat mixture evenly over the pears and bake until the top is golden brown and the pears are tender, 40–45 minutes. (If the crisp is made in advance of serving, rewarm it gently in a 275°F oven for 15 minutes.)

Crisps have a sweet, crumbly topping, made here with oats. They are best when served quite warm, although not piping hot. For variety, you can use other fruits in the filling, including apples, peaches, and nectarines, alone or in combination with fresh berries, nuts, raisins, and dried fruits. You can also replace half of the flour in the topping with shredded unsweetened coconut. A wedge of cheese or a dollop of lightly sweetened whipped cream is good with this dessert.

toasting nuts p. 138

preparing pans p. 70

Cakes
5 and Tortes

Classic American cakes typically consist of two layers of buttery cake, filled and frosted. European cakes, usually referred to as tortes, often have more layers and may include a greater number of elements. Instead of just chocolate butter cake with fudge icing, for example, a European-style torte might include layers of sponge cake, jam, and even meringue. We've all come a long way from the first "cakes," which were really nothing more than grains, perhaps mixed with nuts and fruits, moistened and patted together. Italian bakers are thought to have introduced cakes similar to today's sponge cake in the early seventeenth century. It wasn't until the end of the nineteenth century, however, with the introduction of reliable leaveners and home ovens, that serving cake after a meal became a common habit. Since that time, however, the ability to bake a cake has been a measure of the home baker's prowess.

Mixing cakes

The recipes in this chapter rely upon several mixing methods also used in making quick breads and cookies: the straight mixing method (page 30), the creaming mixing method (page 31), and the foam mixing method (page 33). Cheesecake bears more resemblance to a baked custard than a cake, so it is found with the custards in this book (page 187).

The earliest cakes were leavened only by the air incorporated into the butter or eggs during the mixing process. By contrast, most cakes today include some sort of leavener for a lighter texture: baking soda or baking powder, both chemical leaveners, are typically used in layer cakes and pound cakes. However, as you learn about cake-baking techniques, you will discover that properly mixing air into a batter is still critical to a cake's success.

Prepare and measure out ingredients for a cake batter as directed in the ingredients list before you begin mixing. Ingredients for cake batters should usually be at room temperature so that they mix together easily.

American-style layer cakes, made using the creaming mixing method, often include chemical leaveners, but they also rely upon physical leavening from air that is incorporated into the batter during the creaming of butter. The butter and sugar should be creamed together long enough to make them very light in texture and color—longer than when creaming butter for cookies—in order to incorporate a good amount of air as well as to spread the air and fat evenly throughout the entire batter to make an extraordinarily tender cake with a dense crumb. Both the temperature and the texture of the creamed butter-sugar mixture are important to your success in properly blending in the eggs. Since eggs contain not only protein but also a significant amount of water, they must be added carefully so that they emulsify into the mixture. Having the eggs at room temperature is one part of the equation. The other is adding them one at a time and mixing them in completely before continuing to add more. If the eggs are added all at once, the butter cannot absorb them properly. Since these cake batters also include additional liquid in the form of milk or similar ingredients, the liquid is added after the dry ingredients, usually in two or three steps.

Beaten egg foam, a physical leavener, is what gives angel food, chiffon, and sponge cakes their lightness. When making any of these cakes, you must whip the egg whites long enough for them to fully expand in order for the finished cake to have a light, spongy texture. Adding the dry ingredients and flavorings to the egg foam requires a light touch; use the fewest strokes possible when combining the ingredients to retain the foam's lightness and prevent the cake from becoming tough or rubbery.

Preparing to bake a cake

Angel food and jelly roll cakes should be baked only in the pans suggested. Others, however, can be readily adapted to make layer cakes, Bundt or tube cakes, sheet cakes, or even cupcakes. Adjusting the amount of batter you add to the pan as well as the baking temperatures and times is simple with the aid of the information found on pages 293–95 and the guidelines for filling pans that follow.

Good pan preparation (page 70) is important to getting the cake out of the pan without its sticking or tearing. Often the cake pan requires only a light coating of cooking spray (or smear of soft butter or shortening) and sometimes flour. However, delicate cakes made with a lot of eggs are easier to remove from the pan if you line it with parchment paper. Lining pans with parchment is critical to turning out large, thin jelly roll cakes neatly. Angel food cakes, however, should be baked in ungreased tube pans; leaving the pan ungreased gives the batter something to cling to and climb as the egg whites puff up during baking. For all cakes, follow the directions given in the recipe for the best results.

Baking cakes

Most home ovens preheat in about 10 to 15 minutes, but this varies widely. Be sure to allow your oven enough time to reach the required temperature before putting the cake in the oven. Use an oven thermometer to be certain. If the oven is too cool, the texture and shape of the cake may suffer.

When using a conventional oven, you should position the rack in the middle of the oven for the most even baking. Bake cakes on a single rack with nothing else in the oven, if possible. This improves the circulation of hot air around the cake pan for an even color and a good rise.

Convection ovens are generally not recommended for cakes, because their intense heat can cause overbrowning of sugary batters. The forced movement of air in a convection oven can also give an odd rippled appearance to the cake's top.

If you know that your oven rack is not level or your oven has hot spots (as many ovens do), plan to rotate the pans a half turn and move them from one side of the oven to the other. If you have a rack filled with food above or below your cake, you may need to rotate your cake pans from the lower rack to the higher one, or vice versa, so that the edges or bottom of the cake don't burn.

Avoiding mistakes

Sometimes a cake "falls," or sinks in the middle during or after baking. There are several reasons that a cake may not achieve expected volume. Inaccurate measuring of ingredients may affect the structure of a cake. Or, the leavener used might have lost some of its leavening power. Other reasons that cakes fall have to do with the temperature of the oven, the way the pan is prepared, and the way the cake is cooled.

For example, baking a cake at too high a temperature will cause the sides and top of the cake to set before the interior is fully baked. The cake may rise in the oven and appear to have reached its full volume. However, when you take the cake from the oven to cool, it falls quickly.

Foam cakes, like sponge or angel food cakes, may fall if they are jarred or jostled while they bake. In this regard, they are quite similar to soufflés; even an especially loud noise might make the cake fall. See pages 296–97 for a chart of baking mistakes and their effects.

A very rapid change in temperature may also be responsible for a cake's falling. Opening and closing the oven door too often causes the temperature to drop; this can also lead to a flatter-than-expected cake. A cake transferred directly from the oven to the refrigerator will shrink as it cools, whereas a cake left to cool at room temperature is far less likely to fall.

Finishing cakes

You can serve some of these cakes, like the Sweet Polenta Cake (page 144) and Lemon Buttermilk Cake (page 148), on their own, or with a simple glaze or topping. Or, for additional interest and flavor, you can use techniques such as marbling or adding a streusel filling (page 145). You can slice sponge or butter cakes and fill them with icings, Bavarian creams, whipped soft ganache, or other fillings to make layer cakes, molded cakes, and tortes. With the many recipes for icings, glazes, fillings, sauces, and decorating techniques in the last chapter of this book, you can turn your cake into an elegant dessert.

Serving cakes

Use a large, sharp knife with a thin blade to cut through cakes. Cakes that are frosted and filled can be challenging to slice neatly, unless you are properly prepared for the task. Have a knife, a tall container (such as a pitcher) filled with hot water, and a clean kitchen towel at hand. After you make each cut, dip the knife in the water and wipe away the cake and icing that cling to the blade. Dry the blade before making a second cut. Insert the blade under the slice to lift it and steady the cake against the back of a table fork. Set the cake down on the plate, standing upright, and hold the back of the fork at the wide end of the slice to hold the cake in place as you slide out the knife blade. If the slice of cake is too tall or too thin to stand up, lay it on the plate with one of the cut sides facing down.

Toasting nuts

Toast small amounts of nuts in a dry skillet. For large quantities, use the oven.

1 Toasting methods

For a small quantity of nuts, preheat a dry skillet over medium heat; cast iron is a good choice because it heats evenly. Once the pan is hot, scatter the nuts in a single layer without crowding. Gently swirl the pan or stir the nuts frequently so they toast evenly.

For larger quantities of nuts, preheat the oven to 325°F. Spread the nuts on an ungreased baking sheet and toast them until golden brown and fragrant, 7–15 minutes, depending upon the size of the nut. Stir nuts occasionally as they toast in the oven; those on the edges of the baking sheet will tend to brown more quickly.

Just when the nuts reach the color you want, immediately transfer them from the skillet or baking sheet to a cool container. This keeps them from continuing to brown. Toast nuts before chopping them for the best results.

Separating eggs

Separate eggs carefully to avoid breaking the yolks.

1 Setting up

Eggs can be separated most easily when they are cold, so always keep them in the refrigerator until you are ready to crack them. Have three bowls ready: one to hold the whites, one to hold the yolks, and an empty bowl to crack each new egg over—just in case the yolk breaks as you crack the egg. Note that egg whites that are to be whipped must be free from all fat, whether from a broken yolk or traces of grease in a bowl, because fat inhibits the whites from foaming up to their greatest volume.

2 Separating the eggs

Working with one egg at a time, crack the shell carefully but firmly on the rim of the empty bowl and pull apart the halves, keeping the yolk contained in one shell half. Gently pour the egg yolk from one half to the other, allowing the egg white to fall into the empty bowl. Repeat to separate as much white as possible. Drop the egg yolk into another bowl.

3 Keeping white and yolk separate

After cracking each egg, examine the egg white in the first bowl to be sure that it contains no bits of yolk. If it is clean, transfer it to the egg white bowl. If you see drops of yolk in the white, it cannot be used for whipping. Reserve it for making scrambled eggs, or making egg wash for glazing a pie crust.

Whipping egg whites

Egg whites can be beaten to distinct stages, typically described as soft, medium, hard, and stiff peaks. The foam adds a light texture and leavening power to a wide range of baked goods.

1 Setting up

Egg whites foam best when there are no traces of fat in the whites themselves or on the equipment you use. Separating eggs properly (*left*) ensures that no fat from the yolk mixes in with the whites. Choose a nonaluminum metal bowl large enough to allow the egg whites to triple in volume. Aluminum reacts badly with egg whites, turning them gray, but copper bowls react with egg whites in a beneficial way, to create a foam with good volume and stability. If you have a copper bowl, you can omit the cream of tartar that is typically added to recipes to stabilize the foam. To remove any grease or oil, wipe the bowl and whisk or beaters with lemon juice or white vinegar, then rinse with hot water. You will get the greatest volume if the egg whites are at room temperature when they are whipped. A 10–15 minute rest at room temperature is usually enough time to take the chill off eggs separated while still cold.

2 Whipping to soft peaks

Use a large, round balloon whisk or the wire whisk attachment of a stand mixer to incorporate as much air as possible. Begin whipping at a slow to moderate speed, until the whites loosen and become foamy. Ingredients like sugar or cream of tartar are gradually added starting at this point. Increase the speed to high and continue to whip. As more air is beaten into the whites, the texture becomes very smooth and the foam thickens enough to mound slightly. As you keep whipping, you will see the whisk start to leave track marks in the egg whites. "Soft peak" describes the point at which the foam is still very glossy and moist, and when you pull the whisk out of the bowl and turn it upright, the whites slump over to one side in rounded peaks.

3 Whipping to hard peaks

As you continue to whip egg whites, they reach the "medium peak" stage. You will see distinct tracks left by the whisk or beater as you whip. The peaks formed when the whisk is lifted retain their shape longer, but are still glossy and smooth. This is the ideal stage for foams to be folded into batters or to make soufflés, since the whites are still flexible enough to expand without bursting as they get hot. Once the "hard peak" stage is reached, the tips of the peaks are more pointed and hold their shape for a while before drooping. Beyond hard peak, egg foams approach their maximum volume and are at the "stiff peak" stage. Stiff foams tend to collapse easily, may start to lose their glossy sheen, and will begin to separate if whipping continues.

Egg white foams start to deflate almost the moment you stop whipping them, so they are usually beaten and folded into a dish as the very last step in a recipe, to keep as much air as possible in the foam and the finished dish.

Filling cake pans

Fill cake pans properly for the best texture and appearance in the finished cake.

1 Filling a pan for jelly roll cakes
Jelly roll or roulade-style cakes are thin sponge cakes that are rolled around a filling. Use a jelly roll pan to make the sponge layer; these pans have short sides that permit the cake to rise slightly as it bakes. Fill the pan about three-quarters full. Use an offset spatula (and a very gentle touch) to spread the batter evenly into the corners and along the edges. These cakes bake quickly and tend to dry out, especially in spots where the batter is thinner.

2 Dividing batter for layer cakes
Whether you are baking your cake in a round pan, Bundt pan, rectangular pan, or cupcake tins, the rule of thumb is to fill the pan or tin two-thirds to three-quarters full. This leaves enough room for the cake to expand as it bakes. When the pan is not filled enough, the cake may be dense or flat. If there is too much batter, it will flow over the sides of the pan. To ensure evenly sized layers, weigh the cake pans as you fill them with batter, dividing the batter so that each pan is of equal weight.

3 Using tube pans
Angel food and chiffon cakes are baked in tube pans. The center tube helps the cake bake evenly and keeps the outside from overbaking before the interior is done. Follow the recipe instructions regarding greasing tube pans (or not) so that the cake rises properly. Fill the pan about three-quarters full.

Cooling cakes

Cakes must be completely cool before you fill or frost them.

1 Cooling and unmolding cakes
Cakes need to stay in the pan for a short time after they come out of the oven before they are unmolded. This resting period helps the cake retain its structure. When the cake is finished baking, take it from the oven and set the pan on a wire rack to rest for about 10 minutes. Run a thin blade around the edges of the pan to loosen the cake.

If you are using a standard cake pan, place a wire rack directly against the surface of the cake and invert the pan and rack together to unmold the cake onto the rack. If the cake sticks to the pan, turn it right side up and try to release the cake from the pan with an offset spatula, working gently to avoid tearing the cake. Once the cake is turned out of the pan onto the wire rack, turn it over to cool right side up.

If the cake is in a springform pan, loosen the clamp to open the sides and lift the form away from the cake. Use a spatula to slide the cake off the bottom of the springform pan and slide it onto a cooling rack.

For angel food cakes, turn the cake upside down, still in the pan, when you take it from the oven and let it cool suspended on the neck of a wine bottle or resting on the little "feet" around the rim of some tube pans. This helps the cake retain as much height as possible. Take extra care when loosening the sticky cake from the pan with a knife.

cake layers as needed so that they just touch the sides of the mold. Some molds have tapered or rounded sides; in this case, do the final trimming right in the mold as you stack the layers, using the tip of a paring knife. Another option is to cut smaller pieces of cake and then fit them into the mold or use them to fill any gaps left by layers that don't quite touch the edge of the mold, as you would puzzle pieces.

3 Brushing the layers

As the cake is added to the mold, brush each layer with a little sugar syrup for moistness and flavor. The cake should be brushed with enough syrup to make the cake moist, but not wet. The syrup helps the cake hold together better after unmolding. It also adds flavor and moisture to sponge cake layers, which contain little if any fat for moisture.

4 Layering the cake and chilling

Once the first layer of cake is in place and you've brushed it with syrup, add the filling. Use an offset spatula to gently spread fillings such as Bavarian cream or ice cream into an even layer. Continue layering cake and filling until the mold is filled, ending with a cake layer. Cover the mold tightly with plastic wrap. Refrigerate or freeze the cake until it is firm, at least 3 hours for most cakes. Then unwrap and finish as desired.

Making molded cakes

Molded cakes consist of layers of cake and a filling that is soft enough to pour during assembly. Chill or freeze the filled cake so it can be easily sliced.

1 Preparing the mold

There are many appropriate molds for molded cakes, including footed trifle bowls, large soufflé dishes, and even mixing bowls. Some molded cakes, such as tiramisù, are presented in the mold. Others, like tortes, are prepared in a mold, then removed from the mold to be iced. For these cakes, use a springform pan or a cake ring, available in cookware shops and catalogs. To make it easy to unmold the cake before you serve it, line the mold with plastic wrap. Leave a 2- or 3-inch overhang of plastic wrap to be sure the top of the cake doesn't stick to the mold as you remove the springform or ring.

2 Cutting cake to fit a mold

If your cake mold has straight, symmetric sides, use the mold as a guide to trim large

Assembling a layer cake

Straight edges and a level top give layer cakes an elegant look.

1 Marking layers for slicing

Baked cake layers are sometimes sliced horizontally to make thinner layers for a finished cake. To cut a cake into thinner layers, set the cake on a flat, stable surface. Use a ruler to divide the cake into equal layers and insert toothpicks into the sides of the cake in four or five spots around its circumference to guide your eye and knife as you cut.

2 Slicing layers

Working from one side to the other, cut horizontally through the cake with a serrated knife, using a gentle back-and-forth sawing motion. Rest the hand not holding the knife flat on the top of the cake to help you keep the knife level and the layers evenly thick. Once cut, the layers can be separated by lifting one side and inserting your hand and/or a wide metal spatula to lift the cut layer away and carefully transfer it to a flat plate or cardboard circle. Brush away loose crumbs from each layer using a pastry brush.

3 Trimming layers

Cake layers can also be trimmed to get rid of ragged edges or other unevenness. Take a close look at your cake layers. Some may be thicker or thinner in spots, or when layers were sliced your cut may have been slightly angled. Use the same cutting technique as for dividing the cake into layers. Don't worry about making the layers perfect; some faults can be easily disguised as you put together the cake, by choosing the flattest sides to make the top and bottom, and using extra-thick filling to compensate for uneven layers.

4 Selecting the layers

The bottom surface of an assembled cake should be as level as possible. The top surface should also be even. One way to ensure that the bottom of the bottom layer and top of the top layer of a cake are as level as possible is to use what were the bottom crusts of the cake layers as they baked for these surfaces.

Whether you are assembling the cake directly on a serving plate or have a turntable or cake stand, "cement" the bottom layer to the plate or stand with a dollop of icing. This keeps the cake from shifting around as you work. To keep a serving plate clean of frosting, tuck strips of parchment or waxed paper underneath the edges of the cake before you start to work.

5 Spreading the filling

The best tools for spreading are offset icing spatulas or palette knives. Different fillings have different consistencies, requiring various approaches. For a jam filling, spread an even but rather thin coating over the cake layer. Creamy and foamy fillings, like whipped soft Ganache (page 284) and Italian Buttercream (page 279), are spread in a slightly thicker layer. If the filling layer is too thick, the cake layers may start to slide apart and some of the filling may ooze out of the cake. Leave a rim around the edge of the cake unfilled to allow for the filling to spread after the next layer is placed on it.

6 Evening the layers

Set the next cake layer on top of the filling, line up the edges of the layers so the sides are straight, and very gently press the layer down, so that the top of the cake is level. Keep stacking the layers and the filling to make the appropriate number of layers. The top layer of cake should be very level and straight. Once the layers are straightened and stacked directly on top of each other, use a straight blade or palette knife to remove any filling that squeezed out from between the layers. Let the cake rest for an hour to let the layers settle into position before icing the cake. If the filling contains eggs or cream, store it in the refrigerator.

For detailed instructions on icing a cake, see page 265.

Sweet Polenta Cake

Cooking spray for greasing

¾ cup all-purpose flour plus extra for dusting

1 tsp baking powder

½ tsp salt

3 large eggs

6 large egg yolks

½ tsp vanilla extract

1 cup (2 sticks) unsalted butter, at room temperature

1 cup sugar

½ cup yellow cornmeal, medium or coarse grind

Makes one 8-inch cake layer

Preheat the oven to 350°F. Spray an 8-inch round cake pan with cooking spray and flour lightly.

Sift the flour, baking powder, and salt into a bowl and set aside. In another bowl, whisk together the eggs, egg yolks, and vanilla extract.

In a stand mixer fitted with the paddle attachment, cream together the butter and sugar on medium speed, scraping down the bowl with a rubber spatula as needed, until the mixture is smooth and light in texture, about 5 minutes.

Add the egg mixture to the butter mixture in 3 additions on low speed, scraping down the bowl as needed, until evenly blended, 3–4 minutes. Add the sifted flour mixture and the cornmeal; mix on low speed just until the batter is evenly moistened.

Pour the batter into the prepared pan. Gently tap the filled pan to release any air bubbles. Bake until a skewer inserted near the center of the cake comes out clean, 50–60 minutes.

Remove the cake from the oven and cool completely in the pan on a wire rack. Release the sides and bottom of the cake from the pan with a narrow metal spatula or a table knife before unmolding and serving.

Polenta is the Italian word for cornmeal, and also the name of a dish of cornmeal cooked with liquid. Polenta, like cornmeal, is available in a variety of textures. For this recipe, medium or coarse grind is best.

This very simple cake tastes like sweetened corn bread. Slice and serve at room temperature with Tropical Fruit Salsa (p. 236), fruit coulis (p. 273), or Chantilly Cream (p. 281).

the creaming mixing method p. 31

cooling cakes p. 140

Sour Cream Streusel Pound Cake

All-purpose flour for dusting

Streusel Filling

⅓ cup tightly packed light brown sugar

¼ cup chopped toasted walnuts

¼ cup mini semisweet chocolate chips

1 tsp cocoa powder

½ tsp ground cinnamon

1½ cups cake flour, sifted

1 tsp baking powder

½ tsp baking soda

8 Tbsp (1 stick) unsalted butter, at room temperature, plus extra for greasing

¾ cup granulated sugar

½ tsp salt

½ cup sour cream

2 large eggs

1 tsp vanilla extract

Makes 1 loaf cake

Preheat the oven to 350°F. Lightly butter and flour an 8½-inch loaf pan.

To prepare the streusel, toss together the brown sugar, walnuts, chocolate chips, cocoa powder, and cinnamon until evenly blended. Set aside.

Sift the cake flour, baking powder, and baking soda into a bowl and set aside.

In a stand mixer fitted with the paddle attachment, cream together the butter, granulated sugar, and salt on medium speed, scraping down the bowl with a rubber spatula as needed, until the mixture is smooth and light in texture, 4–5 minutes.

In a separate bowl, blend the sour cream, eggs, and vanilla extract. Add the egg mixture to the butter mixture in 3 additions, alternating with the sifted dry ingredients. After the last addition of the egg mixture, mix on low speed until just blended, scraping down the bowl as needed, 1 minute.

Pour half of the batter into the prepared pan. Scatter the streusel filling evenly over the batter. Spoon the remaining batter over the streusel and carefully spread into an even layer. Bake until a skewer inserted near the center of the cake comes out clean, 50–55 minutes.

Remove the cake from the oven and cool completely in the pan on a wire rack. Release the sides of the cake from the pan with a narrow metal spatula and unmold. Slice and serve at room temperature.

Instead of layering it as suggested in the recipe, the streusel filling mixture can also be folded into this cake for a swirled effect. To do this, scatter the streusel mixture over the batter while it's still in the bowl. Use a broad, flat spoon or rubber spatula to fold the streusel. Two or three strokes will streak it throughout the batter without blending it in completely.

This cake is good with a simple accompaniment, such as fruit coulis (p. 273) or Chantilly Cream (p. 281).

toasting nuts p. 138

preparing pans p. 70

VARIATION

Marble Pound Cake

After mixing the batter, remove one-third of the batter to a separate bowl and add 2 oz melted and cooled bittersweet chocolate (page 242), combining thoroughly with a rubber spatula. Gently pour the chocolate batter into the bowl holding the plain batter. Using the handle end of a wooden spoon, gently swirl the batters with 3 or 4 strokes. Do not overblend. Pour into the pan and bake as directed above.

Yellow Butter Cake

Cooking spray for greasing

3½ cups cake flour

2 cups sugar

1 Tbsp baking powder

½ tsp salt

1 cup (2 sticks) unsalted butter, diced, at room temperature

1 cup whole or low-fat milk (divided use)

4 large eggs

2 large egg whites

2 tsp vanilla extract

Makes two 8-inch layers

Preheat the oven to 350°F. Coat two 8-inch cake pans lightly with cooking spray.

Sift the flour, sugar, baking powder, and salt into the bowl of a stand mixer fitted with the whisk attachment or a large mixing bowl. Add the butter and ½ cup of the milk. Mix on medium speed until smooth, about 4 minutes, scraping down the bowl with a rubber spatula as needed.

In a separate bowl, blend the eggs, egg whites, the remaining ½ cup milk, and the vanilla extract. Add to the batter in 3 additions, mixing for 2 minutes on medium speed after each addition. Scrape down the bowl between additions.

Divide the batter evenly between the 2 pans. Bake until the layers spring back when touched lightly in the center, 35–40 minutes.

Remove the layers from the oven and cool completely in their pans on wire racks. Release the sides and bottom of the layers from the pans with a narrow metal spatula or a table knife before unmolding and finishing with fillings and icings.

This cake has a dense texture and keeps well, thanks to its special mixing method, known to pastry chefs as the high-ratio method. Instead of creaming together the butter and sugar as a first step, you blend together all of the dry ingredients with all of the butter and a bit of the liquid. Precise mixing times and speeds are important for success, as is careful scraping of the mixing bowl to be sure the batter is evenly blended.

Fill and frost this cake with whipped soft Ganache (p. 284), plain or flavored Buttercream (p. 276), Chocolate Sabayon filling (p. 283), or Raspberry Curd Filling (p. 235).

assembling a layer cake p. 142

separating eggs p. 138

VARIATION

Chocolate Butter Cake

Replace ¾ cup of the flour with Dutch-process cocoa powder and proceed as directed.

Any flavor of Italian Buttercream (p. 279) or Devil's Fudge Icing (p. 278) is a good match for this cake. Also try pairing it with White Chocolate–Cream Cheese Icing (p. 278), Raspberry Curd Filling (p. 235), or Bavarian Cream filling (p. 275).

Lemon Buttermilk Cake

2⅔ cups all-purpose flour plus extra for dusting

½ tsp baking soda

¼ tsp salt

1 cup (2 sticks) unsalted butter plus extra for greasing

1¾ cups granulated sugar

1 Tbsp grated lemon zest

4 large eggs

1¼ cups buttermilk

5 Tbsp freshly squeezed lemon juice (divided use)

¾ cup confectioners' sugar plus extra as needed

1 Tbsp hot water plus extra as needed

Makes one 9-inch Bundt cake or 36 cupcakes

Preheat the oven to 350°F. Lightly grease and flour a 9-inch Bundt pan or line 36 muffin tins with paper liners. Sift the flour, baking soda, and salt into a bowl and set aside.

In a stand mixer fitted with the paddle attachment, cream together the butter, granulated sugar, and lemon zest on medium speed, scraping down the bowl with a rubber spatula as needed, until the mixture is smooth and light in texture, about 5 minutes. Add the eggs one at a time, beating well and scraping down the bowl after each addition.

Alternate adding the sifted dry ingredients and buttermilk to the creamed mixture in 3 additions, mixing on low speed until just incorporated. Increase the speed to medium and mix until very light and smooth, another 2 minutes. Add 4 Tbsp of the lemon juice last and blend just until evenly mixed, 30 seconds.

Pour the batter into the prepared Bundt pan or fill each muffin cup two-thirds full with batter. Bake until the center of cake springs back when touched and a skewer inserted near the center of the cake comes out clean, 65–75 minutes. For cupcakes, bake until the cupcakes rise in a dome shape and spring back when lightly pressed with your fingertip, 16–20 minutes.

Remove the cake from the oven and let cool completely in the pan on a wire rack. Release the sides and bottom of the cake from the pan with a narrow metal spatula or a table knife. Invert the pan and turn out the cake. Place a wire rack in a baking pan and set the cake, right side up, on the rack.

Combine the confectioners' sugar, hot water, and the remaining 1 Tbsp lemon juice and stir until very smooth. Add a little more confectioners' sugar or water as necessary to achieve a good glazing consistency (similar to that of honey). Spoon the glaze evenly over the cake. When the glaze has firmed, transfer the cake to a plate. Slice and serve at room temperature.

Buttermilk and other cultured dairy foods are often used in cakes and quick breads leavened with baking soda. The acid in the buttermilk neutralizes the alkali present in baking soda, making the baking soda more effective at lightening the batter as it bakes. If you do not have buttermilk on hand, you can simply "sour" milk by blending 1 Tbsp of lemon juice or vinegar, or 1¼ tsp cream of tartar, into a cup of whole milk.

If making cupcakes, frost with White Chocolate– Cream Cheese Icing (p. 278) if desired.

the creaming mixing method p. 31

filling cake pans p. 140

Vanilla Sponge Cake

2 cups cake flour

6 Tbsp (¾ stick) unsalted butter plus extra for greasing

1 Tbsp vanilla extract

1¼ cups sugar

5 large eggs

5 large egg yolks

Makes two 8-inch layers

Preheat the oven to 375°F. Lightly butter two 8-inch cake pans and line with parchment paper.

Sift the flour twice and set aside. Melt the butter in a saucepan over low heat. Remove from the heat, add the vanilla extract to the melted butter, and stir to combine. Set aside to cool.

Combine the sugar, eggs, and egg yolks in the bowl of a stand mixer and set the bowl over a pan of barely simmering water. Whisking constantly with a wire whisk, heat until the mixture is warm to the touch or reaches 110°F on a candy thermometer.

Remove the bowl from the heat and attach it to the stand mixer fitted with the whisk attachment. Whip the eggs on medium speed until the foam is 3 times the original volume and no longer increasing in volume, about 5 minutes.

Fold the flour into the egg mixture using a rubber spatula. Blend a small amount of the batter into the melted butter and then fold the tempered butter into the remaining batter.

Fill the prepared cake pans about two-thirds full. Bake until the top of each layer is firm to the touch, about 30 minutes.

Let the layers cool in the pans for a few minutes before turning out onto wire racks. Let cool completely before finishing with frosting and filling.

Sponge cake, whether you know it as génoise or *pan di Spagna*, is a light, sweet, delicate cake rich in eggs. These cakes are made from egg foams with very little or no added fat. To add moisture, sponge cakes are often liberally brushed with sugar syrup.

Fill the cake with Chocolate Sabayon (p. 283) or whipped soft Ganache (p. 284), or make a simple filling by spreading lightly sweetened whipped cream and sliced or diced fresh fruits between layers. Add a final layer of whipped cream on top and garnish with a few perfect fresh berries or slices of fruit.

using a double boiler
p. 167

the foam mixing method
p. 33

VARIATIONS

Chocolate Sponge Cake

Replace ½ cup of the cake flour with cocoa powder. Sift the cake flour and cocoa together twice. Proceed as directed.

Nut Sponge Cake

Replace 1 cup of the cake flour with ¾ cup finely chopped toasted (page 138) almonds, hazelnuts, walnuts, or pecans. Use a food processor to grind the nuts very finely. Proceed as directed.

Devil's Fudge Cake

Flourless cooking spray
for greasing

All-purpose flour for dusting

2½ cups cake flour

1¾ cups sugar

1½ tsp baking powder

½ tsp baking soda

½ tsp salt

3 large eggs

¾ cup (1½ sticks) unsalted
butter, melted, plus extra for
greasing

1½ cups warm water

1 cup Dutch-process cocoa
powder, sifted

Makes two 8-inch layers

Preheat the oven to 350°F. Coat two 8-inch cake pans lightly with cooking spray and dust lightly with all-purpose flour.

Sift the cake flour, sugar, baking powder, baking soda, and salt into the bowl of a stand mixer fitted with the whisk attachment. On low speed, add the eggs one at a time, beating well and scraping down the bowl with a rubber spatula after each addition. Add the butter and blend until smooth, about 2 minutes. Add the water and blend until a smooth batter forms, another 2 minutes. Add the cocoa powder last, mixing on medium speed until evenly blended, 2–3 minutes. Scrape down the bowl as needed while you mix.

Divide the batter evenly between the pans. Bake until a skewer inserted near the center of each comes out clean, 40–50 minutes.

Cool the layers in the pans for a few minutes before turning out onto wire racks. Cool completely before filling and icing.

Devil's fudge cake gets its name from the reddish brown color it develops during baking. The color is the result of a chemical reaction between cocoa powder (a naturally acidic ingredient) and baking powder (an alkaline ingredient). Fill and frost with Devil's Fudge Icing (p. 278), White Chocolate–Cream Cheese Icing (p. 278), or Simple Buttercream (p. 276).

using chemical leaveners p. 69

filling cake pans p. 140

Angel Food Cake

1 cup cake flour

1¼ cups sugar (divided use)

½ tsp salt

12 large egg whites

2 Tbsp water

1 tsp cream of tartar

1 tsp vanilla extract

Chantilly Cream (p. 281)
for serving

Makes one 9-inch tube cake

Preheat the oven to 350°F. Sift the flour, ¼ cup of the sugar, and salt twice onto parchment or waxed paper and set aside.

In a stand mixer fitted with the whisk attachment, whip the egg whites and water on low speed until foamy, 2 minutes. Add the cream of tartar and continue to whip until the egg whites form soft peaks, 2 minutes. Add the vanilla extract, then gradually add the remaining 1 cup sugar while whipping. Continue until the egg whites are glossy and form medium peaks, 3–4 minutes.

With a rubber spatula or wide spoon, gently fold the sifted flour and sugar mixture into the egg whites. Spoon the batter into an ungreased 9-inch angel food cake pan, run a butter knife through the batter once to ensure that there are no air pockets, and smooth the top. Bake until golden brown on top, 40–45 minutes.

Turn the cake pan upside down and let it cool completely before turning out. Use a spatula or thin knife to release the cake from the sides of the pan and turn out carefully. Serve at room temperature with Chantilly cream.

In order to reach a lofty height, angel food cake needs to cling to the sides of the pan, both as it bakes and while it cools. This is why the pan is ungreased and the cake is cooled upside down. Some angel food cake pans have little "feet" on the rim to hold the cake above the tabletop or counter. If your pan has no feet, place the inverted pan on a bottle with a long, relatively thin neck.

Other good accompaniments for this cake include fruit coulis (p. 273), Lemon Verbena Sauce (p. 271), and Tropical Fruit Salsa (p. 236).

foam mixing method p. 33

filling cake pans p. 140

Carrot Cake

Unsalted butter for greasing

1⅔ cups sugar

½ tsp salt

1⅔ cups bread flour plus extra for dusting

2 tsp ground cinnamon

1 tsp baking soda

½ tsp baking powder

3 large eggs

⅔ cup vegetable oil

2 cups grated carrots

½ cup chopped toasted walnuts

Makes one 10-inch tube cake

Preheat the oven to 350°F. Lightly grease and flour a 10-inch tube pan or Bundt pan.

Sift the sugar and salt into a bowl and set aside.

In another bowl, sift together the flour, cinnamon, baking soda, and baking powder and set aside.

In a stand mixer fitted with the whisk attachment, whip the eggs on medium speed, scraping down the bowl with a rubber spatula as needed, until thick, about 3 minutes. Increase the speed to high and continue whipping until the eggs fall in thick ribbons from the whisk, about 4 minutes. Gradually add the oil while continuing to whip until evenly blended.

Add the sifted sugar mixture slowly to the whipped egg mixture while continuing to whip at medium speed until blended.

Add the sifted flour mixture to the batter, mixing on low speed until just incorporated. Fold in the carrots and walnuts by hand using a rubber spatula.

Pour the batter into the prepared pan. Bake until a skewer inserted near the center comes out clean, 45–50 minutes.

Cool the cake in the pan for a few minutes before turning out onto a wire rack. Cool completely before icing and slicing.

If you have a Mouli-style rotary grater or grating and shredding disks for your food processor, you can select how coarse or fine you want your grated carrots to be. The more finely you grate your carrots, the finer the texture of the finished cake will be. Coarsely grated carrots remain more visible in the baked cake, for an appealing flecked appearance and a delightfully rustic texture.

Serve warm slices of this cake with Custard Sauce (p. 274) or a dollop of Chantilly Cream (p. 281). If made in a straight-sided tube pan, the cake may be iced with White Chocolate–Cream Cheese Icing (p. 278).

toasting nuts p. 138

Orange Chiffon Cake

Cooking spray for greasing

All-purpose flour for dusting

2¼ cups cake flour

1½ cups granulated sugar (divided use)

1 Tbsp baking powder

1 tsp salt

1 cup freshly squeezed orange juice

½ cup vegetable oil

5 large egg yolks

2 Tbsp grated orange zest

8 large egg whites

½ tsp cream of tartar

Confectioners' sugar for dusting

Makes one 10-inch tube cake

Preheat the oven to 350°F. Coat a 10-inch tube pan with a removable bottom lightly with cooking spray and dust lightly with flour, tapping out the excess.

Sift the flour, 1¼ cups of the granulated sugar, the baking powder, and salt into a large mixing bowl and set aside.

In a separate bowl, whisk together the orange juice, oil, egg yolks, and orange zest. Mixing by hand with a spoon or rubber spatula, blend the wet ingredients into the dry ingredients. Continue to mix until the batter is smooth and evenly blended, about 2 minutes.

In the clean bowl of a stand mixer fitted with the whisk attachment, whip the egg whites on medium speed until they are foamy. Add the remaining ¼ cup granulated sugar and the cream of tartar. Continue to whip until the whites form medium peaks when the beater is lifted, about 4 minutes.

Using a rubber spatula, fold the whipped whites into the batter in 2 or 3 additions.

Pour the batter into the prepared tube pan and bake until a skewer inserted near the center of the cake comes out clean and the cake springs back when lightly pressed with a fingertip, 55–60 minutes.

Remove the pan from the oven and carefully invert on a funnel or the neck of a wine bottle to cool. When cool, release the cake from sides of the pan with a table knife or thin palette knife and unmold.

Dust the cake with confectioners' sugar before slicing and serving.

Chiffon cakes, like angel food cakes, are light, delicate, and airy. Unlike angel food cakes, however, they contain both egg yolks and some oil, giving the cake a finer, more tender crumb as well as a moister texture.

While chiffon cakes are wonderful "as is," without any more topping or adornment than a dusting of confectioners' sugar, you may choose to serve slices in a pool of Lemon Verbena Sauce (p. 271) or fruit coulis (p. 273).

filling cake pans p. 140

cooling cakes p. 140

VARIATIONS

Lemon or Lime Chiffon Cake

Replace the orange juice with 10 Tbsp water and 6 Tbsp freshly squeezed lemon or lime juice. Replace the orange zest with lemon or lime zest. Continue as directed.

Mocha Torte

Coffee Syrup

¾ cup strong brewed coffee or espresso

¼ cup Kahlúa or other coffee-flavored liqueur

¼ cup sugar

Two 8-inch layers Vanilla Sponge Cake (p. 149)

4½ cups Chocolate Italian Buttercream (p. 279)

1 cup chopped bittersweet chocolate, melted (p. 242) and cooled (optional)

10 chocolate-covered coffee beans or marzipan coffee beans (p. 259) (optional)

Makes one 8-inch torte

To make the coffee syrup, combine the coffee, Kahlúa, and sugar in a small saucepan and bring to a simmer over medium heat. Simmer until the sugar is completely dissolved and the syrup has reduced slightly, about 3 minutes. Remove the syrup from the heat and let cool to room temperature.

Slice each of the sponge cake layers into 2 even layers.

Place one layer of the sponge cake on a cake plate and brush it evenly with enough coffee syrup to moisten the layer, about ¼ cup. Spread ¾ cup of the buttercream in an even layer over the cake. Repeat this sequence with the next 2 layers of cake, pressing the layers gently into position. Add the last layer of cake, press down gently, and brush it with ¼ cup syrup.

Spread 1½ cups of the buttercream evenly over the top and sides of the cake. If using, drizzle the melted and cooled chocolate over the top, creating a random pattern. Fill a pastry bag fitted with a small star tip with the remaining ¾ cup buttercream and pipe 10 rosettes of buttercream at even intervals around the cake's edge. Place a coffee bean in the center of each rosette, if desired.

Note: If the cake is not going to be served right away, wrap it carefully or place it in a covered container to preserve the decoration, and store in the refrigerator. Let the cake return to room temperature before serving it, however, so that the buttercream is not too hard to cut easily.

A torte is a European-style pastry typically made with layers of sponge cake, a jam or cream filling, and a frosting. These rich and complex desserts are often enjoyed in the middle of the afternoon, served with coffee or tea, rather than as a dessert following dinner.

assembling a layer cake p. 142

piping p. 266

Tiramisù

1 cup espresso

½ cup Kahlúa or other coffee-flavored liqueur

1½ cups granulated sugar (divided use)

6 large egg yolks

1 large egg

26 oz mascarpone cheese

1 tsp vanilla extract

3 large egg whites

48 slightly stale ladyfingers (p. 127)

¼ cup cocoa powder

2 Tbsp confectioners' sugar

Makes 8 servings

Combine the espresso and Kahlúa in a small bowl to make a syrup. Set aside.

Whisk together 1 cup of the granulated sugar, the egg yolks, and the egg in the bowl of a stand mixer and set over simmering water. Continue to whisk until the volume nearly doubles and the mixture becomes a light lemon yellow, 4–5 minutes.

Transfer the bowl to a stand mixer fitted with the whisk attachment and whip on high speed until the mixture has cooled to room temperature, 8–10 minutes. Add half of the mascarpone and the vanilla extract and blend on low speed until very smooth, scraping down the bowl with a rubber spatula as needed. Add the remaining mascarpone and mix just long enough to combine evenly.

Beat the egg whites with the remaining ½ cup granulated sugar in a clean bowl to medium peaks, 5–6 minutes. Fold the beaten egg whites into the mascarpone mixture in 3 separate additions.

Place 16 ladyfingers in a 2½-qt dish or a 9 x 13–inch baking pan. Brush the ladyfingers evenly and liberally with the espresso syrup. Spread one-third of the mascarpone filling in an even layer over the ladyfingers. Repeat this layering sequence twice to use the remaining ladyfingers, espresso syrup, and mascarpone filling, ending with mascarpone filling.

Dust the entire surface of the tiramisù with the cocoa powder and the confectioners' sugar. Wrap and chill for at least 3 hours or up to overnight to allow the flavors to blend. Cut into portions and serve directly from the dish or pan.

Note: You may prefer to use pasteurized egg whites in this recipe to eliminate any food safety concerns.

Tiramisù is one of the most famous Italian dessert concoctions. Some have opined that its name, which translates as "pick me up" or "carry me up," refers to the caffeinated lift it gave to the courtesans of Treviso (the town near Venice where the dish is said to have been created). Others prefer to think the name reflects the fact that it is so delicious it will "carry you up" to heaven.

using a double boiler
p. 167

whipping egg whites
p. 139

Flourless Chocolate Soufflé Cake

5 oz bittersweet chocolate, chopped

¾ cup (1½ sticks) unsalted butter plus extra for greasing

10 large eggs (divided use)

⅔ cup sugar (divided use)

¼ cup Grand Marnier or other orange-flavored liqueur

Makes one 8-inch cake

Preheat the oven to 375°F. Grease the bottom of an 8-inch round cake pan and line with parchment paper. Use another piece of parchment paper to form a collar around the inside edge of the pan, allowing the paper to extend 3 inches above the top of the pan. Secure the collar in place with tape. Butter the paper generously.

Stir the chocolate and butter together in the top of a double boiler until melted and smooth, or melt them in the microwave on low power in 15- to 20-second increments (page 242). There may be a few lumps left, but they will melt as the chocolate cools to room temperature.

Separate 9 of the eggs. Set aside.

In a stand mixer fitted with the whisk attachment, beat the 9 egg whites on medium speed until frothy. Gradually add ⅓ cup of the sugar. Whip the whites on high speed until medium peaks form, about 4 minutes. Transfer the meringue to a separate bowl.

Rinse out the mixing bowl and return it to the mixer. With the whisk attachment, beat the 9 egg yolks, the remaining whole egg, and the remaining ⅓ cup sugar on medium speed until a dense foam that falls in ribbons from the whisk forms, scraping down the bowl with a rubber spatula as needed, about 5 minutes. Add the Grand Marnier and the cooled chocolate mixture. Continue whipping until the batter is evenly blended, 1 minute.

Remove the bowl from the mixer and fold half of the meringue into the yolk mixture until the batter is evenly blended, lighter in texture, and smooth. Fold in the remaining meringue, folding only until blended evenly.

Pour the batter into the prepared pan and bake until the cake just starts to pull away from the sides and the center no longer jiggles when the pan is gently shaken, 45–50 minutes.

Let the cake cool completely in the pan on a wire rack before turning out by placing a serving plate over the pan and inverting. Turn the cake upright before slicing and serving.

Although the CIA does not recommend the use of a collar when making a hot dessert soufflé, a collar is useful here, to give the cake something to cling to as it cools, for a more delicate texture.

Serve with whole or sliced fresh berries or fruit coulis (p. 273) made with berries. Custard Sauce (p. 274) or Chocolate Sauce (p. 270) would also make a fine accompaniment.

using a double boiler p. 167

separating eggs p. 138

Apricot Jelly Roll

Flourless cooking spray
as needed

All-purpose flour for dusting

5 large eggs, separated

¾ cup granulated sugar
(divided use)

⅔ cup cake flour, sifted twice

1 tsp vanilla extract

½ tsp salt

½ cup confectioners' sugar plus
extra for dusting

1 cup strained apricot preserves
(divided use)

2 cups Chantilly Cream (p. 281)

Makes about 8 servings

Preheat the oven to 375°F. Coat a jelly roll pan lightly with cooking spray and line with parchment paper. Spray the paper with cooking spray and dust with all-purpose flour, tapping out any excess.

Combine the egg yolks and ½ cup of the granulated sugar in the bowl of a stand mixer fitted with the whisk attachment and whip the egg yolks on high speed until the foam is 3 times its original volume and falls in thick ribbons when the whisk is lifted, 4–5 minutes. Transfer to a large mixing bowl and set aside.

In a clean bowl and with a clean whisk attachment, beat the egg whites on medium speed until they are frothy, 2 minutes. Add the remaining ¼ cup of granulated sugar gradually while whipping. Continue to whip until medium peaks form when the beater is lifted, 3 minutes.

Fold the meringue into the yolk mixture with a rubber spatula in 2 or 3 additions. Scatter the flour, vanilla extract, and salt all at once over the batter and fold into the batter just long enough to blend the flour evenly. Pour the batter into the prepared jelly roll pan and gently spread into an even layer with an offset spatula.

Bake until the top of the cake is golden brown and the edges are just starting to pull away from the sides of the pan, 12–15 minutes. While the cake is baking, lay a clean flat-weave towel on a work surface and sift the confectioners' sugar over it.

When the cake is finished baking, invert it onto the sugar-coated cloth. Remove the pan and parchment paper and, starting at a long edge, roll the cake into a log (the cloth will be inside the roll). When the cake is cool, unroll it and spread it with ¾ cup of the apricot preserves, covering the cake evenly. Spread the Chantilly cream over the preserves. Use the cloth to lift the long edge and roll the cake up gently without the cloth. Spread the remaining ¼ cup apricot preserves over the top of the cake, transfer to a platter, and chill for at least 1 hour before dusting with confectioners' sugar, slicing into 2-inch pieces, and serving.

Jelly roll cakes, or roulades, are made by baking and rolling a thin layer of sponge cake around a filling. Jelly is traditional, but you can certainly replace the jelly with fresh fruits, softened ice cream, mousse, or pudding. The trick to keeping the cake from cracking is to carefully "mold" it before you fill and roll it. Turn the cake out of the pan while it is still hot onto a sugar-coated towel and roll it up to keep it from drying out as it cools. Another important tip for making a nice moist cake with no dry spots is to spread it into an even layer in the pan, paying close attention to the edges and corners.

You can substitute Bavarian Cream (p. 275) or whipped soft Ganache (p. 284) as the filling.

the foam mixing method
p. 33

separating eggs p. 138

Warm Apple Charlotte

15 slices fine-grain sandwich bread

½ cup (1 stick) unsalted butter, melted, plus 2 Tbsp unsalted butter (divided use)

4½ cups Granny Smith apples, peeled, cored, and very thinly sliced

½ vanilla bean

¼ cup tightly packed light brown sugar

½ tsp ground ginger

¼ cup apricot jam

¼ cup brandy

1 Tbsp freshly squeezed lemon juice

Makes 8 servings

Preheat the oven to 375°F. Remove the crust from the bread and cut 11 slices of the bread in half diagonally into 2 triangles each. Cut the remaining 4 slices in half to make 2 rectangles each. Brush all of the pieces of bread with some of the ½ cup melted butter. Line the sides of a 1½-qt soufflé dish with the rectangles, overlapping them slightly, and then use 11 triangles to line the bottom of the dish in an overlapping spiral pattern. Fill the hole in the center of the spiral with a bit of scrap bread left over from trimming. Brush with butter once again. (It is important to line the sides of the mold before the bottom because the bottom layer of bread should sit slightly inside the sides. If the bottom is put in first and the sides are layered on top of it, there is a greater chance that the bottom will stay in the dish when the charlotte is unmolded.)

Heat the 2 Tbsp butter in a large sauté pan over medium heat and add the apples. Split the vanilla bean in half lengthwise and scrape out the seeds. Add the vanilla seeds, brown sugar, and ginger to the pan. Sauté, stirring frequently, until the apples are evenly coated with sugar and ginger. Add the apricot jam, brandy, and lemon juice. Simmer over medium heat, stirring occasionally, until nearly all the liquid has evaporated, 15–20 minutes.

Fill the lined soufflé dish with the apple filling, pressing it gently to pack it lightly. Top the charlotte with the remaining 11 triangles of bread in an overlapping spiral pattern and brush the top with the remaining melted butter.

Bake until the top crust is golden brown and the apples are very tender, 35–40 minutes. Cool slightly before inverting onto a cake plate and cutting into pieces. Serve warm.

The first known printed apple charlotte recipe appeared in 1796. It may have been named after Queen Charlotte of England, who was the wife of King George III and a supporter of apple growers. Charlottes are traditionally made in a basin-shaped mold with sloping sides and a flat bottom, and usually a tight-fitting lid. There are two types of charlotte fillings: baked and unbaked. For both, a casing or crust encloses a sweet filling, which may be made with other flavors besides apple.

Accompany warm slices of charlotte with Custard Sauce (p. 274), Caramel Sauce (p. 271), or French Vanilla Ice Cream (p. 199).

cooling cakes p. 140

Angel Food Summer Pudding

2 cups stemmed and quartered strawberries

2 cups blackberries

2 cups raspberries

½ cup sugar

2 Tbsp freshly squeezed lemon juice

2 Tbsp framboise or other raspberry liqueur (optional)

2 Tbsp honey, or to taste

Angel Food Cake (p. 151)

Chantilly Cream (p. 281) for serving

Makes 6 servings

Combine the berries with the sugar and lemon juice in a saucepan and simmer over low heat for 5 minutes.

Remove the berries from the heat and stir in the framboise and honey. Use a slotted spoon to lift the berries out of the syrup and set berries and syrup aside separately.

Line six 10-oz soufflé dishes with plastic wrap.

Slice the angel food cake into ½-inch-thick slices. Cut slices to fit the sides and bottoms of the soufflé dishes. Dunk the slices in the berry syrup, turning to coat evenly. Line the bottom and sides of the dishes completely with slices of the cake. Spoon the berries into the center, dividing them evenly among the molds. Lay a syrup-soaked slice of cake on top of each of the molds.

Fold the plastic wrap over the puddings and press down gently. Chill the puddings for at least 3 hours or up to overnight.

To unmold the puddings, pull back the plastic wrap and invert onto dessert plates. Spoon or pipe a dollop of Chantilly cream onto each pudding before serving.

Note: This dessert can also be made using a prepared angel food cake, and frozen berries can be used if fresh berries are unavailable.

Summer puddings are made by soaking cake slices in a flavored syrup and filling them with poached or fresh fruits. Unlike traditional steamed puddings, they are not cooked, but they look quite similar because of the way they are molded. To make a single large pudding instead of individual ones, use a clear glass bowl or footed trifle dish. Since you'll serve a large summer pudding directly from the mold, there is no need to line it with plastic wrap before you layer the cake and fruit.

piping p. 266

Chocolate Sabayon Torte

Simple Syrup

½ cup water

½ cup sugar

One 8-inch layer Chocolate Sponge Cake (p. 149), sliced in half horizontally (p. 142)

1 recipe Chocolate Sabayon (p. 283), prepared after simple syrup and cake-lined ring are ready

1 recipe soft Ganache (p. 284)

Makes one 8-inch torte

To make the simple syrup, combine the water and sugar in a saucepan over medium heat and bring to a boil. Remove the pan from the heat and cool to room temperature.

Choose a cake ring or springform pan between 7 and 8 inches in diameter. Line with plastic wrap. (If you are using a cake ring, set it on a baking sheet.) After trimming 1 of the chocolate sponge cake layers as needed to just fit the mold, set the layer in the ring and brush with about ¼ cup of the simple syrup.

Prepare the chocolate sabayon as directed. Immediately pour the filling into the cake-lined ring and gently spread into an even layer with a small offset spatula.

Trim and place the second layer of cake over the filling, pressing gently to remove any air pockets and to make the surface level. Brush the second layer with the remaining simple syrup. Cover tightly with plastic wrap and let the cake chill and the filling firm in the refrigerator for at least 3 hours or up to overnight.

When you are ready to finish the cake, unmold it by placing a cake plate over the ring or pan, inverting both together, and removing the ring and plastic wrap.

Whip the ganache in a stand mixer fitted with the whisk attachment on high speed until it has a good spreading consistency, about 5 minutes. Brush away any loose crumbs from the cake and apply a thin crumb coat (page 265). Refrigerate the cake to set the crumb coat, about 1 hour.

To finish the cake, spread most of the ganache evenly over the top and sides of the cake. If desired, use a cake comb to decorate the sides and a pastry bag to pipe the remaining ganache around the rim of the cake to make a decorative border. Wrap and refrigerate until ready to serve.

Tortes usually require some planning. You can bake the cake layers in advance and keep them well wrapped in the refrigerator or freezer. Simple syrup and soft ganache also hold well, so that you can make them when you have time. But, the sabayon filling must be made just before you pour it into the mold so that the gelatin doesn't set up too much.

Stainless-steel cake rings look like cake or tart pans without a bottom and are used to both bake and mold cakes, tortes, and tarts. They are available in various sizes, from 2½ to 12 inches in diameter and from ¾ to 3 inches high.

making molded cakes
p. 141

piping a shell border
p. 268

Custards

and Puddings

Custards and puddings are a study in theme and variation. They are prepared from a limited range of basic ingredients that marry well with both familiar and exotic flavors. They might be served hot or cold. They might be baked, stirred, molded, or chilled. However they are prepared and served, they are characterized by a creamy, rich texture. Mastering the techniques used to make custards and puddings opens the doors to a wide range of delicate sauces, creamy icings and fillings, soufflés, cheesecakes, and even ice creams.

The basic ingredients

Most custards and puddings depend upon the combination of just three simple ingredients: eggs, sugar, and cream or milk. In most puddings, as well as in pastry cream, starches such as cornstarch, flour, rice, or bread supplement or replace the eggs that give custard its body. In other recipes, gelatin provides thickening power.

Eggs thicken and provide structure to custards and puddings as well as add flavor and color. Their delicate proteins cook at a relatively low temperature: whites start to thicken and turn opaque at around 140°F, yolks at 165°F. This means that when making custards and puddings, you must carefully control how fast the eggs cook in order to keep them from overcooking or curdling.

Adding sugar helps. When you blend sugar into eggs, they don't start to solidify until they reach about 185°F. This gives the cook more leeway when heating eggs. Tempering eggs (page 167) is a standard technique used to introduce uncooked eggs into a hot milk or cream mixture without causing the eggs to curdle. Double boilers (page 167) eliminate the hot spots that typically develop when you put a pan directly on a stove-top burner, and hot water baths (page 168) are used to maintain an even gentle heat around custards while they bake in the oven.

Dairy products also contribute to a custard's or pudding's texture. You may choose to substitute whole milk for cream in custard and pudding recipes, but as the amount of butterfat drops, you will notice a difference in the texture and flavor of the finished dish. The higher the butterfat content of the base liquid, the denser and richer the finished item.

Variations in texture

Changing the way you mix and cook the ingredients for a custard also changes the texture of the finished dish. Stirring the ingredients as they cook keeps the eggs and other thickeners moving around so that they don't form a solid network. The end result is a custard, such as pastry cream, that is soft enough to pour, especially while it is still hot. Baking a custard undisturbed instead of stirring it while you heat it allows the proteins to recombine into a relatively strong web with long strands. Baked custards, such as crème caramel, can be cut, sliced, or unmolded and still keep their shape. Cheesecake is essentially a baked custard; it simply replaces the cream with cream cheese for a very dense and creamy texture.

Custard as an element in other preparations

Custard is the base of such cream desserts as mousse, Bavarian cream, or pastry cream. Creams are related to custards in that most dishes that might be described as a cream begin with a base mixture that has the consistency of a stirred custard. Fruit purées and fruit curds, often used as the base for many contemporary creams, are in the same family of texture as a stirred custard. A cream may be thickened with starch, as for pastry cream; blended with gelatin to give it structure and shape; or lightened with foams and chilled, as for a mousse.

From mousse, it's not a big step to soufflés. Soufflés combine whipped egg whites with a pastry cream or fruit purée, then they are baked instead of chilled to give them their final structure and shape.

A word on sugar cookery

Three of the most popular presentations for custard—crème brûlée, crème caramel, and pots de crème—provide some simple lessons in sugar cookery. To make crème brûlée, you scatter sugar in an even layer over a cooked and chilled custard, then caramelize it under a broiler or with a blowtorch to make a crisp, glasslike crust that shatters when a spoon breaks into it. Making crème caramel and pots de crème introduces a second sugar-cooking technique, sometimes called "the dry method." When sugar is carefully heated in a heavy saucepan, it melts, becomes clear, and then gradually takes on a rich amber color. Eventually, it will turn into a deep golden brown caramel. For crème caramel, the caramel layered in the mold liquefies as it absorbs moisture from the baked custard while it chills in its mold overnight. Pots de crème, on the other hand, call for the caramel to be blended into the custard mixture before baking to add a deep and complex flavor.

Molding and presentation options

Some desserts in this chapter, such as crème brûlée and pots de crème, are served in the same container in which they are cooked. Others, like crème caramel, are removed from the mold before serving by running a thin blade around the edge of the mold, then inverting it onto a plate, so that the bottom of the custard is now the top. Some custards benefit from a brief rest after baking so that they can settle; 10 minutes is usually adequate. Soufflés are served hot from the oven, directly in their molds, before they have a chance to sink.

Tempering eggs

Tempering is a technique that allows you to add eggs to a hot liquid without scrambling them.

1 Beating the eggs

Whisk the eggs until they are a uniform golden color. This action breaks up the yolk so that it will blend with hot cream or milk more readily and not overcook upon contact. Adding some sugar also helps to prevent the eggs from overcooking.

2 Stirring in hot liquid

The first addition of hot liquid to eggs should be no more than half the volume of the egg mixture. Pour or ladle the liquid into the eggs while stirring the mixture until it is smooth. This mixture is called a liaison. Once the eggs are slightly warmed in this way, you can add hot liquid in increasingly large increments. Continue until you have added about one-third of the total volume.

3 Stirring the liaison into the pan

The tempered mixture is now hot enough to combine with the remaining base liquid without instantly cooking the eggs into little curds. For a baked custard, add the remainder of the hot milk or cream to the tempered eggs, stirring constantly, before pouring the mixture into a prepared mold or crust. To make a stirred custard or pudding, pour the heated liaison back into the pan that holds the remaining two-thirds of the simmering liquid. Return it to low heat, or simply continue to simmer until the liaison has lightly thickened the base, usually at around 180°F.

Using a double boiler

A double boiler ensures gentle heat, perfect for cooking delicate custards and sauces.

1 Cooking over simmering water

You can either use a set of nested pots specifically designed for use as a double boiler, or create your own setup by selecting a saucepan for the bottom portion of the double boiler and a stainless-steel or glass bowl that will sit snugly atop the pan. Add enough water to the bottom pan to last throughout cooking time, but not so much that the water touches the bottom of the top container. Bring the water just to a simmer. The steam that rises from the water provides the heat to warm or cook the ingredients in the top of the double boiler. Set the top portion of the double boiler over the steaming water. Monitor the heat under the pan as you work to prevent the water from boiling.

For specific information about melting chocolate in a double boiler, see page 242.

Making a hot water bath

Baking in a hot water bath, or bain-marie, prevents egg-rich dishes from overcooking.

1 Setting up the pan

Choose a pan large enough to comfortably hold the egg dish to be baked. There should be enough room for water to be poured halfway up the sides of the dish and circulate around the dish to act as a buffer from the oven's heat. You can also elevate the dish to prevent direct contact with the bottom of the pan, using a wire rack for a single large dish or a folded kitchen towel for custard cups or soufflé dishes, which might shift on a rack.

2 Filling the pan with hot water

Position an oven rack in the center of the oven and pull it out only halfway, so that it doesn't tip as you fill the pan. Set the baking pan with the filled custard dishes on the rack. Carefully pour the hot water into the pan so that it comes one-half (or at least one-third) of the way up the side of the dishes. Push the rack carefully back into the oven. Check the pan periodically. If the water is boiling, lower the oven temperature slightly and replace the water that boiled away.

3 Removing the dishes

When the custard is properly baked, carefully pull the oven rack out halfway. Using an oven mitt or tongs, lift the dish(es) out of the bath and set on a wire rack. Leave the water-filled pan in the oven until it cools.

Making baked custards

Remove baked custards from the oven when they are just softly set. As they cool, residual heat in the custard finishes the cooking process.

1 Testing custards for doneness

Recipes usually indicate about how long a custard needs to cook, but don't rely upon timing alone. Lift the custard from the hot water bath and gently shake the dish. Custards that need to bake longer will have rings moving in concentric circles. A custard that is ready to come out of the oven will have relatively smooth ripples that move back and forth. Let baked custards sit at room temperature for 30 minutes before you put them in the refrigerator.

2 Serving baked custards

Crème brûlée and pots de crème are served in the dish or mold. Crème caramel, however, is traditionally unmolded to let the sauce flow out over the custard. Unmolded custards are usually served cooled or chilled. After the custard is fully baked and chilled, run the thin blade of a knife around the dish to release the custard from the sides. Hold a plate over the top of the cup or dish and invert the plate and cup together. Lift the cup or dish away, leaving the custard behind on the plate. When custards are served hot, they tend to lose their shape as soon as they are cut or unmolded. Let them rest for 10–15 minutes after baking before slicing or scooping them directly from the baking dish or pan.

Making an ice bath

Placing egg-rich dishes in an ice bath speeds the cooling process, preventing overcooking and also shortening the time they sit unrefrigerated.

1 Cooling in an ice bath

Prepare an ice bath before cooking stirred custards or puddings. It is important to start cooling these dishes as soon as they are done cooking or their residual heat might cause them to become overcooked. You can make an ice bath in a large bowl, in the kitchen sink, or in a flat-bottomed roasting pan or deep cake pan for multiple custard cups. If you use a bowl, be sure to choose one that is large enough to hold plenty of cold water and ice as well as the bowl or dish filled with the item you need to cool.

Add ice and then enough cold water to come halfway up the side of the item to be cooled. If the recipe is cooked in a saucepan over direct heat, pour the mixture (through a sieve if the recipe indicates straining) into a glass or metal bowl. Set the bowl in the ice bath and make sure that it doesn't tip over. Stirred custards or puddings should be stirred occasionally to encourage them to release their heat more quickly.

Once custards or puddings have cooled to room temperature, remove them from the ice bath and continue with the recipe or put them in the refrigerator to use or serve later.

Note that baked custards should not be cooled in an ice bath.

Making stirred custards and puddings

Since these dishes are prepared over direct heat, they demand constant attention.

1 Stirring constantly until boiling

During the last stage of cooking a stirred custard or pudding, the liquid is brought up to or very close to a full boil. To prevent eggs from overcooking and starches from sticking to the pan, stir constantly in a figure-eight pattern, reaching into the pan corners with a wooden spoon or silicone spatula.

2 Testing for doneness

Simmer and stir the custard until lightly thickened; this usually happens at around 180°F. This stage is sometimes referred to as "nappé," meaning that the mixture is no longer runny, but coats the back of a wooden spoon in an even layer.

3 Straining and chilling

For a very fine texture, strain the custard to remove any stray bits of egg. Pour the custard through a fine-mesh sieve or cheesecloth-lined colander into a clean bowl. Don't push a custard through with the back of a spoon. (Puddings are usually not strained since they are thick, but if you do need to strain a pudding or pastry cream, you *will* need to use the back of a spoon or a rubber spatula to push it through the sieve.) Use an ice bath *(left)* to cool a stirred custard or pudding quickly. Once cooled to 40°F, custards, creams, and puddings should have parchment paper or plastic wrap placed directly on the surface to prevent a skin from forming. Finish chilling in the refrigerator.

Making steamed puddings

Steamed puddings are richer and denser than other types of puddings, and are actually quite similar to cakes. They may be steamed on the stove top or baked in the oven in a hot water bath.

1 Pudding mold styles

Pudding molds (sometimes referred to as pudding basins) hold the batter as a pudding bakes and give it a special shape. Some molds have deep ridges or other patterns on the sides. Some have rounded bottoms that make a domed pudding when they are unmolded; others, such as soufflé dishes, have flat bottoms.

2 Preparing the mold

Since the pudding is usually unmolded before it is served, it is important to grease the mold liberally. Use cooking spray or softened butter to evenly coat every surface and indentation of the mold. Scattering bread or cake crumbs, granulated sugar, or chopped nuts over the inside surface also helps the pudding release from the mold more easily. If the mold doesn't have a lid, you can protect the upper surface of the pudding as it bakes by covering it with a large piece of buttered parchment paper. Use twine to tie the paper in place.

3 Testing for doneness

Because steamed puddings take a long time to bake, you may need to add more hot water to the hot water bath during baking. Generally, steamed puddings are done when a skewer inserted near the center comes out with just a few moist crumbs clinging to it.

Working with gelatin

Gelatin gives mousses, whipped cream, and other soft, relatively liquid items extra body.

1 Softening or "blooming" gelatin

Gelatin is dehydrated as part of its processing, and must be softened in cool water. Place a small amount of cold liquid in a small bowl (usually about 4 Tbsp for 2¼ tsp, or ¼ oz, powdered gelatin) and scatter the gelatin over the surface. Stir briefly with a fork to break up any clumps. As the gelatin sits in the liquid, it will swell, a process known as "blooming." To use sheet gelatin, substitute an equal weight. Sheets are softened in cool water to cover for about 15 minutes, as opposed to 2 minutes for powdered gelatin.

2 Melting gelatin

After the gelatin has bloomed, melt it in a double boiler over barely simmering water (page 167) until the mixture is clear. Alternatively, microwave it on low power for 20 seconds. Once melted, add it immediately to the liquid to be thickened. Stir it well, or the gelatin may sink to the bottom. The gelatin will gel as the dessert chills; allow at least 3 hours for full thickening. If you want to speed up the gelling, you can stir the mixture over an ice bath (page 169) until it stays slightly mounded when you drop it from a spoon onto itself. Some ingredients, such as raw pineapple and papaya, prevent gelatin from thickening at all. If you want to include them in a dish that calls for gelatin, poach the fruit first.

Brûléeing sugar

There is more than one way to melt and caramelize sugar to a glasslike crust for a cold custard.

1 Scattering the sugar evenly

To make an even layer of sugar on a chilled custard, use your fingertips to scatter pinches of sugar over the custard from a height of 4 inches. A few back-and-forth shakes of the custard cup can help even out the sugar. Superfine sugar works very well for a brûlée topping, although regular sugar works fine, too.

2 Using a kitchen blowtorch

One way to melt the sugar for a crème brûlée is to use a kitchen blowtorch. Move the flame of a blowtorch in a back-and-forth motion over the surface of the crème brûlée 2–3 inches above the sugar.

3 Using a broiler

Alternatively, adjust your broiler rack so that the surface of the crème brûlée will be about 2 inches from the heat. Set the custards in a pan and surround them with crushed ice or ice water before putting the custards under the broiler to brown for 3–4 minutes.

Whichever method you use, look for the sugar to melt, then turn light gold and, soon after, a deep, rich brown. Once the sugar begins to color, it will brown very quickly, so be careful not to burn the sugar. Properly caramelized sugar will set into a hard shiny crust that cracks when you tap it with a spoon.

3 Heating without stirring

As soon as the sugar melts, stop stirring. Instead, very slowly swirl the pan over the heat to keep the temperature even. As the sugar continues to cook, you may smell a change before you start to see it. The first hints of a golden color will start to appear in the melted sugar. From this point on, the caramel will cook quickly, so watch it closely. There may be a slight hint of bitterness in the aroma the sugar gives off. When the sugar reaches the color you want, immediately take the pan from the heat. Set the bottom of the pan in the ice water bath for about 20 seconds to quickly lower the pan's temperature. This keeps the caramel from turning too dark or bitter. The best caramel taste develops when the sugar is cooked until it is a very deep brown. Now you can use the caramel to coat a mold or combine it with other ingredients.

4 Adding liquids

The caramel will thicken as it cools, so it is important to work quickly at this point. Some recipes require you to combine the caramel with cream or other liquids. The safest way to do this is to bring them to a simmer or boil and turn off the heat under them before you start making the caramel. The warm liquid will foam up immediately as it's combined with the caramel and it may splatter. Since the sugar is extremely hot, be sure that you keep your face turned slightly away from the pan. Stir gently until the caramel is dissolved; you may need to return the pan to the heat to melt it completely.

Caramelizing sugar

Some classic custards include sugar syrup cooked to a rich, dark color and a complex flavor.

1 Setting up

Select a heavy pan and dry the inside of the pan thoroughly if needed. Set up an ice bath (page 169) near the stove before beginning; once sugar starts to brown, it can go from perfect to scorched in no time. If you have an ice bath ready, you can stop the cooking at the precise moment you want.

2 Combining sugar with acid

Adding a bit of lemon juice or apple cider vinegar is essential for a flavorful caramel; sugar on its own won't have the depth of flavor it has when acid is added. The acid also helps discourage crystals from forming as the sugar cooks. Set the pan over low heat and stir slowly with a wooden spoon. You will be able to see and hear when the sugar is melted; stir slowly to prevent the sugar from splashing onto the sides of the pan.

Making cheesecakes

Deliciously dense cheesecake is a cross between custard, pie, and cake.

1 Making a crumb crust

Crumb crusts are a classic base for a cheesecake. Gently work together graham cracker or cookie crumbs with a little melted butter until the crumbs are evenly moistened. Spread the crumbs in an even layer in a lightly greased standard or springform cake pan. Use the bottom of a glass or a similar flat surface to press the crumbs down into a compact layer. Although you might form a crumb crust on both the bottom and sides of a pan for pie, cheesecakes usually have only a bottom crust.

2 Tapping to release bubbles

A properly mixed cheesecake batter is very smooth and usually has very little air whipped into it. As you pour the batter into the pan, however, it is possible to trap air in the batter. To settle the cake and release any air bubbles, lift the pan about an inch from the countertop, then drop it carefully onto the counter.

3 Baking cheesecakes

Cheesecakes are baked at a moderate to low temperature so that the eggs bake into a perfectly smooth and dense cake with an even and very moist texture. If the cake puffs up or splits, it may mean that the oven was too hot or that the cake baked for too long. Many recipes suggest using a hot water bath to help keep the heat gentle and even. Wrap springform pans with aluminum foil to keep water from seeping in. The doneness tests for cheesecake are similar to those used for a baked custard. The top and the sides should be quite pale in color. The center of the cheesecake should still be soft and moist; it may not look fully baked. The residual heat will finish the cake as it cools in the pan to room temperature, and firming in the refrigerator overnight produces a creamy, smooth texture.

4 Unmolding cheesecakes

Take the cake from the refrigerator and run a spatula or a thin-bladed knife around the edge to loosen the cake before you loosen the spring on a springform pan. If you used a standard cake pan, cover the top of the cake with plastic wrap after you free the sides of the cake. Hold a flat plate or a wire rack over the cake pan and invert both to get the cake out of the pan. Flip the cake over once more onto a serving plate so that the crust is back on the bottom. Unmolding a cheesecake this way can mar the surface, so you may want to add a glaze or a fruit topping.

the flavor becomes less pronounced with the addition of beaten egg whites. Soufflés made with fruit purées as their base tend to have a more textured upper surface after baking because they contain no starch. The purée should have a consistency similar to that of a pudding. If necessary, simmer the purée over low heat to concentrate the flavor and achieve the correct texture. Whichever kind of base you are preparing, if it is cold from the refrigerator, whisk it until it is smooth and light.

3 Baking in a hot oven

Soufflés need to bake quickly in a preheated oven in order to puff up properly. Don't rely upon the kitchen timer alone. To check the soufflés without cooling the oven, open the door a crack 1–2 minutes before the recipe says the soufflé should be done. (Try not to open the oven door any earlier and limit the number of times you check the soufflé; otherwise the soufflé may fall.) Perfectly baked soufflés rise 2 or more inches above the mold. The upper surface has a deep golden color, while the sides are relatively pale in color and still look slightly moist.

4 Serving soufflés

Custard, chocolate, fruit, and caramel sauces are often served with sweet soufflés to intensify the flavor of this elegant dessert. Have the sauce ready at the right temperature in a small pitcher and add it to the soufflés right at the table. Bring the soufflés directly from the oven to the table. Use a serving spoon to cut an X in the top of the soufflé and spoon the sauce directly into the soufflé.

Making hot soufflés

Hot soufflés demand careful planning and preparation.

1 Preparing the soufflé dish

To prepare the soufflé dish(es), brush or rub with softened butter. Adding a coating of sugar, chopped nuts, or crushed cookies adds flavor and texture, while giving the soufflé traction against the sides of the dish as the egg whites puff up, helping the soufflé rise. To coat the inside well, add a

spoonful of sugar or other dry ingredients to the buttered mold. Twist and turn the mold, rolling the sugar over every surface. Finally, tap the mold on the countertop to loosen the excess. Pour the sugar out of the mold, directly into the next one you need to coat.

2 Preparing the soufflé base

A classic soufflé made from a pastry cream base rises straight and tall with a perfectly flat top. The base should have a relatively heavy consistency and an intense flavor, because

Almond Custard

Flourless cooking spray for greasing

1 cup whole or low-fat milk

¾ cup half-and-half

¾ cup sugar (divided use)

1 vanilla bean

3 large eggs

2 large egg yolks

1 tsp almond extract

6 Poached Peaches in Lemon-Vanilla Syrup (p. 226) (optional)

Makes 6 servings

Preheat the oven to 350°F. Bring a teakettle of water to a boil. Coat six 6-oz ramekins or custard cups lightly with cooking spray.

Combine the milk, half-and-half, and ½ cup of the sugar in a saucepan. Split the vanilla bean in half lengthwise and scrape out the seeds. Add the seeds and the pod to the milk mixture. Bring the mixture to a simmer, stirring until the sugar dissolves. Remove the pan from the heat and let steep for at least 30 minutes. Strain into a clean pan and return to a simmer.

While the milk mixture reheats, blend the eggs and egg yolks with the remaining ¼ cup sugar in a heatproof bowl. Temper the eggs by gradually adding about one-third of the hot milk, whisking constantly. Add the remaining hot milk and the almond extract. Strain the custard through a fine-mesh sieve into a clean container.

Carefully ladle or pour the custard mixture into the prepared ramekins, filling them three-fourths full. Place the ramekins on a kitchen towel in a deep baking pan and place the pan on a pulled-out oven rack. Add enough boiling water to come halfway up the sides of the ramekins. Bake until the edges have set and a nickel-sized spot in the center jiggles slightly when a custard is shaken, 25–30 minutes.

Remove the custard cups from the water bath. Let the custards cool on a rack for 30 minutes, wrap individually, and refrigerate for at least 3 hours or up to 3 days before serving.

To unmold, warm a sharp knife in warm water and run around the edges of each cup. Turn the custards out onto chilled plates. Serve with sliced poached fruit, if desired.

Almond has a sweet, perfumed flavor that pairs well with several fruits, especially stone fruits like peaches, apricots, plums, and cherries, whose pits carry an almondlike flavor. Blending and layering almond and fruit flavors can result in a rich, complex dessert. Instead of the suggested poached peach accompaniment, you can also serve one or more of these fruits in their fresh form with the custard. The fruits' colors, textures, and flavors will contrast with the custard while their flavors complement it.

tempering eggs p. 167

making baked custards p. 168

Lavender Flans

Unsalted butter for greasing

2 cups whole or low-fat milk

½ cup sugar (divided use)

1 Tbsp chopped fresh lavender or 1½ tsp dried

3 large eggs

2 large egg yolks

6 large strawberries, sliced (optional)

Mint sprigs for garnish (optional)

Makes 6 servings

Preheat the oven to 325°F. Lightly butter six 4-oz ramekins or custard cups. Bring a teakettle of water to a boil.

Combine the milk, ¼ cup of the sugar, and the lavender in a nonreactive saucepan and bring to a boil over medium-high heat. Remove the pan from the heat and let steep for at least 30 minutes. Strain into a clean pan and return to a simmer.

While the milk mixture reheats, combine the eggs, egg yolks, and the remaining ¼ cup sugar in a heatproof bowl. Temper the eggs by gradually adding about one-third of the hot milk, whisking constantly. Add the remaining hot milk, stirring constantly. Strain the custard through a fine-mesh sieve into a clean container.

Carefully ladle or pour the custard into the prepared ramekins, filling them three-fourths full. Place the ramekins on a kitchen towel in a deep baking pan and place the pan on a pulled-out oven rack. Add enough boiling water to come halfway up the sides of the ramekins. Bake until the edges have set and a nickel-sized spot in the center jiggles slightly when a custard is shaken, 20–25 minutes.

Remove the flans from the water bath. Let the flans cool on a rack for 30 minutes, wrap individually, and refrigerate for at least 3 hours or up to 3 days before serving.

To unmold, warm a sharp knife in warm water and run around the edges of each cup. Turn the flans out onto chilled plates and, if desired, garnish with strawberries and/or mint sprigs.

Flan and crème caramel (p. 181) are closely related. Both are a type of baked custard, made in a mold with a crust of caramelized sugar. If you grow your own lavender, use fresh lavender flowers to scent the custard. Otherwise, look for lavender flowers in stores that sell bulk spices and herbs. There are a few varieties of lavender and some are more intensely flavored than others. Be sure to check the aroma and adjust the quantity of lavender if needed to keep the custard from tasting too much like a perfume.

making baked custards p. 168

separating eggs p. 138

Milk Chocolate Pudding

¾ cup sugar (divided use)

⅓ cup cornstarch

¼ cup unsweetened cocoa powder

3 cups whole or low-fat milk (divided use)

2 large eggs

2 large egg yolks

4 oz milk chocolate, melted (p. 242)

2 Tbsp unsalted butter

1 tsp vanilla extract

Chantilly Cream (p. 281) for serving (optional)

Chocolate curls (p. 269) for serving (optional)

Fresh raspberries for serving (optional)

Makes 8 servings

In a large bowl, blend ¼ cup of the sugar with the cornstarch and cocoa powder, whisking to break up any lumps. Stir in ½ cup of the milk, the eggs, and the egg yolks and whisk together until smooth. Set aside.

Combine the remaining 2½ cups milk with the remaining ½ cup sugar in a nonreactive saucepan and bring to a boil over medium heat. Temper the eggs by gradually adding about one-third of the hot milk mixture, whisking constantly. Return the tempered egg mixture to the pan with the remaining milk mixture.

Return the pan to medium heat and stir constantly with a wooden spoon until it reaches a boil and is quite thick and very smooth, 4–5 minutes.

Temper the melted chocolate by adding about ½ cup of the hot egg mixture and stirring until very smooth. Return the tempered chocolate to the pan, add the butter and vanilla extract, and stir until well blended.

Pour the pudding into eight 6-oz ramekins or custard cups or a large bowl. Place a piece of parchment or waxed paper directly on the surface of each pudding to prevent a skin from forming; pierce it in 2 or 3 places to the let the heat escape. Chill for at least 2 hours before serving. If desired, garnish with a dollop or rosette of Chantilly cream and chocolate curls and/or raspberries.

Milk chocolate gives this pudding a creamy, mellow flavor, but you can readily substitute other chocolates: semisweet, bittersweet, or white. Use a good quality chocolate for a smooth texture. Chips can be difficult to melt, so opt for bar chocolate if it is available. If you do use chips, melt them either over barely simmering water (p. 242) or in a microwave on a low power setting, working in increments of only 15 to 20 seconds. Stir frequently as the chips melt and stop as soon as they are smooth.

separating eggs p. 138

tempering eggs p. 167

Crème Brûlée

Flourless cooking spray
for greasing

2½ cups heavy cream

¾ cup sugar (divided use)

⅛ tsp salt

½ vanilla bean

5 large egg yolks, lightly beaten

6 Tbsp sugar (superfine if
available)

Makes 6 servings

Preheat the oven to 325°F. Bring a teakettle of water to a boil. Coat six 6-oz ramekins or custard cups lightly with cooking spray and set them on a kitchen towel in a deep baking pan. Combine the cream, ½ cup of the sugar, and the salt in a nonreactive saucepan over medium heat. Split the vanilla bean in half lengthwise and scrape out the seeds. Add the seeds and the pod to the milk mixture. Bring the mixture to a simmer, stirring until the sugar dissolves. Remove the pan from the heat and let the mixture steep for at least 30 minutes. Strain into a clean pan and return to a simmer.

Meanwhile, blend the egg yolks with the remaining sugar. Gradually add about one-third of the hot cream to the yolks, whisking constantly. Add the remaining hot cream and stir. Strain the custard through a fine-mesh sieve into a clean container. Carefully ladle or pour the custard into the prepared ramekins, filling them three-fourths full.

Place the baking pan on a pulled-out oven rack. Add enough boiling water to come halfway up the sides of the ramekins. Carefully slide in the rack and bake until the edges have set and a nickel-sized spot in the center jiggles slightly when a custard is shaken, 20–25 minutes.

Remove the ramekins from the water bath. Let the custards cool on a rack for 30 minutes, wrap individually, and refrigerate for at least 3 hours or up to 3 days before finishing with the brûlée layer.

To finish, evenly coat the top of each custard with a thin layer of sugar, about 1 Tbsp. Use a kitchen blowtorch or the broiler to evenly melt and caramelize the sugar. Serve immediately.

Crème brûlée means "burnt cream" in French, but it's actually a custard topped with a "burnt" coating of sugar. The trick is to quickly cook the sugar into a glasslike crust without overcooking the custard underneath it.

tempering eggs p. 167

brûléeing sugar p. 170

VARIATIONS

Coconut Crème Brûlée

Add ½ cup toasted coconut to the cream in place of the vanilla bean. Strain after steeping for 30 minutes and continue as directed.

Cinnamon Crème Brûlée

Add 3 cinnamon sticks to the cream in place of the vanilla bean. Strain after steeping for 30 minutes and continue as directed.

Coffee Pots de Crème

Flourless cooking spray for greasing

1 cup whole or low-fat milk

1 cup heavy cream

¾ cup sugar (divided use)

2 Tbsp coarsely ground coffee beans

1 large egg

2 large egg yolks

1 tsp vanilla extract

Makes 6 servings

Preheat the oven to 325°F. Bring a teakettle of water to a boil. Coat six 6-oz ramekins or custard cups lightly with cooking spray and set them on a kitchen towel in a deep baking pan.

Combine the milk and cream with ¼ cup of the sugar in a nonreactive saucepan and bring to a simmer over medium heat. Remove from the heat and keep warm.

Place ¼ cup of the sugar in a heavy saucepan and cook over medium heat until the sugar liquefies and turns into a deep golden brown caramel, 4–5 minutes. Add the hot cream mixture to the caramel in 3 additions, bringing to a boil after each addition and stirring to dissolve the caramel, about 5 minutes total. Add the ground coffee and continue to simmer, until the cream is well flavored, about 2 minutes. Strain the cream mixture through a coffee filter into a clean saucepan and return to a simmer.

While the cream mixture heats, blend the egg and egg yolks with the remaining ¼ cup sugar in a heatproof bowl. Temper the eggs by gradually adding about one-third of the hot cream mixture, whisking constantly. Add the remaining cream mixture and stir. Add the vanilla extract to the custard mixture, stir, and strain through a fine-mesh sieve into the prepared ramekins, filling them three-fourths full.

Place the baking pan on a pulled-out oven rack. Add enough boiling water to come halfway up the sides of the ramekins. Cover the pan loosely with parchment paper or aluminum foil and bake until the pots de crème are very glossy on top and jiggle only slightly when shaken, about 20–25 minutes.

Remove the ramekins from the water bath. Let the pots de crème cool on a rack for 30 minutes, wrap individually, and refrigerate for at least 3 hours or up to 3 days before serving in the ramekins.

Pot de crème is a delicate custard that gets its name (literally, "pot of cream") from the lidded cup it was traditionally baked in. The cup usually holds 3 to 4 oz and has a handle. The lid is meant to keep a skin from forming on the custard. Here, the lid is replaced with a sheet of parchment paper or aluminum foil draped loosely over the custards as they bake. The covering traps just a bit of steam for a delicately set, smooth custard. The paper or foil should rest on the rims of the cups and not touch the custard itself.

While the traditional flavor for a pot de crème is vanilla, other flavors—including pumpkin and chocolate—are common.

caramelizing sugar
p. 171

tempering eggs p. 167

Crème Caramel

Flourless cooking spray
for greasing

1 cup sugar (divided use)

⅛ tsp freshly squeezed
lemon juice

3 Tbsp warm water

2 cups whole milk

⅛ tsp salt

3 large eggs

2 large egg yolks

2 tsp vanilla extract

Makes 6 servings

Preheat the oven to 325°F. Bring a teakettle of water to a boil. Coat six 6-oz ramekins or custard cups lightly with cooking spray and set them on a kitchen towel in a deep baking pan.

To make the caramel, combine ½ cup of the sugar with the lemon juice in a heavy saucepan and bring to a boil over high heat, stirring constantly. Once all the sugar has dissolved, stop stirring and start swirling the pan, continuing to cook until the sugar is a rich golden brown, 3–4 minutes. When the caramel has reached the desired color, add the warm water to the caramel and stir over low heat until any hard bits are dissolved. Pour a ⅛-inch layer of caramel into the bottom of each prepared ramekin.

Combine the milk, ¼ cup of the sugar, and the salt in a saucepan over medium heat and bring to a simmer. Remove from the heat and keep warm.

While the milk mixture heats, blend the eggs and egg yolks with the remaining ¼ cup sugar in a heatproof bowl. Temper the eggs by gradually adding about one-third of the hot milk, whisking constantly. Add the remaining hot milk and the vanilla extract. Strain the custard through a fine-mesh sieve into the prepared ramekins, filling each three-fourths full.

Place the baking pan on a pulled-out oven rack. Add enough boiling water to come halfway up the sides of the ramekins. Carefully slide in the rack, and bake until the edges have set and a nickel-sized spot in the center jiggles slightly when a custard is shaken, 20–25 minutes.

Remove the custards from the water bath. Let the custards cool on a wire rack, wrap individually, and refrigerate for at least 24 hours or up to 3 days before unmolding and serving.

To serve, warm a sharp knife in warm water and run around the edges of each ramekin. Turn the custards out onto chilled plates.

Crème caramel is a dessert that produces its own sauce, as long as you are patient with it. After the custard bakes, it needs to cool long enough for two things to happen: the custard must become firm enough to unmold, and the caramel underneath the custard needs time to reabsorb some moisture and turn into a liquid. For both of these things to happen, the custard needs a minimum resting period of 24 hours.

caramelizing sugar
p. 171

making baked custards
p. 168

Riz Maltaise

6 cups whole milk

1 cup medium-grain white rice, such as Arborio

¾ cup sugar (divided use)

1 vanilla bean, split lengthwise

3 large egg yolks

⅓ cup light (golden) raisins

¼ cup dark rum

2 Tbsp finely grated orange zest

1 cup heavy cream, whipped to medium peaks (p. 263)

Makes 6–8 servings

Combine the milk, rice, ½ cup of the sugar, and the vanilla bean in a medium nonreactive saucepan. Bring to a boil over medium heat, reduce the heat to low, and cook, stirring frequently, until the rice is very creamy and tender, about 45 minutes. Remove from the heat. Scrape the seeds from the vanilla bean into the rice.

Meanwhile, stir together the yolks and the remaining sugar. Set aside. Combine the raisins, rum, and orange zest in a small saucepan over low heat. When the rum is just warmed, remove from the heat and allow the raisins to plump for about 10 minutes. Blend the raisin mixture, plus any unabsorbed rum, into the yolks.

Gradually add about one-third of the hot rice mixture to the egg yolks, whisking constantly, and then return the tempered yolks to the rest of the rice. Cook over low heat, stirring constantly, until the mixture just comes to a simmer, about 3 minutes. Remove from the heat, spread in an even layer in a shallow baking pan, and set a piece of parchment or waxed paper directly on the surface. Pierce a few holes in the paper to let the steam escape. Chill completely, about 2 hours.

Fold the whipped cream into the chilled pudding and spoon into six 6-oz molds or cups. Cover and chill for at least 3 hours before serving.

The name for this rice pudding shows a bit of its heritage. The inspiration for this recipe comes from the French classical repertoire. "Maltaise" in the title refers to the oranges of Malta, prized for their intense flavor. A medium-grain rice, like the kind you use for risotto, simmers in milk to a creamy consistency. Riz maltaise builds from the basic rice pudding by folding in whipped cream to make what could be a "nursery dish" into something light, billowy, and elegant.

making an ice bath
p. 169

making stirred custards and puddings p. 169

Panna Cotta

1 package (2¼ tsp) powdered unflavored gelatin

¼ cup cold water

2½ cups heavy cream

1 cup sugar

2⅓ cups buttermilk

¼ tsp salt

2 cups sliced fresh fruit or berries

Makes 8 servings

Sprinkle the gelatin over the cold water in a bowl and stir to break up any clumps. Let the gelatin soften for about 2 minutes. Heat the softened gelatin in a double boiler over simmering water (page 167) or in a microwave for about 20 seconds on low power, until the granules melt and the mixture is clear.

Heat the cream and sugar in a large nonreactive saucepan over low heat, stirring, until the sugar dissolves. Remove the mixture from the heat and stir in the gelatin. Stir in the buttermilk and salt.

Layer the fruit in eight 8-oz cups or a 2-qt serving bowl, filling up to halfway full. Ladle the panna cotta over the fruit. Cover and chill for at least 3 hours or up to 2 days before serving directly in the cups or from the bowl.

To accompany this silky Italian dessert, whose name translates as "cooked cream," use whatever fruit is fresh and ripe at the market, from peaches to mangoes to bananas to gooseberries. If your fruit is very tart, crush and toss it lightly with 2 or 3 Tbsp sugar and let rest for 15 minutes before you start the panna cotta.

working with gelatin
p. 170

Mango Mousse

1 large mango

1 package (2¼ tsp) powdered
unflavored gelatin

¼ cup dark rum or water

2 cups heavy cream

½ cup sugar (divided use)

2 large egg whites

Lime zest for garnish

Makes 6 servings

Peel the mango and cut the flesh away from the pit. Purée the mango
in a food processor or blender until very smooth. You should have
about 1½ cups.

Sprinkle the gelatin over the rum or water in a bowl and stir to break
up any clumps. Let the gelatin soften for about 2 minutes. Heat the
softened gelatin in a double-boiler over simmering water or in
a microwave for about 20 seconds on low power, until the granules
melt and the mixture is clear.

In a chilled deep bowl, whip the cream until it starts to thicken, and then
gradually add ¼ cup of the sugar while whipping to medium peaks.

In the clean bowl of a stand mixer fitted with the whisk attachment,
whip the egg whites on low speed until they are foamy. Increase the
speed to high and gradually add the remaining ¼ cup sugar while
beating. Continue to whip on high speed until the meringue holds
medium peaks.

Stir the melted gelatin into the mango purée. Working by hand with
a spatula, fold the whipped cream into the mango purée until evenly
blended. Add the meringue in 2 additions, folding the mixture just
until blended.

Pipe or spoon the mousse into six 6-oz molds. Refrigerate the mousse
for at least 3 hours or up to 24 hours. Garnish with lime zest just
before serving in the molds.

A small quantity of rum
intensifies the tropical
flavors of this mousse.
Since the rum is not boiled
in this dish and won't lose
any flavor, be sure to
choose a rum with a flavor
you enjoy. Rums that are
golden or dark have more
pronounced flavors
because they are typically
aged longer.

working with gelatin
p. 170

whipping cream p. 263

Warm Gingerbread Pudding

Cooking spray for greasing

1¼ cup crushed gingersnaps (divided use)

1 cup ladyfinger crumbs (p. 127)

6 large eggs

8 Tbsp (1 stick) unsalted butter, at room temperature

½ cup confectioners' sugar, sifted

1 tsp grated lemon zest

1 tsp ground cinnamon

½ tsp ground cloves

¼ tsp ground ginger

⅛ tsp freshly grated nutmeg

⅓ cup granulated sugar

½ cup dried currants

¼ cup candied lemon and/or orange peel (p. 245) plus extra for garnish

Makes 8 servings

Preheat the oven to 350°F. Bring a teakettle of water to a boil. Generously coat a pudding mold or 2-qt soufflé dish with cooking spray and coat with ¼ cup of the crushed gingersnaps. Set the mold on a kitchen towel in a deep baking pan.

Mix the remaining 1 cup crushed gingersnaps and the ladyfinger crumbs together. Set aside.

Separate the eggs (page 138). Set aside.

In a stand mixer fitted with the paddle attachment, cream the butter, confectioners' sugar, lemon zest, and spices on medium speed until light in texture and fluffy, about 2 minutes. Add the egg yolks in 2 or 3 additions, scraping down the bowl with a rubber spatula after each addition and mixing until very smooth, 2 minutes more. Add half of the crumb mixture to the butter mixture and blend on low speed until evenly mixed.

In the clean bowl of a stand mixer fitted with the whisk attachment, whip the egg whites on low speed until frothy. Increase the speed to medium and add the granulated sugar gradually. Increase the speed to high and continue to whip until medium peaks form when the beater is lifted.

Fold the remaining crumb mixture into the egg whites. Fold the egg white mixture into the butter mixture. Finally, fold in the currants and candied citrus peel. Spoon the batter into the prepared dish. Cover the mold with its lid or with aluminum foil or parchment paper tied into place with kitchen string.

Place the pudding mold or soufflé dish in the baking pan on a pulled-out rack in the oven. Add enough boiling water to come halfway up the sides of the mold, carefully slide in the rack, and bake until the pudding is puffy, the sides have begun to pull away from the dish, and a skewer inserted near the center of the pudding has only a few moist crumbs clinging to it, about 1 hour 45 minutes. Serve warm, garnished with candied citrus peel.

Sweet, warm spices like cinnamon, nutmeg, clove, and allspice give ginger-bread and many other baked goods their unmistakable aromas. Spices are generally understood to be dried aromatic ingredients, typically the bark or seeds of a plant; they are sold whole or ground. Whole spices may be toasted, then ground for a more complex flavor: shake them in a dry skillet over low to medium heat until they are richly aromatic.

Serve this pudding with Chantilly Cream (p. 281) or Custard Sauce (p. 274) for a temperature contrast.

whipping egg whites p. 139

making steamed puddings p. 170

Plum Clafouti

4 cups sliced pitted plums

¼ cup plum brandy

Cooking spray for greasing

3 large eggs

6 Tbsp granulated sugar

1¾ cups whole milk

2 Tbsp dark rum

½ tsp vanilla extract

⅛ tsp salt

1½ cups all-purpose flour, sifted

Confectioners' sugar for dusting

Makes 6 servings

Let the sliced plums plump in the brandy for 1 hour. Preheat the oven to 350°F. Coat an 8-inch baking dish lightly with cooking spray. In a stand mixer fitted with the whisk attachment, beat the eggs and granulated sugar on medium speed until foamy, 2 minutes. Mix in the milk, rum, vanilla extract, and salt. With the mixer on low speed, mix in the flour just until moistened. Spread one-third of the batter in the prepared baking dish. Scatter the sliced plums evenly over the batter and drizzle with any unabsorbed brandy. Spread the remaining batter over the plums, covering them evenly. Bake until the crust is a golden brown and a toothpick inserted near the center comes out clean, about 30 minutes.

Dust with confectioners' sugar just before serving. Serve hot, warm, or at room temperature, directly from the baking dish.

Clafouti is a dessert made with a layer of fruit topped with a batter that is baked until puffy. Clafouti is originally from Alsace, a region of France noted for its tree fruits. You will need 6 to 8 good-sized plums for this dish. You can present this rustic custard directly from a ceramic gratin or baking dish at the dinner table or for brunch.

sifting p. 71

Warm Lemon Pudding Cakes

Cooking spray for greasing

4 Tbsp (½ stick) unsalted butter, at room temperature, plus extra for greasing

¾ cup sugar

¼ tsp salt

3 large egg yolks

¼ cup all-purpose flour

2 tsp grated lemon zest

¼ cup freshly squeezed lemon juice

1 cup whole milk

4 large egg whites

1½ cups Custard Sauce (p. 274) (optional)

1½ cups fresh blueberries (optional)

Makes 6 servings

Preheat the oven to 325°F. Coat six 6-oz ramekins lightly with cooking spray and set them on a kitchen towel in a deep baking pan.

In a stand mixer fitted with the paddle attachment, cream together the butter, sugar, and salt on medium speed until smooth, about 2 minutes. Beat in the egg yolks, scraping down the bowl with a rubber spatula as needed, 2 minutes. Add the flour and mix until smooth, 1 minute. Add the lemon zest and juice. Add the milk and mix to make a smooth, light batter, 2 minutes more.

In the clean bowl of a stand mixer fitted with the whisk attachment, beat the egg whites to medium peaks. Fold them into the batter. Ladle the batter into the ramekins, filling them three-fourths full. Place the baking pan on a pulled-out oven rack. Add enough hot water to come halfway up the sides of the ramekins. Bake until the pudding cakes are golden brown and pull away from the edges of the ramekins, about 30 minutes. Remove the ramekins from the water bath. Let the puddings cool on a rack for 10 minutes before serving. To unmold, warm a sharp knife in water and run around the edges of each ramekin. Turn the puddings out onto plates and serve, garnished with custard sauce and blueberries, if desired.

These lemon cakes are more like steamed puddings than true cakes. As with puddings, the pudding cakes are baked in a water bath to keep them tender and light. As the pudding cakes cool, they lose some of their height but gain an extremely moist texture.

whipping egg whites p. 139

making a hot water bath p. 168

Ricotta Cheesecake

1 recipe Graham Cracker Crust
(p. 122)

⅔ cup whole-milk ricotta
cheese

½ cup sugar

1 lb cream cheese

2 large eggs, lightly beaten

1 tsp vanilla extract

1 tsp freshly squeezed
lemon juice

1 Tbsp cornstarch

3 Tbsp bread flour

3 Tbsp unsalted butter, melted
and kept warm, plus extra for
greasing

Makes one 8-inch cake

Preheat the oven to 325°F. Lightly butter an 8-inch springform pan and wrap the outside carefully with aluminum foil.

Prepare the graham cracker crust and press into an even layer in the bottom of the pan using a flat-bottomed glass.

Purée the ricotta and sugar in a food processor until smooth, 3–5 minutes.

In a stand mixer fitted with the paddle attachment, mix the cream cheese with the ricotta mixture on medium speed until smooth, about 10 minutes, scraping down the bowl with a rubber spatula as needed. Add the eggs and mix on low speed until very smooth, scraping down the bowl thoroughly. Add the vanilla extract, lemon juice, cornstarch, and flour to the batter and blend on medium speed until smooth. Gradually add the melted butter, scraping down the bowl as needed, until evenly blended.

Spread the batter in an even layer over the crust. Drop the pan onto the counter from the height of 1 inch to release any air bubbles. Place the pan in a shallow baking dish and place the dish on a pulled-out oven rack. Add about 1 inch of hot water. Carefully slide in the rack and bake until the edges are set (the center should still be soft), the cake starts to pull away from the sides, and the top is just starting to brown, 50–60 minutes.

Remove the pan from the water bath and cool the cheesecake in the pan on a wire rack, then refrigerate for at least 3 hours or up to overnight before unmolding.

To unmold, run a spatula or thin-bladed knife around the inside edge to loosen the cake. Unlatch the clamp to open the sides and lift the form away from the cake. Cut into slices and serve.

Cheese dishes of all sorts have always been popular wherever dairy farming took hold. Some of the earliest cookbooks contain recipes for cheesecake. The ricotta in this recipe gives the finished cheesecake a slightly lighter texture than that of other cheesecakes. Whole-milk ricotta stays tender as it bakes and is worth seeking out for this dish.

making cheesecakes
p. 172

making a hot water bath
p. 168

Sabayon and Fresh Berry Trifle

Sabayon

4 large egg yolks

⅓ cup freshly squeezed orange juice (about 1 orange)

⅓ cup Marsala wine

3 Tbsp sugar

1¼ cups heavy cream

One 8-inch layer Vanilla Sponge Cake (p. 149), cut into 1-inch cubes

2 cups berries, such as raspberries, blackberries, blueberries, strawberries, or a combination, plus berries for garnish

Makes 6 servings

Prepare an ice bath.

To make the sabayon, whisk together the egg yolks, orange juice, wine, and sugar in a stainless-steel mixing bowl and set over a pan of simmering water. Continue to whisk over the hot-water bath as the eggs cook. They will thicken, triple in volume, and become a pale yellow, 15 minutes. The mixture should fall from the whisk in ribbons that hold their shape on top of the sabayon. Remove the bowl from the hot-water bath and set it directly in the ice bath. Continue to whisk until the sauce is cold.

Whip the cream in the chilled bowl of a stand mixer fitted with the whisk attachment until it holds a medium peak when the whisk is turned upright (page 263). Reserve ¾ cup of the whipped cream to garnish the trifle, and refrigerate. Fold the remaining whipped cream into the sabayon and refrigerate for at least 1 hour or up to 4 hours before assembling the dessert.

To assemble individual trifles, place 2 cubes of cake in each of six 6-oz molds, glasses, or dishes. Top with some berries and then a dollop of the cold sabayon. Continue layering cake, berries, and sabayon until the molds are filled. To make a large trifle, layer the cake, berries, and sabayon in a footed trifle dish or a soufflé dish. Cover and chill the trifle for at least 3 hours before serving.

To garnish the trifle, use a pastry bag fitted with a large star tip to pipe a rosette of the reserved whipped cream (page 266) on top of the individual trifles or around the edge of a large trifle, and decorate with berries.

A trifle traditionally includes cake doused with sherry, a custard, and fresh fruit. This trifle introduces an egg-based sauce that the French call *sabayon* and the Italians, *zabaglione*. Marsala, with its rich, raisin-like flavor, gives the custard the same heady aroma that a classic trifle introduces by brushing the cake with sherry.

making an ice bath
p. 169

using a double boiler
p. 167

Raspberry Soufflés

Unsalted butter at room temperature, for greasing

Raspberry Purée

2 cups fresh or thawed frozen raspberries

⅓ cup water

1¼ cups sugar plus extra for dusting

3 large egg whites

Makes 4 servings

Preheat the oven to 350°F. Coat four 8-oz soufflé dishes with softened butter and dust with sugar, making sure to coat the top rim of each dish as well.

To make the raspberry purée, combine the raspberries and water in a saucepan and warm over low heat until the berries are hot, about 4 minutes. Push through a fine-mesh sieve to remove the seeds.

Attach a candy thermometer to the side of a saucepan, making sure that the bulb is not resting on the bottom of the pan. Combine the raspberry purée and sugar in the pan and place over medium heat.

While the raspberry mixture is cooking, put the egg whites in the clean bowl of a stand mixer fitted with the whisk attachment. Begin whipping the whites on medium speed when the raspberry syrup reaches 230°F. (Do not whip beyond soft peak stage.) When the raspberry syrup reaches 240°F, reduce the mixer speed and carefully pour the syrup into the whites in a gradual stream around the sides of the bowl. Continue to whip on medium speed until the whites form medium peaks, about 4 minutes.

Spoon the soufflé batter into the prepared soufflé dishes, filling them each three-fourths full, and set them on a baking sheet before placing in the oven. Bake until the soufflés are very puffy and the tops lightly browned, 18–20 minutes. Serve directly from the oven.

This soufflé is a flavored meringue, baked until puffed and lightly browned. This style of soufflé lets the bright colors and flavors of fresh fruit shine, without making them compete with the pastry cream often used in more traditional dessert soufflés.

Serve the soufflés with Raspberry Coulis (p. 273), Chocolate Sauce (p. 270), or a small amount of framboise (raspberry liqueur) poured into an X cut into the top of the soufflé.

making hot soufflés
p. 173

whipping egg whites
p. 139

VARIATIONS

Strawberry Soufflés

Replace the raspberries with fresh or thawed frozen strawberries. Continue as directed.

Drizzle a little Chocolate Sauce (p. 270) into this soufflé when you serve it, if desired.

Banana Soufflés

Replace the raspberries with 1½ cups puréed bananas (2 firm but ripe bananas mashed with a table fork). Continue as directed.

A little Caramel Sauce (p. 271) drizzled into this soufflé at serving makes a nice addition.

Caramel and Pear Soufflé

Flourless cooking spray for greasing

½ cup sugar (divided use)

1 Tbsp cold water

2 ripe pears, peeled, halved, and cored

¼ cup pear or apple juice

1 small piece cinnamon stick

1 whole clove

1 cup Pastry Cream (p. 282)

3 large egg whites

Makes 4–6 servings

Preheat the oven to 400°F. Coat a 1-qt soufflé dish lightly with cooking spray and set it on a kitchen towel in a deep baking pan. Bring a teakettle of water to a boil.

Combine ¼ cup of the sugar and the cold water in a small saucepan. Cook over medium heat until the sugar liquefies and turns a deep golden brown. Immediately pour the caramel into the prepared soufflé dish, leaving about 2 teaspoons of the caramel in the pan. Add the pears, pear juice, cinnamon stick, and clove to the saucepan used to make the caramel. Bring the mixture to a simmer over medium heat and poach the pears until they are very tender, about 10 minutes. Remove and discard the cinnamon stick and clove. Purée the pears and juice in a blender until very smooth.

Cool the pear purée to room temperature and then stir together the purée and the pastry cream until evenly blended and smooth.

In a stand mixer fitted with the whisk attachment, whip the egg whites until foamy, 2 minutes, then add the remaining ¼ cup sugar. Continue to beat until the egg whites form medium peaks. Fold the egg whites into the pear and pastry cream mixture in 2 additions, blending just until the egg whites are incorporated. Pour the soufflé batter into the caramel-lined soufflé dish.

Place the soufflé dish in its baking pan on a pulled-out oven rack. Add enough boiling water to the pan to come halfway up the sides of the soufflé dish. Carefully slide in the rack and bake until the soufflé has risen and the top is quite golden, 35–40 minutes. Serve the soufflé immediately from the soufflé dish.

Note: If you prefer to make 4 individual soufflés, prepare four 8-oz soufflé dishes by coating each lightly with the cooking spray and pouring a small amount of caramel into each one, turning the mold so that the bottom is evenly coated. The baking time will be reduced to 18–20 minutes.

Bosc pears have a dense flesh that makes them a good choice for baking and cooking, but regardless of what variety you choose, be sure that the pears are ripe. When you press them at the base of their necks, there should be some give. Not all pears change color as they ripen, but their aroma becomes more intense.

To remove the core from a pear, cut it in half from top to bottom, then use a melon baller to scoop out the seeds.

making hot soufflés
p. 173

caramelizing sugar
p. 171

Frozen Desserts

7

Frozen desserts, ices, and even iced dairy treats are mentioned in Chinese literature as early as the twelfth century. It is the Italians, though, who are widely credited with developing ice cream as we know it during the sixteenth century. But ice-cream lovers around the world owe perhaps their greatest debt of gratitude to Nancy Johnson, a Philadelphian who received a patent on September 9, 1843, for her invention: an "artificial freezer" that used a dasher and a crank to allow people to make ice cream at home with greater ease than ever before.

Ice cream does not represent the entire universe of frozen desserts, of course. In this chapter, you will learn the techniques used for making frozen soufflés, parfaits, and granitas, just a few of the frozen desserts you can make even without an ice-cream maker.

Two basic styles: churned and still-frozen

Churned frozen desserts like ice cream, sherbet, and sorbet get their soft, spoonable texture from being stirred with a dasher while they are cooled to below the freezing point in an ice-cream maker. The stirring action ensures that the ice crystals remain tiny and introduces enough air into the mixture that it remains light enough to scoop, even when frozen. Still-frozen desserts are placed into a mold and then allowed to freeze without stirring. Their textures remain light and airy thanks to the whipped cream or whipped eggs they contain. A prime example of a still-frozen dessert is a frozen soufflé.

Ingredients and their roles

The same basic ingredients featured in custards and creams are used to make ice cream, frozen yogurt, sherbet, sorbet, and frozen soufflés: milk (or its close relations, heavy cream, half-and-half, yogurt, and buttermilk), sugar, and, sometimes, eggs.

The butterfat in milk and cream allows the incorporation of air during freezing, in much the same way that heavy cream holds small pockets of air when it is whipped. The milk solids interfere with the formation of ice crystals during freezing, contributing a smoother texture, while natural emulsifiers in milk help to bind together the liquids and fats. The type of milk or cream you use in a recipe determines the consistency of the resulting frozen dessert. Heavy cream has a higher butterfat content than milk, for the smooth and dense texture with smaller ice crystals expected in ice cream. If you choose to substitute milk for some or all of the cream in a recipe, the end result will be more like ice milk or sherbet; it will have an icier, more granular texture.

Sugar and alcohol add flavor to frozen desserts, but they also lower a mixture's freezing point: too much of either will prevent your dessert from freezing into a scoopable consistency.

Eggs make frozen desserts like ice cream richer and smoother because yolks add fat and certain emulsifiers that bind ingredients. Egg white promotes a smoother, less grainy texture, as in sorbet, because of the role its proteins play in keeping the water suspended in the sorbet, so that large crystals don't form as easily. The more moisture trapped by the proteins, especially in ice cream made with a cooked base, the fewer and smaller the ice crystals in the finished dessert. When egg whites are beaten into a meringue, as for a frozen soufflé, they introduce enough air to prevent the mixture from becoming too hard. Other frozen desserts include folding whipped cream for a similar lightening effect.

Making churned frozen desserts

In addition to ice cream, frozen yogurt and sorbet are churned in an ice-cream maker. Whichever type of frozen dessert you are making, it is good practice to refrigerate the base mixture for at least 4 hours and preferably overnight before freezing it. If the base is not chilled completely before you put it into an ice-cream maker, it may not freeze properly.

Likewise, allowing the finished ice cream, sherbet, or sorbet to "ripen" or set in the freezer for at least 3 or 4 hours before you serve it gives the ice cream a chance to fully set. This makes the dessert easier to scoop and slower to melt. Flavor also continues to develop and mellow during ripening.

You can flavor ice cream in a number of ways. Ingredients such as vanilla beans, tea, coffee, or spices are steeped in the dairy used to make a custard base, infusing it with their flavors. Ingredients such as caramel, ganache, nut pastes, or fruit purées are folded into the ice cream at the very end of the churning stage for a rippled or marbled effect. Harder add-ins, from fruits to nuts to chocolate chunks to brownie or cookie pieces, can be folded in just after you take the ice cream from the machine.

Ice creams are sometimes referred to in this country as custard- or French-style and Philadelphia-style. Custard- or French-style ice creams are made by cooking cream, sugar, eggs or egg yolks, and flavorings to make a base. These ice creams have a very rich, smooth texture. Ice cream made without eggs from an uncooked base is called Philadelphia-style ice cream, named for the gastronomic capital of early America where ice cream was always exceedingly popular and produced in great quantity.

Sherbets contain more sugar but less dairy than ice creams. Like Philadephia-style ice creams, they contain no egg yolks, but egg whites may be used. Sherbets may be made using a variety of dairy products, such as whole or reduced-fat milk. Even a cultured milk product like buttermilk can be used to make a smooth and refreshing sherbet (page 202).

Sorbet is made from a concentrated sugar syrup with added flavorings; it never contains dairy. About twice as much sugar is used in sorbet as in ice cream; the additional sugar is necessary to keep these very low-fat or fat-free desserts from freezing into solid cubes. A small amount of egg white may also be added to the sorbet base to give the final product a smoother texture. Flavorings for sorbets range from fresh fruit purées to fruit juices to infusions of tea, sweet basil, or mint.

A granita, known in French as a *granité,* is an Italian ice. Like sorbet, it is a light and refreshing frozen dessert made of sugar, water, and an intensely flavored liquid or purée. A granita does not contain as much sugar as sorbet. This, plus the fact that granitas are not churned constantly as they freeze, results in an icier texture. Stirring the mixture only occasionally, or only at the end of freezing, encourages the formation of large ice crystals. Savory granitas are often served as an intermezzo (between courses), while sweet granitas are served as a dessert, either on their own or paired with richer elements.

Making still-frozen desserts

Still-frozen desserts are molded before they go into the freezer. The mold gives these desserts their distinctive shapes. Frozen soufflés mimic hot soufflés in appearance; a paper collar secured around the mold allows you overfill it, creating the illusion that the mixture has risen like a hot baked soufflé. Parfaits can be piped or spooned into attractive molds; a glass mold practically begs you to use layers of different flavors and colors to make a beautiful presentation. To mold layers of different flavors of homemade ice cream, thoroughly freeze each layer before adding another. Filling cake or loaf pans with a mousse, Bavarian cream, or ice cream—with or without a cake lining—produces a large dessert that can be brought to the table and then cut into slices to serve. Frozen Lemon Savarin (page 212) and Baked Alaska (page 210) are two popular examples.

Serving frozen desserts

To scoop a frozen dessert, make sure that your scoop is clean and dry. If the scoop is wet, it can introduce ice crystals that will give your ice cream or other dessert an unpleasant gritty texture. You can also use a large, sturdy spoon to scrape curls of ice cream from the top of a large block. If your frozen yogurt, ice cream, or sorbet is too firm to scoop or scrape easily, let it rest in the refrigerator for about 30 minutes before serving. Warming frozen desserts in the microwave for 15 or 20 seconds on low power also softens them just enough to scoop.

Fresh or poached fruit, cookies, pies, cakes, and dessert sauces such as chocolate, caramel, and raspberry are all great accompaniments to many frozen desserts. A combination of contrasting flavors and temperatures, as in the Bananas Foster on page 206, is another way to make the most of every nuance of flavor and texture in a frozen dessert.

Using an ice-cream machine

Ice cream, frozen yogurt, and sherbet are easy to make with an ice-cream machine. For the best results, let your ice-cream base mixture ripen, or mellow, overnight to be sure it is very cold.

An ice-cream machine consists of a canister to hold the ice-cream base and a dasher to churn the base as it freezes. Old-fashioned machines and some modern ones are hand-cranked, while other modern machines have motor-driven dashers.

1 Adding the base

The base for ice cream and similar frozen desserts must be very cold when it is added to the canister. If possible, let the base chill and "ripen" for at least 4 hours to be certain that it is properly cooled and also that the sugar is completely dissolved and the flavors fully developed. Do not fill the canister more than two-thirds full to allow space for the base to expand as it freezes.

2 Adding the ice

In old-fashioned ice-cream machines, the canister is surrounded with a mixture of ice and rock salt that lowers the temperature of the ice-cream base enough to freeze it; in modern machines, the canister itself contains a liquid that is frozen first in order to freeze the ice cream. The newer canisters must be left in your freezer for the time directed by the manufacturer to chill them completely.

3 Churning and freezing

As the ice-cream base freezes in the canister, the dasher turns through the mixture, breaking up large ice crystals and preventing

the ice cream, yogurt, or sherbet from freezing solid. The churning motion of the dasher also incorporates air so that the base grows in volume, completely filling the canister. The result is a soft and creamy frozen dessert with a light texture and very fine, barely perceptible ice crystals. The ice cream is properly frozen when it looks like slightly grainy soft-serve ice cream. (This is the perfect texture for ice cream if you want to use it in assembling a cake or other dessert, as described on page 210.) The granules are actually very tiny ice crystals.

Let freshly made ice cream rest in the freezer for at least 3–4 hours before serving. This crucial step, known as ripening, firms the ice cream, makes its texture more creamy, and allows its flavors to blend.

Adding flavorings to ice creams

Add-ins give ice creams, sorbets, and frozen yogurt texture, color, and flavor. Combine them with ice cream at the proper point for best results.

1 Adding liquid flavorings

Liquid flavorings such as liqueurs, fruit purées, or melted chocolate are added to the ice-cream base before freezing. Stir liqueurs or spirits such as rum, brandy, Kahlúa, or amaretto into the custard while it is still very hot; the heat of the base cooks away some of the raw alcohol taste to let the flavor of the liqueur come through. You can add melted chocolate to the base at the same stage; it is best to temper the chocolate by stirring a bit of the base into the melted chocolate before stirring the chocolate into the rest of the base. Purées of raspberries, strawberries, peaches, or other fruit can also be used to flavor and color the custard. For the freshest flavor, add the fruit purée to a cooled ice-cream base.

2 Adding chunks

Pieces of fruit, nuts, chopped chocolate, and crushed candy bars or cookies add an element of texture to ice cream. To make a chunky fruit ice cream, first poach the fruit in a sugar syrup (page 218) or combine sliced fresh fruit with sugar and let rest for a few hours to bring out the flavors. The added sugar keeps the fruit from freezing solid. Then, prepare the base and freeze it in your machine. When it is almost ready to remove from the machine, fold in the prepared fruit. Harder add-ins such as chopped nuts or chocolate might make the dasher stick or jam. It is easiest to add these and similar items after the ice cream has frozen in the machine and before it goes into the freezer to ripen. Transfer the ice cream from the canister to a mixing bowl and fold in the add-in with a rubber spatula.

3 Adding swirls

Swirled, or rippled, ice creams have items like caramel, ganache, fudge, peanut butter, or concentrated fruit purées added in a ribbon throughout the ice cream. The temperature and consistency of the add-in are important. Items like caramel or fudge sauce should be liquid enough to pour but not hot or even warm; if warm, they might melt your ice cream in the machine. If they are too cold, it may be difficult to pour them into the ice cream and you may end up with a few large clumps rather than a swirl. To add ingredients like these, just before the ice-cream mixture is ready to stop churning, drizzle the fudge, caramel, or purée into the machine. The dasher will marbleize the ice cream in 10–15 seconds for machines with an electric motor, or about 30 seconds for hand-cranked machines; longer mixing will produce less distinct ribbons.

Making granitas

A granita is an Italian ice. Its flaky, icy texture is a result of a special freezing technique.

1 Freezing and stirring

Granitas can be made from a variety of ingredients, including fruit juices, brewed tea or coffee, or wine. They contain a large quantity of sugar to keep the liquid from freezing solid. Pour the granita mixture into a shallow pan that fits in your freezer without tilting. There are 2 methods of stirring granitas. You may choose to stir the granita with a fork periodically—usually every hour or so—as it freezes. Then you simply scrape icy, flaky layers from the surface and scoop them into a dish. You may also let the mixture freeze into a large block without stirring. Then, just before you are ready to serve the granita, break it into pieces and chop it in a food processor long enough to crush it, for a texture that is slightly more smooth and light than flaky and icy.

Making molded frozen desserts

You can make a beautiful frozen dessert using ice cream, sorbet, mousse, or Bavarian cream. Choose from a variety of molding options for a dramatic or elegant presentation.

1 Preparing the mold

Some frozen desserts, such as the Nutmeg-Rum Soufflé Glacé (page 207), are served directly in the mold. Others, such as the Frozen Lemon Savarin (page 212), are frozen in the mold and then unmolded before they are served. Mold options include glasses or stemware, loaf pans, bowls, cups, and molds made specifically for frozen desserts. The mold can be treated by spraying it with cooking spray or lining it with plastic wrap so that you can easily unmold the dessert before you serve it. You may line the mold with cake layers as well, as for Baked Alaska (see page 210).

2 Making a collar

Frozen soufflés or parfaits can be molded to look like hot soufflés. Prepare the mold by spraying it with flourless cooking spray. Cut a piece of parchment paper long enough to wrap completely around the outside of the mold; it should rise about 2 inches above the mold. Secure the paper in place with tape or string. Pour the filling into the mold so that it rises above the mold's rim. The parchment holds the filling in place as it freezes.

3 Filling the mold

To fill the mold evenly without any air pockets, be certain the ice cream or mousse is soft enough to pour or spoon easily. Use the back of a spoon or a small palette knife to spread the mixture in an even layer and press out any air bubbles. You can add a variety of ice creams and mousses with different flavors and colors to create a variegated frozen dessert, or add layers of garnish items, like crushed cookies, a fruit purée, or ganache. To settle the ice cream or mousse into the mold and fill every corner, gently tap the filled mold on the countertop.

4 Freezing and unmolding

Put the filled mold in the freezer and let the dessert firm up for at least 3 hours; most molded frozen desserts can be held for 2 or 3 days if they are properly wrapped. Be certain that the mold is sitting level on the shelf. Most frozen desserts benefit from a short period of tempering before you serve them. Transfer the frozen dessert to the refrigerator for about 30 minutes so that it softens evenly and the flavors open up. To unmold, fill a big bowl or pan or the sink with a few inches of hot water. Lower the mold into the water for a few seconds, then put a plate over the top of the mold. Hold the plate in place with one hand and invert the plate and mold. Lift the mold up and away from the dessert to release it onto the plate. Peel away the plastic wrap if you used it.

French Vanilla Ice Cream

3 cups heavy cream

1 cup whole or low-fat milk

2 cups sugar (divided use)

1 vanilla bean, split lengthwise

6 large egg yolks

Makes about 1¼ quarts, or
8 servings

Prepare an ice bath (page 169). Combine the cream, milk, 1½ cups of the sugar, and the vanilla bean in a heavy nonreactive saucepan over medium heat and bring to a simmer, stirring constantly.

Whisk together the egg yolks with the remaining ½ cup sugar in a bowl until thick and pale yellow, 2 minutes. Gradually add about one-third of the hot cream mixture, whisking constantly. Pour the tempered mixture back into the saucepan and cook over low heat, stirring constantly, until the custard coats the back of a spoon (about 180°F). Pour the custard through a fine-mesh sieve into a bowl. Set it in the ice bath. Scrape the seeds from the vanilla pod into the custard. Stir the custard every few minutes until cool.

Refrigerate the custard for at least 4 hours or up to overnight before freezing in an ice-cream machine according to the manufacturer's instructions. Pack the ice cream in containers and let ripen in the freezer for 3–4 hours before serving.

This is a classic French-style ice cream, made from a rich base of cooked custard. In some places it is still known as "frozen custard." Vanilla beans are the long, dark pods of an orchid. Tahitian beans have the most subtle flavor, while that of the Madagascar bean is more pronounced. Look for long, glossy, plump beans with a rich aroma and keep beans in a resealable plastic bag or a glass jar with a tight lid, away from moisture and direct light.

making stirred custards and puddings p. 169

using an ice-cream machine p. 196

Chocolate Ice Cream

3 cups whole or low-fat milk

1 cup heavy cream

1½ cups sugar (divided use)

⅛ tsp salt

2 large eggs

2 large egg yolks

6 oz bittersweet chocolate, melted

1 tsp vanilla extract

Makes about 1¼ quarts, or
8 servings

Prepare an ice bath (page 169). Combine the milk, cream, 1 cup of the sugar, and the salt in a heavy nonreactive saucepan over medium heat and bring to a simmer, stirring constantly.

Whisk together the eggs and egg yolks with the remaining sugar in a bowl until thick and pale yellow, 2 minutes. Gradually add about one-third of the hot milk mixture, whisking constantly. Pour the tempered mixture back into the saucepan and cook over low heat, stirring constantly, until the custard coats the back of a spoon (about 180°F). Pour the custard through a fine-mesh sieve into a bowl. Set in the ice bath. Add some of the custard to the melted chocolate and then pour the tempered chocolate and vanilla extract into the custard and stir until blended. Stir the custard every few minutes until cool.

Refrigerate the custard for at least 4 hours or up to overnight before freezing in an ice-cream machine according to the manufacturer's instructions. Pack the ice cream in containers and let ripen in the freezer for 3–4 hours before serving.

You can add virtually any type of add-in you like to this ice cream, including crushed or chopped cookies, brownies, chocolate bits, nuts, hard candy, and marshmallows. Gather your add-ins and have them ready to fold gently into the ice-cream base just after removing it from the ice-cream machine and before you pack the ice cream away to ripen in the freezer.

melting chocolate p. 242

using an ice-cream machine p. 196

Coffee Ice Cream

3 cups heavy cream

1 cup whole milk

1½ cups sugar

¾ cup coarsely ground coffee beans

⅛ tsp salt

1 tsp vanilla extract

Makes about 1¼ quarts, or 8 servings

Combine the cream, milk, sugar, ground coffee, and salt in a heavy nonreactive saucepan over medium heat and bring to a simmer, stirring occasionally. Remove the pan from the heat, cover, and let steep for 30 minutes. Stir in the vanilla extract.

Strain through a coffee filter into a container. Refrigerate the ice-cream base until thoroughly chilled, at least 4 hours or up to overnight before freezing in an ice-cream machine according to the manufacturer's instructions. Pack the ice cream in containers and let ripen in the freezer for 3–4 hours before serving.

Freshly ground coffee gives this Philadelphia-style ice cream a bold flavor. Coffee beans are sold by variety or as a blend, and in varying degrees of "roast," from a light, or American, roast to inky black and shiny espresso roast. Coarsely grinding the coffee beans right before you use them permits them to infuse the hot cream and milk mixture with a rich, full-bodied coffee flavor. The darker the bean's roast, the more intense the ice cream's flavor will be. Decaffeinated beans may be used as well as regular ones.

using an ice-cream machine p. 196

VARIATIONS

Chunky Coffee Ice Cream

When you remove the finished coffee ice cream from the ice-cream machine, transfer it to a bowl and fold in 1 cup of the following: crushed Toffee (page 251) or purchased toffee candy bars (with or without chocolate coating, such as Heath Bar), chunks of Fudge Brownies (page 97), or peanut butter cup candy (such as Reese's). Pack into containers and let ripen as described above.

Espresso Ice Cream with Armagnac Prunes

Replace the ground coffee with ½ cup coarsely ground espresso-roast beans. While the ice-cream base is chilling, soak 12 pitted prunes in ½ cup Armagnac, cognac, or brandy mixed with 2 teaspoons grated lemon zest. While the ice cream is being churned in the ice-cream machine, drain the prunes, chop coarsely, and fold into the ice cream directly after you remove it from the machine. Pack into containers and let ripen as described above.

Buttermilk Sherbet

1 qt buttermilk

1½ cups light corn syrup

½ cup sugar

½ cup freshly squeezed lemon juice

2 tsp vanilla extract

Makes about 1¼ quarts, or 8 servings

Prepare an ice bath (page 169). Combine the buttermilk, corn syrup, and sugar in a nonreactive saucepan. Heat over low heat, stirring, just until the sugar dissolves, about 2 minutes. Stir in the lemon juice and vanilla extract. Immediately pour the mixture through a fine-mesh sieve into a bowl. Set the bowl in the ice bath. Stir the mixture every few minutes until it is quite cool.

Refrigerate the mixture for at least 4 hours or up to overnight before freezing in an ice-cream machine according to the manufacturer's instructions. Pack the sherbet in containers and let ripen in the freezer for 3–4 hours before serving.

Corn syrup helps prevent the sugar in this recipe from forming crystals that could give the sherbet a grainy texture. This is especially helpful in a recipe like this one, with virtually none of the butterfat that keeps ice creams smooth and soft. The lemon juice in this recipe serves the same function as salt in other recipes to balance and enhance flavors of other ingredients.

using an ice-cream machine p. 196

making an ice bath p. 169

Pear Sorbet

3 large pears, peeled, cored, and sliced ¼ inch thick

⅔ cup sugar

½ cup water

⅛ tsp salt

⅓ cup pear wine or dry white wine

Makes about 1¼ quarts, or 8 servings

Combine the pears, sugar, water, and salt in a saucepan. Bring to a simmer over medium heat, reduce the heat to low, cover the pan, and poach until the pears are very tender, 6–8 minutes.

Purée the pears with their poaching liquid in a food processor or blender until very smooth. Stir in the wine.

Refrigerate for at least 4 hours or up to overnight. Freeze in an ice-cream machine according to the manufacturer's instructions. Pack the sorbet in containers and let ripen in the freezer for 3–4 hours before serving.

Pear wine adds depth to this delicate sorbet, but if you can't find a good pear wine, you can use a tablespoon or two of a pear brandy or eau de vie, such as Poire Williams, to replace some of the white wine.

poaching p. 218

Champagne and Lemon Sorbet

2 cups water (divided use)

1½ cups sugar

1½ cups Champagne, other dry sparkling white wine, or water

2 Tbsp grated lemon zest

½ cup freshly squeezed lemon juice

Makes about 1¼ quarts, or 8 servings

Bring 1 cup of the water and the sugar to a boil in a nonreactive saucepan over medium heat, stirring occasionally, until the sugar is dissolved. Remove from the heat and let cool to room temperature, about 1 hour.

Stir in the remaining 1 cup water, the Champagne, lemon zest, and lemon juice.

Refrigerate for at least 4 hours or up to overnight. Freeze in an ice-cream machine according to the manufacturer's instructions. Pack the sorbet in containers and let ripen in the freezer for 3–4 hours before serving. (It keeps very well in the freezer for up to 1 month.)

Serve this sorbet between courses, to cleanse the palate, or as a dessert. For an elegant presentation, scoop the sorbet into chilled champagne flutes or saucers.

zesting and juicing citrus p. 69

Strawberry Frozen Yogurt

3 cups sliced hulled strawberries

1½ cups sugar (divided use)

1 Tbsp freshly squeezed lemon juice

3 cups whole or low-fat plain yogurt

Makes about 1¼ quarts, or 8 servings

Toss the strawberries with ½ cup of the sugar and let them sit, covered, at room temperature for 1 hour.

Purée 2 cups of the strawberries along with any syrup released by the fruit until very smooth in a food processor or blender. Reserve the remaining cup of berries to add later.

Stir the purée, the remaining 1 cup sugar, and the lemon juice into the yogurt and stir until the sugar is completely dissolved.

Refrigerate the mixture for at least 4 hours or up to overnight. Freeze in an ice-cream machine according to the manufacturer's instructions. Transfer the frozen yogurt from the machine to a large bowl and fold in the remaining sliced strawberries. Pack the frozen yogurt in containers and let ripen in the freezer for 3–4 hours before serving.

Choose the ripest, most flavorful strawberries for this yogurt. Hull, rinse, and slice them just before you are ready to make the frozen yogurt. To remove the hulls, use a huller (a tweezerlike tool that pinches out the hull) or the tip of a paring knife to cut around the hull. Slice the berries rather thinly, so that the sugar can pull out the juices; the juices will dissolve the sugar for a smoother finished texture.

using an ice-cream machine p. 196

zesting and juicing citrus p. 69

Caramel Swirl Ice Cream

4 cups half-and-half

2 cups sugar (divided use)

1 vanilla bean, split lengthwise

6 large egg yolks

½ cup Caramel Sauce (p. 271), at room temperature

Makes about 1¼ quarts, or 8 servings

Prepare an ice bath. Combine the half-and-half, 1½ cups of the sugar, and the vanilla bean in a heavy nonreactive saucepan over medium heat and bring to a simmer, stirring constantly. Whisk the yolks with the remaining sugar until thick and pale yellow, 2 minutes.

Temper the egg yolks by gradually adding about one-third of the hot half-and-half mixture, whisking constantly. Pour the tempered mixture back into the saucepan and cook over low heat, stirring constantly, until the custard coats the back of a spoon (about 180°F). Pour the custard through a fine-mesh sieve into a bowl. Set it in the ice bath. Scrape the seeds from the vanilla pod into the custard. Stir the custard every few minutes until quite cool.

Refrigerate the custard for at least 4 hours or up to overnight before freezing in an ice-cream machine according to the manufacturer's instructions. Just before the ice cream is ready to stop churning, drizzle the caramel sauce into the ice cream with the dasher turning. As soon as the caramel is swirled throughout the ice cream, stop churning immediately. Pack the ice cream in containers and let ripen in the freezer for 3–4 hours before serving.

To get the best ripple in a swirl ice cream, be sure the caramel, or other sauce, is cooled to the right temperature. It should still be soft enough to pour but just slightly thicker than honey so that it falls in a steady stream. It should also be cool enough not to warm up the ice cream.

making an ice bath p. 169

adding flavorings to ice creams p. 197

Goat Cheese Ice Cream

2½ cups whole or low-fat milk

1 cup sugar (divided use)

¼ tsp salt

5 large egg yolks

½ tsp vanilla extract

12 oz fresh goat cheese, crumbled, at room temperature

Makes about 1¼ quarts, or 8 servings

Prepare an ice bath (page 169). Combine the milk, ½ cup of the sugar, and the salt in a heavy nonreactive saucepan over medium heat and bring to a simmer, stirring constantly. Whisk the yolks with the remaining sugar until thick and pale yellow, 2 minutes.

Temper the eggs by gradually adding about one-third of the hot milk mixture, whisking constantly. Pour the tempered mixture back into the saucepan and cook over low heat, stirring constantly, until the custard coats the back of a spoon (about 180°F). Pour the custard through a fine-mesh sieve into a bowl. Set it in the ice bath. Stir in the vanilla extract. Stir the custard every few minutes until quite cool.

Refrigerate the custard for at least 4 hours or up to overnight. Whisk the goat cheese into the chilled base. Freeze in an ice-cream machine according to the manufacturer's instructions. Pack the ice cream in containers and let ripen in the freezer for 3–4 hours before serving.

As this ice-cream base freezes, the goat cheese is worked evenly throughout the base for a smooth consistency. Choose soft, young fresh goat cheese without any herbs or other flavorings. Some goat cheeses are aged, which changes their texture and sharpens their flavor. Fresh goat cheese is mild and soft enough to mash with a fork, while aged goat cheeses are firm enough to grate.

using an ice-cream machine p. 196

Hazelnut Parfait

1 recipe Nut Brittle
(p. 252) with hazelnuts or
Toffee (p. 251)

2 cups heavy cream

8 large egg yolks

¾ cup sugar

6 Tbsp water

5 Tbsp plus 8 tsp Frangelico or
other hazelnut-flavored liqueur
(divided use)

Makes 8 servings

Break the brittle into small pieces or pulse in a food processor until coarsely broken up but not pulverized.

Place eight 8-oz parfait glasses, molds, or ramekins in the freezer to chill.

Whip the cream in a chilled bowl until it holds a medium peak when the whisk is turned upright. Refrigerate until ready to use.

In a stand mixer fitted with the whisk attachment, whip the egg yolks on medium speed until thick and pale yellow, 2 minutes. Meanwhile, combine the sugar and the water in a small saucepan and bring to a full boil. Slowly add this sugar syrup to the yolks with the mixer on low. Increase the mixer's speed to medium and continue whipping until the mixture cools to room temperature. Fold in 5 Tbsp of the Frangelico. Add one-third of the reserved whipped cream to the egg yolk mixture and gently fold until incorporated. Fold in the remaining whipped cream. Spoon the mixture into the molds, alternating layers of cream with layers of brittle. Freeze for 3–4 hours.

To serve, temper the parfaits in the refrigerator for 30 minutes. Pierce 2 holes in the top of each parfait and pour in 1 tsp Frangelico.

Frozen in layers and presented in a long, slender glass, "parfait" is both the name of a dessert and the name of the glassware it's served in. This rich frozen dessert comes close to ice cream in texture and flavor. Instead of requiring an ice-cream machine, however, this recipe simply calls for some level space in your freezer.

whipping cream p. 263

making simple syrup p. 244

Bananas Foster

3 Tbsp unsalted butter

2 Tbsp sugar

½ tsp freshly squeezed
lemon juice

2 medium-ripe bananas, sliced
½ inch thick on the bias

3 Tbsp dark or light rum

1 Tbsp banana liqueur

2 cups French Vanilla Ice Cream
(p. 199) or 1 pint purchased

Makes 4 servings

Heat the butter in a large skillet over medium-high heat. Add the sugar and cook until the sugar has started to darken slightly, about 2 minutes. Add the lemon juice and continue to cook until the sugar is completely dissolved, 2 minutes more. Add the bananas and cook over medium heat until they give off a good aroma and have started to soften, 2–3 minutes.

Remove the pan from the heat and pour in the rum and banana liqueur. Return to the heat and let come to a simmer, 2–4 minutes.

Scoop the ice cream into bowls or dishes. Spoon the bananas and their cooking liquid over the ice cream. Serve at once.

Bananas for this dish should be entirely yellow, with no green on the skin. However, they should not have ripened to the point that the skins have brown spots. The fruit should be ripe enough to be flavorful but still firm enough to hold its shape as it is sautéed.

caramelizing sugar p. 171

Nutmeg-Rum Soufflé Glacé

2 cups heavy cream

8 large egg yolks

¾ cup granulated sugar

6 Tbsp water

5 Tbsp plus 8 tsp dark rum (divided use)

2 tsp freshly grated nutmeg

2 tsp grated orange zest

Cocoa powder for dusting

Confectioners' sugar for dusting

Makes 8 servings

Wrap eight 6-oz ramekins with a parchment paper collar that extends 2 inches above the rim. Set on a baking sheet.

Whip the cream in a chilled bowl until it holds a medium peak when the whisk is turned upright. Refrigerate until ready to use.

In a stand mixer fitted with the whisk attachment, whip the egg yolks on medium speed until thick and pale yellow, 2 minutes. Meanwhile, combine the granulated sugar and water in a small saucepan and bring to a full boil. Slowly add this sugar syrup to the yolks with the mixer on low. Increase the mixer's speed to medium and continue whipping until the mixture cools to room temperature. Fold in 5 Tbsp of the rum, the nutmeg, and the orange zest.

Add one-third of the reserved whipped cream to the yolk mixture and gently fold until incorporated. Fold in the remaining whipped cream. Spoon the mixture into the ramekins to a height of 1 inch above the rim of each ramekin. Freeze for 3–4 hours.

To serve, unwrap the collars from the ramekins. Pierce 2 holes in the top of each parfait and pour in 1 tsp rum. Use a sieve to dust with cocoa powder and confectioners' sugar and serve immediately.

Soufflés, whether hot or cold, are light, delicate desserts. Hot soufflés are the inspiration for *soufflés glacés,* or frozen soufflés. A parchment paper collar wrapped around a soufflé dish allows the frozen mousse to be mounded high, mimicking the height of a hot soufflé just taken from the oven. Even the dusting of confectioners' sugar and cocoa pays tribute to the rituals of serving a hot soufflé.

making molded frozen desserts p. 198

whipping cream p. 263

Peach Melba

6 cups raspberries

½ cup sugar

2 Tbsp framboise or other raspberry-flavored brandy

2 tsp lemon juice

4 Poached Peaches in Lemon-Vanilla Syrup, drained (p. 226)

4 cups French Vanilla Ice Cream (p. 199) or 2 pints purchased

½ recipe Chantilly Cream (p. 281)

2 Tbsp toasted sliced unsalted almonds

Makes 8 servings

Chill 8 champagne saucers or ice-cream dishes.

Combine the raspberries and sugar in a blender and purée until smooth. Stir in the framboise and lemon juice. Pour ¼ cup of the raspberry sauce into each of the chilled saucers. Place a peach half, flat side up, in each champagne saucer. Place a scoop of ice cream on top of each peach half. Top with Chantilly cream and garnish with almonds. Serve immediately.

In 1894, when opera singer Nellie Melba appeared in London, she stayed at the Savoy Hotel, where Auguste Escoffier was the executive chef. Escoffier was so impressed by her performance that he created this peach and ice cream dessert in her honor. When the new Ritz Carlton Hotel opened in London a few years later, the dish reappeared with a rich raspberry sauce and bearing the name Pêche Melba.

toasting nuts p. 138

whipping cream p. 263

Orange Granita

2 cups freshly squeezed orange juice

¾ cup white wine

3 Tbsp Grand Marnier or other orange-flavored liqueur

¼ cup sugar

1 Tbsp grated orange zest

Makes about 4½ cups, or 6 servings

Prepare an ice bath (page 169). Combine all the ingredients in a nonreactive saucepan and warm over low heat just until the sugar dissolves, about 4 minutes. Set the saucepan in the ice bath and stir occasionally until the mixture is cold.

Pour the mixture into a shallow metal or glass container and place it in the freezer. Stir the mixture with a small spoon or fork once every hour until it is completely frozen, 2–3 hours. The granita will have a very granular consistency. Or, you can opt to let the mixture freeze without stirring it so that it freezes into a large block. Then, just before you are ready to serve the granita, break it into pieces and chop it in a food processor just long enough to make it flaky.

With a sturdy serving spoon, scrape out the granita into chilled serving bowls or wineglasses.

You could serve this refreshing citrus granita as a palate cleanser between courses. It would also be delightful after a rich main course of duck or lamb. Add it to a plate of sliced fresh seasonal fruit, or serve it in a simple glass dish or bowl with a few plain but buttery cookies and some citrus zest garnish.

making granitas p. 198

zesting and juicing citrus p. 69

Chianti Granita

¾ cup warm water

1 cup sugar

1½ cups Chianti or other light-bodied red wine

⅓ cup freshly squeezed lemon juice

⅓ cup freshly squeezed orange juice

Makes about 4½ cups, or 6 servings

Prepare an ice bath (page 169). Combine the warm water and sugar in a large nonreactive bowl. Stir until the sugar dissolves, 3–4 minutes. Add the wine, lemon juice, and orange juice. Set the bowl in the ice bath and stir periodically until the mixture is cold.

Pour the mixture into a shallow metal or glass container and place it in the freezer. Stir the mixture with a small spoon or fork once every hour until it is completely frozen, 2–3 hours. The granita will have a very granular consistency. Or, you can opt to let the mixture freeze without stirring it so that it freezes into a large block. Then, just before you are ready to serve the granita, break it into pieces and chop it in a food processor long enough to make it flaky.

With a sturdy serving spoon, scrape out the granita into chilled serving bowls or wineglasses.

You often read that for cooking, you should choose wines that you enjoy drinking. That's especially good advice here, where the light-bodied red wine is barely warmed as you combine it with fruit juices and sugar. Since the flavors of this granita resemble those of a classic sangría, you might try a fuller-bodied Spanish Rioja instead of a Chianti.

making an ice bath p. 169

making granitas p. 198

Baked Alaska

1 recipe French Vanilla Ice
Cream base (p. 199)

1 recipe Vanilla Sponge Cake
(p. 149)

6 cups Common Meringue
(p. 234)

¼ cup rum or brandy (optional)

Makes 8 servings

Prepare the vanilla ice cream (or use another flavor, if you prefer) as directed in the recipe, up through refrigerating the custard. Before you put the custard in the ice-cream machine, line a 2½-qt bowl or similar mold with plastic wrap. Cut the sponge cake into ½-inch-thick pieces to line the bottom and sides of the mold, overlapping the cake to cover any gaps. Reserve enough cake to cover the top of the mold once the ice cream has been added.

Freeze the custard in an ice-cream machine according to the manufacturer's instructions. Instead of transferring it to a storage container, transfer it to the cake-lined mold. Top with the reserved sponge cake, pressing gently to work out any air pockets. Cover with plastic wrap and freeze for at least 4 hours or up to 2 days before unmolding.

When you are ready to serve the dessert, set the rack in the upper third of the oven and preheat the broiler or have ready a kitchen torch. (The top of the dessert should be at least 8 inches from the heating element. If your broiler is not large enough, use a kitchen torch.) Prepare the meringue according to the recipe, continuing to whip until the meringue holds stiff peaks.

Remove the molded cake and ice cream from the freezer. Remove the plastic from the top of the mold, then invert the cake and ice cream onto an ovenproof platter. Cover with the meringue either by spreading and swirling it over the entire surface with the back of a spoon or by piping it over the cake. Put the baked Alaska under the broiler until the meringue browns, about 5 minutes, or pass the flame of the blowtorch evenly over the meringue until it browns.

Warm the rum or brandy, if using, in a small saucepan over low heat. Flame the alcohol *(right)* and drizzle the warm flamed rum or brandy over the meringue. Serve at once.

Also known as a Norwegian omelet, this showy dessert takes some advance planning, but it makes a dramatic end to your dinner party. Be sure to warm the alcohol before igniting it, if you choose to use it. Tilt the pan slightly so the alcohol will pool at one side. Use a long wooden match and hold the flame just above the rum or brandy. When it flames, level the pan out. Shaking the pan will make the rum flare up again, so be sure you don't shake hard enough to spill over the edge. Let the flames die down on their own or use a pan lid to extinguish them.

making molded cakes
p. 141

piping p. 266

Frozen Pumpkin Terrine

1 recipe Angel Food Cake
(p. 151)

2 Tbsp dark rum, apple cider,
or water

1 package (2¼ tsp) powdered
gelatin

2 cups Custard Sauce (p. 274),
chilled

1 cup fresh, frozen, or canned
pumpkin purée

1½ tsp ground cinnamon

½ tsp ground ginger

¼ tsp ground cloves

¼ tsp salt

1 cup heavy cream, chilled

1 cup Caramel Sauce
(p. 271)

Makes 8–10 servings

Line a terrine mold or loaf pan with plastic wrap, leaving an overhang on all sides. Cut the cake into slices about ¼ inch thick and line the bottom and sides of the mold completely with the cake. Reserve enough sliced cake to cover the top of the mold after the filling is added.

Put the rum in small bowl. Scatter the gelatin evenly over the surface and stir if necessary to break up any clumps. Let the gelatin soften until it swells, about 2 minutes.

While the gelatin softens, stir together the custard sauce, pumpkin purée, cinnamon, ginger, cloves, and salt until evenly blended.

Warm the gelatin mixture in the microwave until the gelatin melts and the mixture is translucent, about 20 seconds. Stir into the pumpkin mixture until evenly blended.

Whip the heavy cream to medium peaks. Fold the whipped cream into the pumpkin mixture in 2 or 3 additions until it is evenly blended. Spoon the mixture into the lined mold, spreading it gently to remove any air pockets. Top the pumpkin cream with the reserved sliced cake.

Fold the plastic wrap over the top of the terrine to completely cover it. Freeze until firm, at least 4 hours or up to overnight. Let the terrine soften in the refrigerator for 1 hour before slicing and serving with warm caramel sauce.

Note: To make fresh pumpkin purée, halve a baking pumpkin and roast at 350°F cut side down in ½ inch water until tender, about 45 minutes. Scoop out and discard the seeds and fiber, then scoop out the flesh and purée in a food mill or food processor.

Terrine is the name for both the earthenware mold used to make loaf-style dishes as well as for the food prepared in the mold. Savory terrines are typically made in a dish that is lined with snowy white fatback. In this sweet version, we replaced the fatback with a delicate white angel food cake and replaced the meat filling with a pumpkin cream. Whether you use fresh or frozen pumpkin purée, you can intensify its flavor by cooking it over medium heat until the purée thickens slightly and takes on a slightly browner color. Be sure to let the purée cool to room temperature before you add it to the custard sauce.

making molded frozen desserts p. 198

whipping cream p. 263

Frozen Lemon Savarin

Flourless cooking spray for greasing

½ cup sugar

2 Tbsp light corn syrup

¼ cup cold water (divided use)

3 large egg whites

1 tsp powdered unflavored gelatin

⅓ cup freshly squeezed lemon juice

2 Tbsp grated lemon zest

⅓ cup plain whole or low-fat yogurt

1 cup heavy cream

Makes 1 large savarin, 8 individual savarins, or one 8-inch terrine

Lightly coat an 8-cup savarin mold, eight 6-oz savarin molds or ramekins, or an 8-inch loaf pan with cooking spray.

Combine the sugar, corn syrup, and 2 Tbsp of the water in a small, heavy saucepan. Attach a candy thermometer to the side of the pan, making sure that the tip is submerged but not resting on the bottom of the pan. Bring the mixture to a boil over medium heat. Continue to cook without stirring until the mixture reaches 240°F.

While the sugar mixture is coming to the proper temperature, in a stand mixer fitted with the whisk attachment, whip the egg whites on medium speed until they form medium peaks when the whisk is lifted (page 139); reduce the speed to low if the sugar mixture is not ready.

As soon as the sugar mixture reaches 240°F, add it to the egg whites in a slow, steady stream while whipping on low speed. Once all of the sugar mixture has been incorporated, increase the speed to high and continue to whip until the meringue has cooled to room temperature, about 5 minutes.

Sprinkle the gelatin over the remaining 2 Tbsp cold water in a small bowl and stir to break up any clumps. Let the gelatin soften until it swells, about 2 minutes. Heat the softened gelatin over simmering water or in a microwave for about 20 seconds on low power until the granules melt and the mixture is clear. Stir the lemon juice and lemon zest into the gelatin.

Remove the bowl of cooled meringue from the mixer. Using a rubber spatula, fold the lemon mixture into the meringue, and then fold in the yogurt.

Whip the cream in a chilled bowl until it holds a medium peak when the whisk is turned upright (page 263). Add the whipped cream to the meringue in 2 or 3 additions, folding gently just until the mousse is evenly blended.

Spoon or pipe the mousse into the prepared mold(s). Wrap well and freeze for at least 3 hours or up to 2 days before serving. Before unmolding, let the mold(s) temper in the refrigerator for 30 minutes. To unmold, dip the mold in a bowl of hot water for a few seconds then place the chilled dessert plate over the mold, invert, and lift away the mold.

The term *savarin* is often associated with a yeast-raised cake that is served with a syrup. These cakes are baked in special molds, called savarins, and by extension any dish made in such a mold may also be called a savarin. A savarin mold is a ring shape, 1½ to 2 inches deep. The unique savarin shape is part of what makes this frozen dessert so appealing once it has been unmolded.

working with gelatin p. 170

making meringue p. 219

8 Pastries

When is a baked good more accurately called a pastry? It's hard to define this category with precision because it contains so many items, from delicate cream puffs dipped in chocolate ganache to napoleons made with puff pastry, strudel made with phyllo, and even crisp shells of meringue filled with fresh fruits or mousse.

Pastries differ from other desserts because they typically call for at least two distinct elements: a crust or shell—such as pie dough, short dough, pâte à choux, meringue, or puff pastry—and a filling or topping of some sort. And although it is true that cakes and tortes often combine at least two elements, pastries usually share another distinguishing feature. While pies, tarts, and cakes are generally prepared as a single, large item that you cut into individual portions, pastries are more often made in miniature or single-serving sizes. But not all pastries are meant to satisfy a craving for sweets. Sharp cheeses, ham or prosciutto, and even vegetables or mustard turn items made with pastry dough into savory hors d'oeuvres.

Pastry doughs

Pastry making involves several distinct types of dough, as well as a variety of techniques necessary to work with them effectively. In this chapter, you can choose among recipes that feature puff pastry, phyllo dough, and pâte à choux, a cooked dough that is used to make éclairs, cream puffs, and profiteroles. Short dough, featured in tarts, is also used in pastries as the base for bite-sized tartlets, baked in miniature tins. And, although it is not a pastry dough, meringue comes into play as a base to hold a filling.

Puff pastry, known to professionals as a "roll-in" or "laminated" dough, consists of many layers of dough separated by layers of butter. By carefully controlling the temperature of both dough and butter and using a specific folding sequence, the baker ends up with a dough that rises to a spectacular height when baked. Although this pastry is really no more complex in terms of technique than a pie dough, it does require a significant amount of time and refrigerator space so that the dough can relax and firm up between the folding and layering steps. It can take up to 2 days to prepare. For most home bakers—and even most professional chefs—it is more practical to buy frozen prepared puff pastry sheets or precut shells than to make puff pastry from scratch.

Phyllo dough is made from a simple mixture of flour and water. The dough is worked until it develops enough gluten to stretch into very thin sheets, sometimes called leaves. Although it doesn't rise quite as dramatically as puff pastry, stacking sheets up with a layer of melted butter in between each sheet gives the finished pastry a similarly flaky texture. Phyllo dough is readily available frozen.

Pâte à choux, whose name means "cabbage pastry," is a cooked dough that is used to make cream puffs and similar small, hollow puffs with irregular, cabbage-like shapes.

Meringues can be made using the common, Swiss, or Italian technique. Swiss meringue, featured in Raspberry Meringue Tartlets (page 235), calls for egg whites and sugar to be cooked together over hot water until they reach 110–120°F, hot enough for the sugar to dissolve completely and for the proteins in the egg whites to start to unfold, making it easier to create a foam with a good volume. An Italian meringue, featured in Frozen Lemon Savarin (page 212) and again in Italian Buttercream (page 279), calls for a hot sugar syrup to be beaten into medium-peak egg whites. Both Swiss and Italian meringues have a drier texture than common, or regular, meringue, which is used as a topping for pies, tarts, and Baked Alaska (page 210). When baked into layers or shells, Swiss and Italian meringues provide a delightful crunchy contrast to a smooth filling. Meringue can be piped into a variety of shapes to create a shell. Baked meringue shells store well at room temperature, if it's not too humid.

Pastry fillings

Several pastries in this chapter rely upon the flavor, texture, and color of fruits for their success. The flavor of any fruit varies greatly depending upon the season, the way it was grown, and the region. Fruits frozen without sugar, such as strawberries, blueberries, and raspberries, can often be used for cooked fillings or purées, but once thawed their texture may not be suitable for uncooked fillings.

Cream-based fillings, such as Pastry Cream (page 282), Bavarian Cream (page 275), and Diplomat Cream (page 282), build on the methods used to make custards and creams. Pastry cream is a custard sauce that is thickened with flour. It can be used as a filling on its own, or lightened with whipped cream, to become a diplomat cream. To make a Bavarian cream, a custard sauce is folded together with whipped cream. Both diplomat and Bavarian creams can be stabilized with gelatin to make a filling that holds its shape when piped into a pastry. Plan to make cooked fillings in advance so that they have time to cool properly. Give the assembled or filled pastry a little time to settle before serving for a good texture and flavor, but avoid storing for too long. Eventually, the moisture in the filling turns pastries soft.

If you made a pastry ahead of time and want to serve it warm, put it on a baking sheet in a moderate oven (300°F) just until the pastry feels warm, usually about 5 minutes. Serve individual pastries or slices on plates that have been properly heated or chilled. You can enhance pastries easily by adding a bit of sauce to the plate. Chocolate Sauce (page 270), Custard Sauce (page 274), or Raspberry Coulis (page 273) are a few options that give the presentation more color and flavor.

Using puff pastry

Puff pastry dough is readily available in the freezer case, both as sheets and as pastry shells.

1 Thawing and rolling out

Frozen puff pastry thaws in about 8 hours in the refrigerator. Thawing it at room temperature can cause the butter in the dough to warm too much. If you do need to thaw it at room temperature, return it to the refrigerator for 15–20 minutes to let it firm slightly before using the dough. Keeping the pastry cold ensures that it will puff up dramatically and have a crisp texture.

To work with puff pastry, dust a flat work surface very lightly with flour. If your recipe requires rolling the puff pastry, lightly dust the top of the pastry sheet and your rolling pin with a little additional flour. Roll with even pressure over the entire surface of the dough, rolling up to but not over the edges. Once the dough is rolled, put it back in the refrigerator to rest before cutting with a sharp knife or pastry cutter. Letting the shaped pastry chill once more before baking gives the layers of dough a chance to relax and the butter a chance to firm up, for the crispest, tallest, flakiest result.

Note that puff pastry to be used as a layer in items like the Berry Napoleon (page 223) is liberally docked, or pierced, with a docker or fork to keep the pastry level and flat. You may also top the pastry with a piece of parchment paper and/or a baking sheet to weigh it down as it bakes. Remove the paper and the baking sheet to allow the pastry to brown during the last few minutes of baking.

Using phyllo dough

Phyllo dough is available in the freezer section of well-stocked supermarkets and from Greek or Middle Eastern groceries.

1 Thawing and layering

Thaw frozen phyllo dough either in the refrigerator overnight or at room temperature for 2 hours. Once thawed, the individual sheets should pull apart easily and be very flexible. However, contact with the air soon dries out phyllo unless it is covered. Set up your work area so that your phyllo stays moist and flexible as you work with it. Place a large baking sheet or a piece of plastic wrap on your work surface, remove the phyllo from the box, and unroll enough sheets to make your recipe. Set the sheets flat on the baking sheet or plastic wrap. Cover the sheets completely with another large piece of plastic wrap, then lay lightly dampened paper towels or a barely moistened kitchen towel over the plastic to keep the air around the phyllo moist.

Transfer one sheet of the phyllo at a time to your flat work area and immediately re-cover the remaining sheets. Brush or spray the entire sheet with butter or oil. For a very flaky texture and extra flavor in the finished dish, you can scatter bread crumbs or sugar over the sheet next. Keep working this way, one sheet at a time, until you have the correct number of layers for your recipe. If necessary, cut the phyllo stack into shapes such as large squares to make a Beggar's Purse (page 228). Let the shaped or filled phyllo chill in the refrigerator before baking for the lightest, flakiest layers.

Making pâte à choux

Pâte à choux puffs up as it cooks to create a crisp, hollow shell, perfect for filling, as for cream puffs and éclairs.

1 Heating the ingredients

Combine the liquid—water, milk, or both and the butter in a large saucepan and bring it to a rolling boil over high heat. Add the sifted flour to the mixture all at once and stir constantly with a wooden spoon over medium heat. At first, the mixture will be lumpy, but as you stir it, the dough will become smooth and eventually pull away from the sides of the pot.

2 Adding the eggs

Cool the flour mixture slightly before you add the eggs; otherwise, the eggs could overcook before the pastry even goes into the oven. Remove the pan from the heat or transfer the dough to a mixing bowl. Stir it until it is nearly at body temperature. Add the eggs to the flour mixture one at a time and stir until the dough is smooth.

3 Piping and baking

A pastry bag and round tip are helpful for making even shapes, as for éclairs (page 233). For gougères, cream puffs, or profiteroles (pages 230–31), you may prefer to simply drop the batter onto baking sheets with 2 spoons. Make regular, even shapes, spacing them about 2 inches apart. For a very crisp, light, and dry pastry, lower the oven temperature after the initial puffing and browning and continue to bake until there are no beads of moisture visible on the pastry's sides.

Making crêpes

Crêpe batter is similar to pancake batter, but more liquid. Whisk well to remove any lumps, then let the batter rest for 30–60 minutes to moisten and soften the flour for the most tender crêpes.

1 Preparing the pan

Crêpes are typically prepared in a small, flat, round pan with short, sloped sides. Small nonstick skillets also work well for making crêpes. Before starting to cook, have ready a small bowl of melted butter. Heat the pan over medium heat and brush the pan with butter to prevent sticking (or, in the case of nonstick pans, to add flavor).

2 Ladling the batter

If the batter is not perfectly smooth after resting, strain it through a fine-mesh sieve. With a ladle or small measuring cup, quickly pour a small amount of batter into the pan. Immediately tilt and swirl the pan to spread the batter in a thin, even layer that just covers the bottom of the pan.

3 Determining doneness

Cook for a few minutes, then check the doneness of a crêpe by carefully lifting one edge with a small spatula and looking underneath it for a golden color with specks of light brown. Loosen the edge of the crêpe from the pan, turn it with the spatula, and cook it on the other side until golden. Do not worry if the first one or two crêpes are "practice" crêpes; the subsequent ones will improve in appearance.

Poaching

This gentle cooking method is used for a range of delicate foods, from meringue to fresh fruit.

1 Cooking gently

Poached foods are cooked in enough liquid to keep them submerged. The liquid is kept just below a true simmer, 160–180°F. Choose a large pot to avoid crowding the items to be poached. This technique is used to prepare "eggs" of meringue (page 236) and fruits for a filling or element in a pastry (page 226).

The first step when poaching any fruit is to taste the fruit and assess its flavor and texture. This will help you decide how much sugar you should add to the poaching liquid. Cut back on the sugar when the fruit is very sweet; add more when it is not. The amount of sugar in the poaching liquid will also have an effect on the fruit's shape after cooking. More sugar results in a firmer poached fruit.

If your poaching syrup is already at a bare simmer when you add the fruit, more flavor will stay in the fruit. If the poaching liquid is barely warm when you add the fruit, some of the fruit's flavor will infuse the liquid so that it can be served as part of a dessert.

Consult a recipe to determine whether you should peel, core, or slice the fruit before you poach it. Poach most fruits until they are tender enough to pierce easily with a fork or a skewer. Once they are poached, you may opt to let them cool directly in the liquid. Use a slotted spoon to lift the fruit gently from the poaching liquid to maintain its shape.

Making meringue

Adding sugar to egg whites as you whip them allows them to be folded into a flavorful base or piped without losing too much volume. For basics on whipping egg whites, refer to page 139.

1 Making common meringue

For a common meringue, begin by beating the egg whites alone in a bowl on low to medium speed. Once the whites are broken up and look frothy, add the sugar gradually, with the mixer running or while whipping by hand. Once all of the sugar is added, increase the mixer speed to high.

2 Making Italian meringue

To incorporate a hot sugar syrup into egg whites for an Italian meringue, you should also begin by whipping the egg whites on low speed until loosened. Increase the speed to medium and whip to medium peaks. Reduce the speed to low and add the hot sugar syrup in a thin stream. Once the syrup is added, increase the speed to medium or high.

3 Making Swiss meringue

For a Swiss meringue, sugar is blended and warmed with the egg whites before you start to whip. Stir the mixture with a whisk to heat the whites evenly as well as to be sure that the sugar is thoroughly dissolved. Then, whip the meringue on medium to high speed.

For every style of meringue, continue to whip the meringue until medium or stiff peaks form (as for cream page 263), as directed in a recipe. Medium peaks are preferred when you want to fold the meringue into a dish. Stiff peaks pipe well and hold their shape.

Making meringue shells

Swiss and Italian meringues are excellent for making shells or layers. These meringues will hold their shape after they are piped and during baking.

1 Preparing the guides

To keep meringue from sticking to baking sheets, line the sheets with parchment paper. Trace an outline for your meringue shell or layer on the back of the parchment paper. Drawing guides in advance makes it easier to make multiple shells consistent in size.

2 Piping bases and walls

Using your outlines as guides, pipe the base of the shell using a pastry bag and a plain tip (page 266). Work in a spiral from the center outward, holding the tip just above the surface of the paper. Next, pipe rings of meringue to create a wall on the outer rim of the spiral, until the wall of the shell is the desired height.

3 Drying in the oven

Meringues need to dry out in a low oven. As the meringues bake, the moisture in the egg whites evaporates, leaving behind a crisp, foamy shell. Start the meringues at around 250°F and bake until they look dry on the outside, then lower the temperature to 180°F and bake until they are dry, light, and crisp, then turn off the heat. Open the oven door a little and leave the meringues in the oven after it is turned off to help dry them a bit more. Meringues should be perfectly dry but without any color.

Paillettes

1 sheet prepared puff pastry, thawed

Egg wash (1 large egg whisked with 2 Tbsp cold milk or water)

½ cup grated Parmesan cheese

Sweet or hot paprika to taste

Makes 36 pieces

Preheat the oven to 400°F. Line a baking sheet with parchment paper. Lay a piece of parchment on a work surface and place the pastry on it. Brush one side of the pastry sheet with the egg wash. Sprinkle the cheese and paprika evenly over the pastry. Use a rolling pin to press the cheese into the surface without rolling over the edges. Chill the pastry for about 15 minutes to let it firm and to allow the egg wash to dry slightly.

Remove the pastry from the refrigerator and cut it lengthwise into ¼-inch-wide strips with a pizza cutter or sharp knife. Holding the ends of a strip in each hand, twist your hands in opposite directions to twist the strips and transfer them to the prepared baking sheet, leaving an inch of space between each strip to allow them to expand. Bake in batches as needed until golden brown, about 10 minutes. Transfer to a wire rack and let cool completely before serving.

These puff-pastry cheese sticks are a quick and simple way to add a festive touch to your table. Cajun spice blend, cayenne, poppy seeds, and sesame seeds may also be used to flavor the sticks. Paprika is available in sweet (mild) and hot styles, and Hungarian paprika is considered the best. You can use either type here, depending upon your personal tolerance for heat.

using puff pastry p. 217

Palmiers with Prosciutto

1 sheet prepared puff pastry, thawed

6 Tbsp tomato paste

1 Tbsp water

5 oz prosciutto, very thinly sliced (about 12 slices)

¼ cup finely grated Parmesan cheese

Makes 36 pieces

On a lightly floured surface, roll the puff pastry sheet into a 9-inch square. Blend the tomato paste and water. Brush one side of the pastry with the tomato paste mixture.

Lay the prosciutto slices over the tomato paste in a single layer, completely covering the puff pastry, then sprinkle with an even layer of the Parmesan cheese.

Roll 2 sides of the pastry in toward the center until they meet (this is known as a palmier shape). Wrap the roll with plastic wrap and refrigerate until firm, at least 15 minutes.

Preheat the oven to 400°F. Line a baking sheet with parchment paper. Unwrap the puff pastry roll and slice it into ¼-inch-thick slices with a serrated knife. Lay the slices on the prepared baking sheet about 1 inch apart. Place a second sheet of parchment paper on top of the palmiers to help them stay flat as they bake. (If the slices are no longer cool, you should chill them again to firm before baking.) Bake until light golden brown, 6–7 minutes. Remove the top sheet of parchment paper for the last few minutes of baking for a deeper brown color. Serve warm or at room temperature.

This is a savory variation of a classic French pastry made of puff pastry sprinkled with granulated sugar. The name *palmier* reflects the palm-leaf shape of the pastry. These *palmiers* are lined with prosciutto, and a dusting of Parmesan cheese replaces the sugar.

using puff pastry p. 217

Blackberry and Apricot Turnover

½ cup granulated sugar

3 Tbsp cornstarch

2 cups fresh blackberries or one 12-oz bag frozen unsweetened blackberries, thawed

2 medium apricots, peeled, pitted, and chopped

½ tsp grated lemon zest

¼ tsp ground cinnamon

⅛ tsp ground nutmeg

⅛ tsp ground cardamom

2 sheets prepared puff pastry, thawed

Egg wash (1 large egg whisked with 2 Tbsp cold milk or water)

3–4 Tbsp coarse sugar

Makes 8 servings

In a medium saucepan, stir together the granulated sugar and cornstarch to break up any clumps. Add the blackberries and apricots to the sugar mixture and toss to coat evenly. Let rest for 5 minutes to draw the juices from the fruit. Place over low heat and bring to a simmer. Simmer until thickened, 6–8 minutes, stirring frequently. Remove from the heat and stir in the lemon zest, cinnamon, nutmeg, and cardamom. Transfer to a bowl and let the blackberry mixture cool, covered, in the refrigerator, for at least 2 hours or up to 1 week.

Preheat the oven to 400°F. Line 2 baking sheets with parchment paper or aluminum foil.

Working with 1 sheet of pastry at a time on a lightly floured surface, roll the puff pastry sheet into a 12-inch square. Cut into 4 squares and lightly brush the edges of each square with egg wash. Spoon about ¼ cup of the blackberry mixture onto the center of each square and fold the pastry in half diagonally to make a triangle. You can seal the edges by pressing with the tines of a fork or making small slits along the edge with a paring knife, or by simply pressing the edges with your fingertips. Transfer to a prepared baking sheet. Use a sharp knife to poke 2 or 3 holes in the top of each pastry. Keep refrigerated while rolling and filling the second puff pastry sheet. (Chilling the turnovers before baking for at least 15 minutes will improve their appearance and texture.)

Brush the turnovers with egg wash and scatter with coarse sugar. Bake until the pastry is evenly golden and very flaky, 20–22 minutes.

Remove the turnovers from the pans, cool briefly on a wire rack, and serve warm or at room temperature.

If you can find coarse sugar, it makes a more dramatic decoration than regular table sugar since the crystals are about four times as large as those of regular sugar. This style of sugar may also be labeled "sugar crystals" or "crystal sugar." Look for it with other baking items or at shops specializing in ingredients for baking and pastry.

using puff pastry p. 217

zesting and juicing citrus p. 69

Berry Napoleon

2 sheets prepared puff pastry, thawed

1 recipe Crème Légère (p. 283) or Diplomat Cream (p. 282)

6 cups fresh raspberries

Confectioners' sugar for dusting

8 lemon balm sprigs or mint leaves

Makes 4 servings

Line 2 baking sheets with parchment paper. Working with 1 sheet of pastry at a time, cut the sheet into thirds along the fold lines. Place on a prepared baking sheet and prick all over a pastry docker or fork. Cover the pastry with a second piece of parchment paper (and, if you have enough baking sheets, top with a second baking sheet). Repeat with the second sheet of pastry. Chill the puff pastry in the refrigerator for at least 15 minutes or up to 12 hours.

Preheat the oven to 375°F. Bake the puff pastry until it is lightly browned and crisp, 20–25 minutes. Remove the pastry from the oven and remove the top baking sheet and parchment paper. Return the pan to the oven and bake until evenly golden and dry, 3–4 minutes more. Cool the pastry completely on a wire rack. Cut each strip of puff pastry into 2 rectangles with a serrated knife.

Assemble the napoleons up to 3 hours ahead of serving them: Place the crème légère in a pastry bag fitted with a large plain or star tip. Reserve 4 of the best-looking rectangles of puff pastry for the napoleon tops. Reserve some of the best-looking raspberries for garnish. Place 4 rectangles of puff pastry on the work surface. Cover each rectangle with berries and pipe the crème légère over the berries. Top each napoleon with a second layer of pastry and another layer of berries and crème légère. Top each napoleon with one of the reserved rectangles. Dust with confectioners' sugar and garnish with the reserved raspberries and lemon balm or mint. Refrigerate until ready to serve.

The classic napoleon pastry is known as *mille-feuille* in France. It consists of layers of flaky puff pastry and a rich cream. The Danes say that a Danish royal pastry chef in Copenhagen first invented the dessert in the 1800s for a state visit between the Emperor Napoleon and the King of Denmark. Some believe that the chocolate lines that sometimes garnish the pastry appear to form the letter "N" for Napoleon.

If lemon balm is available, use it instead of the more common mint sprig to add a hint of citrus to the plate. To keep mint or lemon balm fresh, make a bouquet of the herb and set it in a tall glass or pitcher. Add cold water, then cover the top of the herbs loosely with plastic wrap, and keep refrigerated. Replace the water and trim about ¼ inch from the bottom of the herbs every day or so for longer life.

using puff pastry p. 217

piping p. 266

Cheese-Filled Crêpes with Blueberry Coulis

Crêpe Batter

1 cup all-purpose flour

2 Tbsp sugar

¼ tsp salt

1 large egg

1 cup whole or low-fat milk

1 Tbsp unsalted butter, melted

¼ tsp vanilla extract

Melted unsalted butter for greasing and drizzling

Cheese Filling

2 cups cottage cheese

3 oz cream cheese

2 Tbsp sugar

1 large egg

½ tsp vanilla extract

Blueberry Coulis (p. 273), warmed

Makes 12 crêpes, or 6 servings

To make the crêpe batter, sift the flour, sugar, and salt into a bowl and set aside. Combine the egg, milk, butter, and vanilla extract in another bowl and stir until smooth. Add this mixture to the dry ingredients and stir just until the ingredients are blended into a relatively smooth batter. Let the batter rest for 30 minutes in the refrigerator. (The batter may be prepared to this point and stored in the refrigerator for up to 12 hours.) Strain the batter to remove any lumps if necessary before preparing the crêpes.

Heat a crêpe pan or small skillet over medium heat. Brush the pan with melted butter. Pour a scant ¼ cup batter into the crêpe pan, swirling and tilting the pan to coat the bottom. Cook, reducing the heat if necessary, until the first side is set and has a little color, about 2 minutes. Use a thin metal or heatproof rubber spatula to loosen the crêpe, and turn it over. Cook on the other side until set and very lightly colored (the crêpe will not be as dark on the second side as on the first), 1 minute more. Stack the crêpes between layers of parchment or waxed paper as you cook.

To make the cheese filling, purée the cottage cheese and cream cheese in a blender until very smooth. Transfer to a bowl and stir in the sugar, egg, and vanilla extract by hand. Keep refrigerated until you are ready to finish the crêpes.

Preheat the oven to 400°F. Lightly brush a medium baking dish with melted butter.

Spoon or pipe about 2 Tbsp of the cheese filling onto each crêpe. Fold each crêpe into quarters, or fold the sides in to the center, then roll each crêpe up. Place the crêpes seam side down in the prepared baking dish. Drizzle with melted butter and bake until very hot, 8–10 minutes.

Serve immediately, 2 crêpes per serving, with warm blueberry coulis.

Crêpe pans resemble skillets with short, sloping sides. A well-seasoned cast-iron crêpe pan will help prevent these thin pancakes from sticking.

Crêpes are easily made in advance. Make stacks of 5 or 6 crêpes, separating them with parchment or waxed paper between each one. They may then be wrapped well in plastic wrap and refrigerated or frozen for later use. Thaw frozen crêpes before filling and folding.

making crêpes p. 218

piping p. 266

Crêpes with Poached Peaches in Lemon-Vanilla Syrup

Poached Peaches in Lemon-Vanilla Syrup

4 peaches or 8 apricots

1½ cups water

½ cup granulated sugar

2 tsp freshly squeezed lemon juice

Two 2-inch-square pieces lemon zest

1 vanilla bean, split lengthwise

2 Tbsp unsalted butter

¼ cup tightly packed light brown sugar

½ cup late-harvest Gewürztraminer, Muscat, or other sweet dessert wine

12 crêpes, cooked and stacked (p. 225)

2 Tbsp peach or apricot brandy

2 cups Chantilly Cream (p. 281) or Custard Sauce (p. 274)

Makes 4 servings

To make the poached peaches, prepare an ice bath (page 169). Bring a large saucepan of water to a rolling boil over high heat. Drop a few peaches or apricots at a time into the boiling water for 30 seconds. Using a slotted spoon, transfer the fruit to the ice bath until cool to the touch. Peel, cut in half, and remove the pit. Set aside.

Combine the water, granulated sugar, lemon juice, lemon zest, and vanilla bean in a large saucepan over medium heat. Bring the mixture to a boil and cook for 5 minutes to make a syrup.

Add the peach or apricot halves to the syrup. Adjust the heat to maintain a bare simmer and poach gently until the peaches or apricots are cooked through (15–20 minutes for peaches, 6–8 minutes for apricots). Remove from the heat and let the fruit cool in the syrup to room temperature. Remove the lemon zest and discard; the vanilla bean should remain in the syrup. (Store the fruit in the syrup in a clean, covered container for up to 10 days in the refrigerator.)

To assemble the dessert, heat the butter in a wide sauté pan over medium-high heat. Add the brown sugar and cook until the sugar is melted. Add wine and simmer until the mixture is thickened and very hot, 3–4 minutes. Working with 1 crêpe at a time, place the crêpe flat in the pan (still over medium-high heat). Turn the crêpe once to coat evenly, then (still in the pan) fold the crêpe into quarters using a serving spoon and table fork. Transfer to a baking dish to keep warm or put it directly on a warmed dessert plate. Continue until all the crêpes are coated and folded, keeping the folded crêpes warm. Drain and add the peaches or apricots to the same pan and toss gently over medium heat until warmed through, 3–4 minutes. Add the peach brandy and cook until hot. For each serving, plate 3 crêpes and 2 peach halves or 4 apricot halves and top with some Chantilly cream or custard sauce.

Poaching is a great way to coax extra flavor from fruits. Adding sugar to the poaching liquid helps the fruit keep its shape. You may like to experiment with other spices and flavorings in the poaching liquid, including a piece of cinnamon stick, some lavender flowers or seeds, a clove, or a piece of star anise.

poaching p. 218

making crêpes p. 218

Winter Fruit Strudel

¼ cup chopped pitted prunes

¼ cup chopped dried apricots

¼ cup dark raisins

2 Tbsp brandy or dark rum

¼ cup water

4 Granny Smith apples, peeled, cored, and diced

2 Anjou pears, peeled, cored, and diced

¼ cup tightly packed light brown sugar

2 Tbsp chopped toasted pecans or walnuts

¾ tsp ground cinnamon

¼ tsp freshly grated nutmeg

⅛ tsp salt

8 sheets prepared phyllo dough, thawed

4 Tbsp (½ stick) unsalted butter, melted

Makes 8 servings

Preheat the oven to 375°F. Combine the prunes, apricots, and raisins in a small pan. Add the brandy and water and bring just to a simmer over low heat. Remove the pan from the heat and allow the fruit to plump for about 30 minutes.

Combine the apples, pears, brown sugar, nuts, cinnamon, nutmeg, and salt in a large bowl and toss to coat the fruit with the sugar and spices. Add the dried fruit and its plumping liquid and toss until blended. Spread this mixture in an even layer in a baking pan and cover loosely with parchment paper or aluminum foil. Bake until the fruits are very tender, 35–40 minutes. Remove from the oven and let cool.

Leave the oven at 375°F. Line a baking sheet with parchment paper.

Meanwhile, place the thawed phyllo sheets on a baking sheet or piece of plastic wrap. Cover the phyllo with another piece of plastic wrap and then a layer of barely moistened paper towels. Uncover the stack, remove 1 sheet to a piece of plastic wrap placed on a work surface, and re-cover the stack. Brush the first sheet lightly with the melted butter. Repeat this sequence, placing each new sheet of phyllo atop the buttered one and keeping the unused phyllo covered so it doesn't dry out or crack, until all the phyllo sheets are stacked and brushed with butter.

Mound the fruit filling along one of the long edges of the dough and use the plastic wrap to help roll the phyllo dough around the filling, being careful not to roll the plastic into the filling. The phyllo dough should overlap itself by about ½ inch. Use the plastic to help lift the strudel onto the prepared baking sheet, placing it seam side down. Brush the strudel with a little butter, and use a sharp knife to very lightly score the top 7 times, to mark the cutting lines for individual portions.

Bake the strudel until the dough is golden brown and crisp, about 25 minutes. Let cool slightly before slicing and serving.

Note: The strudel can be prepared up to the point of baking, and then wrapped and frozen. Without thawing, bake the strudel at 375°F for 30 minutes, then increase the oven temperature to 425°F for the final 10 minutes of baking.

The dried fruits in this recipe can be varied to suit your taste. Try adding a few dried cranberries or blueberries, or add chopped dried apple rings to give the strudel a deeper apple taste. The small amount of salt in the filling goes a long way to bring out the fruits' flavors. Whipped cream, vanilla ice cream, or frozen yogurt make perfect accompaniments to this dish.

toasting nuts p. 138

using phyllo dough p. 217

Baked Fig Beggar's Purses

Vegetable oil for greasing

6 fresh, ripe medium figs, stemmed

3 Tbsp packed almond paste

6 sheets prepared phyllo dough, thawed

4 Tbsp (½ stick) unsalted butter, melted

Confectioners' sugar for dusting

Makes 6 servings

Preheat the oven to 300°F. Lightly oil a baking sheet. Score the top third of each fig with an X. Roll the almond paste into 6 equal balls. Press 1 piece of almond paste into the center of each fig.

Place the thawed phyllo sheets on a baking sheet or piece of plastic wrap. Cover the phyllo with another piece of plastic wrap and then a layer of barely moistened paper towels. Working with 1 sheet at a time, cut into quarters. Brush each quarter with melted butter and place another quarter on top, staggering the corners in a pinwheel arrangement. Brush the top sheet with melted butter and place a fig in the center of the stack. Pull the pastry up around the fig and pinch together at the top, making a beggar's purse. Brush the outside with melted butter and transfer to the prepared baking sheet. Repeat with the remaining figs and phyllo.

Bake until the figs are soft and the phyllo is golden brown, about 30 minutes. Serve warm, dusted with confectioners' sugar.

Beggar's purses on the menu appear to have originated with a special appetizer that featured caviar. The name comes from the appearance of the dish, which resembles the small gathered sack that a hobo or beggar might have tied on the end of a stick. This is a fantastic dessert to try when fresh figs are available, late June through mid-August and sporadically throughout the fall. Peeled and cored pears or apples can be used when figs are not available.

using phyllo dough p. 217

Date and Pistachio Kataifi

1½ cups Pastry Cream (p. 282)

1 cup chopped pitted dates plus extra for garnish

⅔ cup chopped shelled unsalted pistachios plus extra for garnish

1 Tbsp Pernod or other anise-flavored liqueur

8 oz *kataifi* or shredded prepared phyllo dough

4 Tbsp (½ stick) unsalted butter, melted

1 cup Lemon Verbena Sauce (p. 271)

Makes 4 servings

Preheat the oven to 400°F. Line a baking sheet or jelly roll pan with parchment paper. Fold together the pastry cream, dates, pistachios, and Pernod with a rubber spatula in a bowl until evenly blended.

Place a piece of plastic wrap 14 inches long on the work surface. Arrange the *kataifi* on top of the plastic wrap in a rectangle about 12 inches long and 4 inches wide. Use a pastry brush to coat the top of the *kataifi* with the melted butter.

Spread the pistachio-date filling along the long edge of the *kataifi* closest to you, or pipe using a ¾-inch plain round tip. Use the plastic wrap to help roll the *kataifi* around the filling, being careful not to roll the plastic into the filling. The *kataifi* should overlap itself by about ½ inch. Use the plastic wrap to help transfer the *kataifi* roll carefully onto the prepared baking sheet, seam side down.

Bake the roll until golden brown, about 30 minutes. Cool slightly before cutting into four 3-inch slices. Serve warm, on plates garnished with scattered chopped dates and pistachios. Pool the lemon verbena sauce on the side.

Kataifi is shredded phyllo dough. If you can't find it in your grocery store or a Middle Eastern market, use phyllo sheets instead. Take thawed sheets of phyllo, roll them into a cylinder, and cut them crosswise into fine shreds with a pizza cutter, chef's knife, or kitchen scissors. Keep the shreds well covered as you would regular phyllo sheets so they don't dry out too much.

piping p. 266

using phyllo dough p. 217

Gougères

1 cup water

8 Tbsp (1 stick) unsalted butter

½ tsp salt

1 cup bread flour, sifted

4 large eggs

¾ cup grated Gruyère cheese

Makes about 50 pieces

Preheat the oven to 400°F. Line baking sheets with parchment paper.

Combine the water, butter, and salt in a saucepan over high heat and bring to a boil. Reduce the heat to medium, add the sifted flour all at once, and stir well. Cook, stirring constantly with a wooden spoon, until the dough begins to come away from the sides of the pan, about 5 minutes.

Transfer to the bowl of a stand mixer fitted with the paddle attachment and beat on medium speed until cooled to body temperature. Add the eggs one at a time, beating well after each addition, to achieve a stiff but pliable texture. Add the grated cheese and continue mixing for 1 minute more.

Transfer the dough to a pastry bag with a plain round tip and pipe into balls (or other shapes as desired) about ½ inch in diameter and about 2 inches apart onto the prepared baking sheets. (Alternatively, use 2 spoons to drop the dough onto the baking sheets.)

Bake until the gougères are golden brown, about 5 minutes, then lower the oven temperature to 325°F and continue to bake until they are puffy with no beads of moisture on the sides, 15–17 minutes more. Cool slightly on wire racks, then serve warm.

Note: Gougères are best when served warm from the oven, but they an also be cooled, held in an airtight container, and served at room temperature. This recipe makes a large quantity because it is difficult to make a smaller batch of dough, but you can freeze any that you won't eat within a few days. To reheat, defrost at room temperature for 10 minutes, then crisp in a 350°F oven for 5–10 minutes.

Pâte à choux, used to make classic gougères, is made by vigorously stirring flour into boiling liquid to develop the flour's gluten. The eggs added to this recipe create a great deal of steam as they bake. Since the gluten in the flour allows the batter to expand without bursting, pâte à choux puffs up as it cooks.

In addition to being a delightful hors d'oeuvre item, these Gruyère cheese puffs lend texture as a garnish for cream soups or purée soups.

making pâte à choux
p. 217

piping p. 266

Cream Puffs

Pâte à Choux

1 cup whole or low-fat milk

8 Tbsp (1 stick) unsalted butter, diced

2 Tbsp granulated sugar

½ tsp salt

1 cup bread flour, sifted

3 large eggs

1 large egg white

Egg wash (1 large egg whisked with 2 Tbsp cold milk or water)

½ cup sliced blanched almonds

2 cups Pastry Cream (p. 282) or Diplomat Cream (p. 282)

Confectioners' sugar for dusting

Makes 20 cream puffs

Preheat the oven to 375°F. Line baking sheets with parchment paper.

To make the pâte à choux, combine the milk, butter, granulated sugar, and salt in a saucepan over high heat and bring to a boil. Reduce the heat to medium, add the sifted flour all at once, and stir well. Cook, stirring constantly with a wooden spoon, until the dough begins to come away from the sides of the pan, about 5 minutes. Transfer to the bowl of a stand mixer fitted with the paddle attachment and beat on medium speed until cooled to body temperature. Add the eggs one at a time, beating well and scraping down the bowl with a rubber spatula after each addition. Beat in the egg white.

Transfer the pâte à choux dough to a pastry bag with a plain round tip. Pipe or spoon the dough into 20 equal-sized balls (about the size of a golf ball) onto the prepared baking sheets about 2 inches apart. Brush the unbaked puffs very lightly with egg wash. Scatter the puffs with the sliced almonds.

Bake until the pastries are puffy and lightly browned, about 20 minutes. Lower the oven temperature to 325°F and continue to bake until the puffs appear dry and a rich golden brown, another 20–25 minutes. Remove from the oven and cool completely on wire racks before splitting and filling.

When the pastry has cooled, slice off the top ½ inch from each cream puff. Pipe a dollop of pastry cream onto each base. Replace the top of the cream puff and dust with confectioners' sugar before serving.

Note: Cream puffs can be assembled and refrigerated up to 4 hours ahead.

For the greatest volume and the best texture, these pâte à choux pastries are baked at a high temperature for the first part of cooking, then the heat is lowered to finish baking them through. A high initial baking temperature makes the puffs expand rapidly; the lower temperature helps to dry the puffs so that they are crisp and light.

making pâte à choux p. 217

piping p. 266

VARIATION

Profiteroles

Prepare the dough as directed above. Pipe or spoon into 24 large marble–sized balls and omit the almond garnish. Bake for 10 minutes at 375°F and then 10–12 minutes at 325°F. Split as directed above, but fill with tempered French Vanilla Ice Cream (recipe on page 199; see also Serving Frozen Desserts, page 195); replace the pastry tops and drizzle with warmed Café au Lait Glaze (page 285) or Chocolate Glaze (page 284), scatter with toasted (page 138) sliced almonds.

Chocolate Éclairs

1 cup whole or low-fat milk

8 Tbsp (1 stick) unsalted butter, diced

2 Tbsp sugar

½ tsp salt

1 cup bread flour, sifted

3 large eggs

1 large egg white

1½ cups Diplomat Cream (p. 282)

2¾ cups Chocolate Glaze (p. 284), warmed

Makes 12 éclairs

Preheat the oven to 375°F. Line 2 baking sheets with parchment paper. Combine the milk, butter, sugar, and salt in a saucepan and bring to a boil over high heat. Reduce the heat to medium, add the flour all at once, and stir well. Cook, stirring constantly with a wooden spoon, until the dough begins to come away from the sides of the pan, about 5 minutes.

Transfer to the bowl of a stand mixer fitted with the paddle and beat at medium speed until cooled to body temperature. Add the eggs one at a time, beating well and scraping down the bowl with a rubber spatula after each addition. Beat in the egg white.

Transfer the dough to a pastry bag with a plain round tip. Pipe the dough into 5-inch-long cylinders on the parchment-lined baking sheets about 2 inches apart.

Bake the éclairs until they are puffed and light golden brown, 20 minutes. There may be beads of moisture on the sides. Lower the oven temperature to 325°F and continue to bake until the éclairs look dry, 20 minutes more. Transfer the éclairs to wire racks and let cool completely before filling.

Pierce a hole in both ends of each cooked éclair using a skewer or chopstick. Fit a pastry bag with a ⅛-inch plain tip. Fill the pastry bag with the diplomat cream and pipe into the éclair from each end.

Dip the top of each éclair in the warm glaze, removing any excess with a small metal spatula, and transfer to a rack set over a baking sheet. Refrigerate until the glaze firms, then serve.

Note: An alternative method for filling the éclairs is to slice them in half horizontally and pipe the diplomat cream in a spiral over the base of the éclair using a plain pastry tip. Dip the top of the pastry in warm glaze, removing any excess with a small metal spatula, and place it on top of the cream. Chill to firm the glaze as directed above.

The shape of a baked éclair depends upon the shape it is given before baking. It is easiest to make a nice, round éclair using a pastry bag, but you can also drop the batter from a spoon. Use a table knife dipped in water to smooth out any tails or peaks on the surface of the éclair before it goes into the oven. To be sure that your éclairs are all about the same size, use a pencil to trace templates onto the sheets of parchment paper before you place them, pencil-marked side down, onto baking sheets.

making pâte à choux p. 217

piping p. 266

Common Meringue

4 large egg whites

1 cup sugar

Makes about 6 cups

Put the egg whites in the clean, grease-free bowl of a stand mixer fitted with the whisk attachment and blend briefly on low speed. Increase the speed to medium and beat until the egg whites are loose and foamy, about 2 minutes. Increase the speed to high and gradually add the sugar, a few tablespoons at a time, until it is completely incorporated and the meringue is thick and glossy and has the desired peak (soft, medium, or stiff) according to its intended use.

Note: You may prefer to use pasteurized egg whites in this recipe to eliminate any food safety concerns.

Meringue is a thickly whipped foam of egg white blended with sugar. Common meringue is the quickest to prepare, since the egg whites and sugar are simply combined without heat. It is used as a topping for pies and in Baked Alaska (p. 210).

separating eggs p. 138

making meringue p. 219

Swiss Meringue

4 large egg whites

1 cup sugar

Makes about 6 cups

Put the egg whites and sugar in the clean, grease-free bowl of a stand mixer fitted with the whisk attachment and stir together until the sugar is blended into the whites. Place the bowl over a saucepan of simmering water and stir frequently until the mixture reaches 110–120°F. Transfer the bowl to the mixer and beat on high speed until the meringue is thick and glossy and has the desired peak (soft, medium, or stiff) according to its intended use.

Note: You may prefer to use pasteurized egg whites in this recipe to eliminate any food safety concerns.

Warming egg whites and sugar before you beat them into a meringue dissolves the sugar completely for a smooth texture and keeps the foam slightly more stable. In a Swiss meringue, the eggs and sugar are warmed together before beating.

using a double boiler p. 167

Italian Meringue

Cooking spray for greasing

¾ cup sugar (divided use)

¼ cup water

5 large egg whites

Makes about 7 cups

Grease a heatproof glass measuring cup. Combine ½ cup of the sugar with the water in a heavy saucepan. Cook over medium-high heat without stirring until the mixture reaches 230°F. At that time, place the egg whites in the bowl of a stand mixer fitted with a whisk attachment and whip on medium speed until frothy. Add the remaining ¼ cup of sugar and beat the meringue to medium peaks. When the sugar mixture reaches soft ball stage, 240°F, pour it into the measuring cup, then into the meringue in a slow, steady stream on low speed. Increase the speed to high and whip until the meringue cools to room temperature and has the desired peak.

A meringue made with a cooked sugar syrup is known as Italian meringue. This stable foam works well for piping meringue shells (p. 219) or for making Italian Buttercream (p. 279).

Raspberry Meringue Tartlets

Meringue Tartlet Shells

1 recipe Swiss or Italian Meringue (p. 234)

Raspberry Curd Filling

1 package (2¼ tsp) powdered unflavored gelatin

¼ cup cold water

½ cup Raspberry Purée (p. 190)

2 large egg yolks, lightly beaten

1 large egg, lightly beaten

½ cup sugar

8 Tbsp (1 stick) unsalted butter, diced

2 Tbsp Chambord or other raspberry-flavored liqueur

Makes 8 individual tartlets

Preheat the oven to 250°F. To prepare the tartlet shells, draw eight 3½ x 2–inch ovals on 2 pieces of parchment paper, leaving a 3-inch space between each oval. Flip the parchment paper and place on baking sheets, pencil-marked side down.

Fill a pastry bag fitted with a plain round tip with the meringue. Pipe the meringue in a spiral motion, beginning at the center of each oval and moving toward the outer edge, keeping the tip just above the parchment paper while piping. Once you reach the outer edge of the oval, pipe rings of meringue to create a wall on the outer rim of the spiral, until the wall of the shell is 1¼ inches tall.

Bake until the exteriors of the meringues appear dry. Lower the oven temperature to 180°F and continue to bake until the meringues are completely dry and crisp throughout, about 1½ hours. Leaving the meringue shells in the oven, turn off the oven and allow the shells to cool completely before filling.

To prepare the filling, sprinkle the gelatin over the cold water in a small bowl and stir to break up any clumps. Let the gelatin soften in the water for about 5 minutes.

Meanwhile, combine the raspberry purée, egg yolks, egg, and sugar in a saucepan over medium heat and bring the mixture to a boil while stirring constantly.

Remove the pan from the heat and whisk in the butter a few pieces at a time until it is all incorporated and the curd is quite thick. Stir in the Chambord.

Heat the softened gelatin over simmering water or in a microwave until the granules melt and the mixture is clear, about 20 seconds on low power. Stir the melted gelatin into the raspberry curd.

Carefully spoon the curd into the meringue shells. The curd should come to the top edge of the shells. Refrigerate for 2 hours before serving.

Chambord is a French liqueur flavored with black raspberries. The black raspberries are steeped in aged Cognac. After the Cognac is infused with the black raspberry flavor, extracts from red raspberries, currants, and blackberries are added. When the liqueur is nearly completed, mace, cinnamon, ginger, cloves, and vanilla are added, along with several herbs, orange, and lemon. Acacia honey is also included before the entire mixture is aged in barrels and bottled.

working with gelatin
p. 170

making meringue shells
p. 219

Poached Meringue Eggs with Tropical Fruit Salsa

Tropical Fruit Salsa

¼ cup freshly squeezed orange juice

¼ cup passion fruit juice

2 Tbsp sugar

1 cup finely diced mango

1 cup finely diced pineapple

½ cup thinly sliced star fruit

½ cup finely diced papaya

⅓ cup finely diced kiwi

1 Tbsp freshly squeezed lime juice

2 Tbsp minced fresh mint

1 recipe Common Meringue (p. 234), prepared just before assembling dessert

3 cups whole or low-fat milk

¼ cup sugar

8 mint sprigs

Makes 8 servings

To make the tropical fruit salsa, combine the orange and passion fruit juices with the 2 Tbsp sugar in a small saucepan and simmer over medium heat until reduced by half, about 20 minutes. Remove the pan from the heat and let the syrup cool to room temperature. Toss the fruits together gently in a bowl and pour the cooled syrup over them. Add the lime juice and mint and toss gently just until evenly coated. Cover and refrigerate the salsa until ready to use, up to 24 hours.

Cut out 4 circles of parchment or waxed paper 10 inches in diameter.

When ready to finish the dessert, make the meringue and work quickly once it is prepared.

Combine the milk and ¼ cup sugar in a straight-sided pot that is wider than it is tall. Attach a candy thermometer to the side of the pot, making sure that the tip is submerged but not resting on the bottom of the pot. Warm over low heat until the mixture reaches 140°F. There should be no bubbles visible, and a small amount of steam should be rising from the surface.

Using 2 large spoons or an oval ice cream scoop, shape some of the meringue into 6 egg shapes and place them on one of the parchment paper circles. Flip the circle over into the hot milk and peel back the paper to release the "eggs." Poach the "eggs" for about 2 minutes on each side. Using a slotted spoon, carefully remove them and place on paper towels to drain slightly. Repeat with the remaining meringue to make 24 "eggs." Cover and chill the "eggs" for at least 2 hours before serving.

Divide the fruit salsa among 8 dessert plates or soup plates and place 3 "eggs" on each bed of salsa. Garnish with a mint sprig.

These poached meringue eggs harken back to a classic French dessert, *oeufs à la neige,* or "eggs in snow." In the traditional recipe, poached meringues, shaped like eggs, are served atop a rich custard sauce with a cage or nest of spun sugar. This version is updated and simplified for today's tastes.

poaching p. 218

making meringue p. 219

Chocolates
9 and Confections

Candy is different from naturally occurring sweets like honey, dates, or dried fruits because it is prepared, or manufactured—although often using these same naturally sweet ingredients. The first items categorized as candies were whole fruits cooked in a sugar syrup. By the nineteenth century, the term "confection" referred to a wide array of sweetened dishes, including preserves of fruits in syrups or jellies, candies, wines, and liqueurs. Candies of the time included hard candies, marzipan shapes, taffy, toffee, pralines, and dragée-style nuts. Chocolate had become more widely available and was starting to be used in candies and confections such as fudge and chocolate-covered cream centers.

The building blocks of confections

Confectionary work prior to the eighteenth century was actually considered part of the druggist's work. Sugar and chocolate, the basis for all the recipes in this chapter, have traditionally been used as both foodstuffs and medicines, carefully measured and handled by cooks and chemists alike. Sugar, the sine qua non of all candies, was so valued in some parts of the world until well into the eighteenth century that it was considered a curative rather than the commonplace ingredient we blithely measure out into our recipes today. Chocolate, another valued commodity used as currency long ago in South America, was once considered food fit for the gods and royalty.

There are few other ingredients that exhibit such a complexity of flavor and texture, as well as such an astonishing range of uses. Sugar, for instance, is a preservative, a sweetener, and a tenderizer. It can be used in its granular form, dissolved into syrups, or cooked into a wide range of confections and candies. Chocolate, too, has uses you might not have considered. For example, chocolate is a great source of antioxidants, making it a valuable component in a healthful diet. It also acts as a thickener, and when it is applied as a glaze or coating, it seals in moisture and keeps out air to preserve the food it coats.

Both granular sugar and chocolate have a crystalline structure. By manipulating this aspect of these ingredients, candy makers can produce an array of textures, from the glasslike hardness of toffee and brittles to the creaminess of taffy and soft caramels to the distinct and appealing graininess of fudge. Some candy-making methods are designed to encourage crystals to form. For example, first heating the candy to just the right temperature, then letting it cool and stirring it until thickened produces fine, even crystals and a smooth creamy candy such as fudge. If the candy is too hot when you start to stir it, fewer but larger crystals will form, making a grainy candy. Other methods are meant to prevent the formation of crystals entirely. For these candies, such as toffee or brittle, the sugar syrup is heated to the correct temperature, then poured from the pot into shapes or molds and allowed to cool without being stirred at all. Some recipes include corn syrup; the molecular structure of the syrup makes crystals less likely to form. Efforts are made to eliminate any conditions that might promote the formation of crystals: the sides of the pot are washed down to prevent crystals from forming on the side of the pan; metal spoons, which can encourage the formation of crystals, are not used for stirring; all tools, including the thermometer and spoons, are kept very clean as you work; and the candy is cooled as quickly as possible, either by forming it into small clusters or by spreading it in a thin layer.

Chocolate styles

Chocolate derives from the seeds, or beans, of the cacao plant. The beans are fermented, dried, roasted, cracked, and the parts of the bean containing cocoa butter are ground. The resulting chocolate liquor may now be sold as unsweetened or baking chocolate, used as an ingredient in baking; it is quite bitter and unpleasant to eat out of hand. Bittersweet and semisweet chocolates are made by adding more cocoa butter and sugar to the chocolate liquor, and they are used for both baking and eating. Milk chocolate has a percentage of milk solids added as well. Cocoa results when all the cocoa butter is extracted from the chocolate liquor, and the cocoa butter may be sweetened and flavored to create white chocolate. Cocoa powder that is processed with an alkali to intensify the flavor and deepen the color is referred to as Dutch-processed.

Solid chocolate should be stored at cool room temperature, well wrapped, for up to 1 month; if left in the original packaging, chocolate may last up to 2 years. (If you live in a very hot and humid climate, keep chocolate in either the refrigerator or freezer.) Cocoa powder can be stored on the shelf for up to a year.

Working with chocolate

Chocolate is often used to decorate cookies, cakes, and pastries. You can drizzle melted chocolate from the end of a spoon, or put it in a parchment paper cone (page 268) and use it to write a message on top of a cake, or even on a plate. You can also pipe delicate filigrees or designs onto parchment paper. Once they harden, you can use them to decorate almost any dessert, or you can store them between layers of parchment or waxed paper to use later. Use a vegetable peeler to shave flakes of chocolate from a larger bar or a grater to dust desserts with a powdery coating.

Tempering is a process chocolate undergoes so that, as it hardens, it has a good texture (sometimes referred to as "snap") and an appealing shine. The chocolate you buy has already been tempered, but in order to coat foods with chocolate, it must be melted. Heating the chocolate enough to melt it takes it out of temper, but you can re-temper chocolate at home for beautiful, glossy chocolate coatings.

And although tempering chocolate is an exacting exercise in temperature control, you can be successful even without an elaborate tempering machine. All you really need is a good setup for melting the chocolate over simmering water (either a double boiler or a metal bowl set snugly over a saucepan of simmering water), an accurate candy thermometer, and plenty of chocolate. If tempering chocolate is more than you want to take on, however, there are plenty of recipes in this chapter that call for simple melted chocolate.

Working with sugar

Candy makers must understand how sugar cooks and how it looks and behaves at various temperatures. The common names for the stages that sugar goes through on its way to becoming candies of various sorts include thread, soft ball, firm ball, hard ball, fudge, soft crack, brittle, hard crack, and caramel. The names refer to the way the cooked sugar acts after it has been chilled in cold water. Each stage also represents a specific temperature, but you can use the old-fashioned test of dropping a little of the sugar mixture into ice-cold water as well. For example, if, after dropping the sugar in water, you can gather it into a ball that holds its shape only briefly, it is at the soft ball stage. If it keeps its shape after gathering, then it has reached hard ball stage, and so on. See the chart at right for descriptions and temperature requirements for each stage.

Cooking sugar requires patience; there can be a seemingly interminable wait as the water cooks away and the syrup concentrates enough to move through each stage. However, once the sugar begins to color, the changes occur rapidly. Undercooking sugar usually results in confections that won't set properly as they cool, or, in the case of fudge, candy that won't form crystals of the right number and size. Overcooking sugar can lead to a bitter taste and may cause the candy to set up too quickly to be properly shaped.

An advanced degree in chemistry is certainly not a prerequisite for making candy. Simple marzipan confections are as easy to make as the clay sculptures you made in grade school. And making candied citrus peel, with or without a chocolate coating, doesn't even require a candy thermometer. Even when you embark upon creating sugar- or chocolate-based confections and candies, the essentials are a good thermometer, a careful reading of the recipe, and a little patience.

Cooking sugar to stages

STAGE	DESCRIPTION OF SUGAR	TEMPERATURE
Simple syrup	sugar dissolves	212°F (100°C)
Thread	sugar forms soft 2-inch-long thread between the index finger and thumb when dropped into and removed from water	215–230°F (102–110°C)
Soft ball	sugar forms soft ball that flattens by itself when dropped into and removed from water	240°F (116°C)
Firm ball	sugar forms a firm but pliable ball when dropped into and removed from water	245°F (118°C)
Hard ball	sugar forms a rigid ball when dropped into and removed from water	250–260°F (121–127°C)
Soft crack	sugar separates into rigid but still pliable threads when dropped into and removed from water	265–270°F (129–132°C)
Hard crack	sugar separates into brittle threads when dropped into and removed from water	295–310°F (146–154°C)
Light caramel	sugar becomes a transparent, pale golden color	320°F (160°C)
Medium caramel	caramel darkens to a deep beige or light tan	346°F (174°C)
Dark caramel	caramel becomes dark or reddish brown	350°F (177°C)

Using pectin

Pectin is a thickener derived from fruits such as tart apples or citrus. It is used to make jams and jellies as well as candies.

1 Thickening with pectin

In order for pectin to gel and thicken a mixture, the recipe must have the proper balance of acids and sugar. Since fruits contain varying amounts of acids and sugar, depending upon their variety, the season, and growing conditions, cooking with pectin can be challenging. If the fruits do not contain enough acid on their own, the recipe will call for a small amount of lemon juice.

Pectin is sold as a powder and as a liquid. These two forms are not interchangeable in a recipe. Liquid pectin can be added directly to a fruit purée or juice at room temperature. Powered pectin is typically combined with water (about ¾ cup water for 4 tsp powdered pectin) and brought to a boil. The mixture foams up considerably, so choose a pan with tall sides. Cook it at a rapid boil until there is no more foam.

Melting chocolate

Melt chocolate over gentle heat and pay close attention so that it doesn't scorch or seize.

1 Preparing the chocolate

Chop chocolate finely before melting it, in order to speed the melting process and prevent scorching.

2 Melting in a double boiler

Using a double boiler (page 167) is one option for melting chocolate. However, if any moisture comes into contact with the chocolate, it causes the chocolate to stiffen and develop grains or lumps, a situation referred to as "seizing." (A relatively large amount of liquid combined with the chocolate as it melts does not have this effect.) To prevent seizing, be sure that the water in your double boiler is at a bare simmer and that the top of your double boiler fits snugly, so that no steam escapes. Also make sure that the container for the chocolate and the spoon or spatula you use are perfectly dry.

3 Melting in a microwave

Chocolate melted in the microwave is less likely to come in contact with moisture. However, a common problem is that the chocolate overheats and scorches. Place the chopped chocolate in a nonmetal bowl and set the power to low. Microwave the chocolate in 15- to 20-second increments, until it appears slightly glossy but still holds its original shape. Stir the chocolate to evenly distribute the heat. If necessary, continue to melt in the microwave, but remember that the chocolate's residual heat will melt smaller pieces even after removal from the oven.

Tempering chocolate

Heat chocolate to a specific temperature, then cool and hold it at a stable temperature for a glossy coating.

1 Heating to a specific temperature

One classic method for tempering chocolate calls for heating chopped chocolate first to 110–120°F for dark chocolate and 105–110°F for milk or white chocolate. Once that temperature is reached, a portion of the chocolate is removed from the heat, poured onto a marble slab, and repeatedly spread and folded over on itself until it reaches 78–80°F. The cooled chocolate is added back to the warm chocolate and the mixture is stirred until it reaches the correct temperature: 86–90°F for dark chocolate or 84–87°F for milk or white chocolate. It is now ready to use as a coating.

You can also achieve good results with a quick method that involves "seeding" melted chocolate with unmelted chocolate. Reserve one-third of the total amount of chocolate (either chopped or in a large piece) in a dry bowl and place the rest in the top of a double boiler (page 167). Set over simmering water and melt the chocolate, stirring often with a rubber spatula. Do not let any steam or moisture come in contact with the chocolate. Once the chocolate is melted, add the reserved chocolate. Stir until it cools to 86–90°F for dark chocolate or 84–87°F for milk or white chocolate.

To keep chocolate in temper as you work with it, set it over a bowl of warm water about 2°F warmer than the tempered chocolate.

Dipping in chocolate

Use plenty of tempered or melted chocolate for best results when dipping items.

1 Setting up

Clear a large area on a flat work surface. Let foods come to room temperature before you dip them. Set up trays lined with parchment or waxed paper to hold the chocolate-dipped candies. Arrange trays, tools, and chocolate in a logical order; you should be able to work in a single direction without doubling back.

2 Dipping in chocolate

Dipping tools and forks have long handles and an open "cradle" or long prongs, similar to the tines on a table fork, but a little longer. You can use ordinary forks as well, or break the middle tines out of a plastic fork. Set the item you want to dip on the tool or fork. Lower it into the chocolate until it is completely submerged, then lift it up out of the chocolate and drain away the excess. As you move the item away from the pan holding the chocolate, gently scrape or tap the tool against the edge of the pan to remove any drips. Finally, tip the tool or fork so the chocolate-dipped item rolls onto the lined tray or use another tool to gently push it onto the tray.

3 Letting the chocolate set

Let chocolate harden at room temperature if possible. If your kitchen is especially hot or humid, you may need to let the chocolate harden in the refrigerator for about 15 minutes. Chocolate coatings that have been refrigerated, however, can sometimes appear streaky or lose some of their sheen.

Making simple syrup

When you heat sugar and water, you increase the amount of sugar that can be dissolved into the water. Making a syrup is the first step on the way to making confections and many other desserts.

1 Combining sugar and water

If you are making confections, you may have a relatively large amount of sugar in relation to the amount of water. If you are making a simple syrup for other desserts or a poaching liquid, you'll have less sugar or more liquid. It is a good practice to put the sugar in the pot first and then gradually pour the liquid over it, washing down any sugar that splashes onto the pot's sides as you add it. Put the pot over low heat until the sugar mixture turns clear. Then raise the heat and bring to a boil. Once the mixture comes to a full boil, remove it from the heat.

2 Infusing syrups with flavor

You may want to add spices or citrus to the sugar and water mixture before putting it on the heat, to extract the most flavor from these items. You can add a variety of other flavorings to the syrup after it has come to a boil. Add fresh herbs such as mint or lemon verbena to a syrup when it is still very hot; cover the syrup and let the herbs steep into the syrup, then strain out the herbs. Flavored cordials and liqueurs such as Kahlúa, Grand Marnier, amaretto, Frangelico, or Chambord should be added after the syrup has cooled for the most intense flavor.

Cooking sugar to stages

As you gradually cook the water out of a sugar solution, you control the texture and flavor of your confection by controlling the sugar's temperature, the ingredients you add, and the way you handle the sugar as it cooks.

1 Combining sugar, water, and acid

Place the sugar in a heavy saucepan. Pour the water over it and stir gently so that you don't splash too much sugar on the sides of the pan. If the recipe calls for an acid, like lemon juice or cider vinegar, add it now for flavor and to help prevent the sugar from recrystallizing as it melts. Attach a candy thermometer to the side of the pan, making sure that the bulb is submerged but not resting on the bottom of the pan.

2 Heating the sugar mixture

Cook the sugar-water mixture over high heat, stirring with a nonmetal spoon. If there is a lot of foam on the surface, skim it away. Once it reaches a boil, stop stirring to avoid splashing sugar crystals on the sides of the pan. If there are sugar crystals clinging to the sides of the pan, wash the sides down using a pastry brush dipped in water. Since this added water will increase the time it takes to reach the desired temperature, use as little water as possible. Hot sugar can cause especially serious burns; never touch it.

3 Removing from the heat

Cook the sugar syrup to the appropriate stage required by the recipe. (see chart, page 241). Remove the pan from the heat a degree or two before it reaches the target temperature; it will continue to cook off the heat.

Candied Almonds

¾ cup sugar

3 Tbsp water

3½ cups (1 lb) whole blanched almonds

1 Tbsp unsalted butter

Makes 2 pounds

Line a jelly roll pan with a silicone mat or parchment paper.

Combine the sugar and water in a heavy saucepan and stir until the sugar is evenly moistened. Bring to a boil over high heat, stirring constantly. Cook the mixture to 230°F. Remove from the heat. Add the almonds and stir vigorously until the sugar crystallizes and makes a white crusty coating on the almonds.

Return the pan to the heat and stir constantly until the sugar melts and caramelizes, making a coating on the nuts. The nuts will become shiny and smooth, with a very dark caramel coating. Remove the pan from the heat, immediately add the butter, and quickly stir it.

Pour the nuts onto the prepared pan, immediately using the tip of an oiled or buttered knife to separate them. Let the nuts cool completely before serving.

A texture contrast between a nut and a crisp coating of caramelized sugar is part of this confection's appeal. Stirring the nut and sugar mixture as it cools gives the sugar a better chance to change into crystals that adhere to the nuts and then turn into a caramel as the nuts are cooled.

cooking sugar to stages
p. 244

Candied Citrus Peels

3 navel oranges or 4 large lemons, preferably organic

2 cups granulated sugar

1½ cups water

⅓ cup light corn syrup

3 cups superfine sugar

Makes about 100 pieces

Cut the citrus into quarters. Remove the pulp, leaving as much pith (the white portion under the peel) on the peel as possible. Place the peels in a medium saucepan and cover with cold water. Bring to a boil, then drain the water. Repeat this process 3 more times, or until the peels can be easily pierced with a knife. Drain thoroughly.

Meanwhile, combine the granulated sugar, water, and corn syrup in a large, heavy saucepan and bring to a boil over high heat, stirring from time to time until the sugar is completely melted.

Add the blanched peels to the sugar syrup and bring to a simmer. Reduce the heat to low and gently simmer, uncovered, for 1 hour, or until the peels appear somewhat shiny and slightly translucent. Transfer the peels and syrup to a medium bowl and let cool to room temperature.

Remove the peels from the syrup with a slotted spoon. Pat dry with a cloth towel and cut into slivers about ⅜ inch wide and 2 inches long. Toss the peels in the superfine sugar, transfer to a baking sheet, and let them air dry for a day. Store the peels in an airtight container in a cool dry place for up to 2 weeks. Do not refrigerate.

Other citrus fruit may be substituted for the oranges or lemons in this recipe. Try grapefruit, tangerine, lime, or pomelo. You'll need a total of about 2½ cups of peel pieces.

Candied peel may be used in fruitcakes, mincemeat pie, and steamed puddings.

making simple syrup
p. 244

Truffles

1 doubled recipe hard Ganache
(p. 284), chilled

4 cups chopped semisweet
chocolate (divided use)

Makes about 48 truffles

After preparing the ganache, cover tightly and refrigerate until firm, at least 8 hours or up to overnight.

Line baking sheets with parchment paper. Scoop the ganache using a 1-inch-diameter melon baller onto the prepared pans. Roll the truffles into round balls (they need not be perfectly even). Let the truffles firm in the refrigerator if the kitchen or your hands are warm, then let them come just back to room temperature before coating.

Line more baking sheets with parchment. To temper the semisweet chocolate, attach a candy thermometer to the side of the top pan of a double boiler (page 167), making sure that the bulb is not resting on the bottom of the pan. Melt 3 cups of the chopped chocolate in the double boiler over barely simmering water. When it reaches 115°F, remove it from the heat. Add ½ cup of the remaining chopped chocolate and stir until the chocolate cools to 90°F. Set the pan in a bowl of 92°F water.

Spread a small amount of tempered chocolate in the palm of your hand or on a nonporous work surface such as marble, stainless steel, or china and gently roll the truffles one at a time in the chocolate until evenly coated. Transfer to the prepared baking sheets and continue until all of the truffles are coated. (This precoating helps the final chocolate layer to adhere better and prevents the ganache from melting when the final layer is applied.) Reserve the melted chocolate for applying a final coat. Let the coating firm at room temperature until set.

Repeat the tempering procedure: Reheat the reserved chocolate over simmering water to 115°F, remove from the heat, and stir in the remaining ½ cup chopped chocolate. Stir until the chocolate cools to 90°F. Set the pan in a bowl of 92°F water. Using a dipping tool or fork, dunk the truffles in the tempered chocolate to apply a final coat. Transfer the truffles to the clean prepared baking sheets and let the chocolate set. (To store, transfer the truffles to storage containers and separate the layers with parchment or waxed paper.)

Chocolate truffles are so named for the resemblance they bear to the sought-after edible fungus: round, slightly knobby, and deep, earthy brown in color. And, like their mushroom counterparts, truffles have a distinctive aroma and texture. Dipping truffles in tempered chocolate for a shiny coat makes them perfect for gift giving, but for spur-of-the-moment candy making, truffles can be simply coated with cocoa powder, shredded coconut, or chopped toasted nuts.

dipping in chocolate
p. 243

tempering chocolate
p. 243

Fudge

Flourless cooking spray for greasing

¾ cup heavy cream

½ cup milk

2¼ cups sugar

⅓ cup light corn syrup

1 Tbsp unsalted butter

¼ tsp salt

4 oz unsweetened, semisweet, bittersweet, or white chocolate, finely chopped, or ½ cup peanut butter

2 tsp vanilla extract

1 cup chopped toasted walnuts, black walnuts, Brazil nuts, or macadamia nuts (optional)

1 cup marshmallow bits, toffee bits, and/or dried fruits such as cherries or raisins (optional)

Makes 2 pounds

Cut two 9 x 14–inch rectangles of parchment paper. Lightly coat a 9-inch square baking pan with cooking spray. Lay one strip of the parchment in the baking pan, pressing it to the bottom and sides. Lightly coat the parchment with cooking spray. Lay the second parchment rectangle across the pan in the opposite direction to form a cross. Press the parchment to the bottom and sides of the pan and lightly coat with cooking spray. You should have a few inches of paper overhang on each side of the pan.

Combine the cream and milk in a measuring cup and pour half of the mixture into a heavy saucepan. Add the sugar and corn syrup. Stir until the sugar dissolves. Attach a candy thermometer to the side of the pan, making sure that the bulb is submerged but not resting on the bottom of the pan. Heat the mixture over medium heat, stirring occasionally to keep the mixture from scorching. If there are sugar crystals on the sides of the pan, brush them away with a pastry brush dipped in water, using as little water as possible.

When the mixture reaches 230°F, add the butter and salt and stir to blend. Slowly add the remaining milk and cream mixture and continue to cook until the mixture reaches 240°F, stirring only enough to prevent scorching. Add the chopped chocolate and vanilla extract. Stir just enough to blend in the chocolate, and pour into a clean, dry bowl.

Attach the candy thermometer to the side of the bowl and let the fudge cool to 110°F without stirring. Once the mixture reaches 110°F, stir the fudge briefly until it just starts to thicken and lose its gloss. At this point add the nuts and other add-ins, if using, continue to stir until blended, and immediately pour the fudge into the prepared pan. Set the pan on a wire rack and let the fudge cool completely before using the parchment to lift it out of the pan and cutting it into pieces.

Note: Not everyone has a marble slab on hand, but if you do, you may prefer to use it instead of a bowl and pan to finish the fudge. Pour the fudge onto a clean piece of marble large enough to hold the entire batch and check the fudge's temperature with a candy thermometer. Once it comes down to 110°F, use a palette knife to lift and fold the fudge over on itself until it begins to thicken. You can then gather the fudge into a slab and let it harden directly on the marble.

Fudge, along with fondant, is a confection cooked to soft ball stage. When a small amount is dropped into cold water and then shaped, it forms a soft ball that flattens by itself when lifted from the water. Fudge is considered a truly American confection, developed at women's colleges like Vassar and Smith. Although a good fudge should be creamy, there is still a fine crystalline structure in the candy. This texture is produced by stirring the fudge only when it cools to 110°F. Since the fudge is already mostly cooled, the crystals that form will be small and regularly spaced.

toasting nuts p. 138

cooking sugar to stages p. 244

Turtles

Unsalted butter for greasing

100 pecan halves (about
1 lb), toasted

One 14-oz can sweetened
condensed milk

1 cup light corn syrup

10 oz bittersweet chocolate,
coarsely chopped

1 Tbsp vegetable oil

Makes 20 pieces

Line baking sheets with parchment paper and coat the paper lightly
with butter. Arrange all of the pecan halves on the parchment paper
in groups of 5, with 1 piece forming the head and 4 pieces as the
legs of a turtle (see photo, page 238). Make sure that all the nuts in
each group touch in the center.

Combine the sweetened condensed milk and corn syrup in a heavy
3-qt saucepan. Cook the mixture over medium heat, stirring constantly
with a wooden spoon, until the mixture turns the color of medium
caramel, a deep beige or light tan. Remove from the heat.

Grease 2 serving spoons lightly. Working quickly, very carefully spoon
1 Tbsp of the hot caramel mixture onto each group of pecans to hold
them together and form the body of the turtle. Let cool thoroughly,
about 1 hour at room temperature.

Melt the chocolate in a double boiler or microwave. Stir in the oil.
Use a spoon or parchment paper cone (page 268) to drizzle or pipe
the chocolate over the caramel, completely covering the caramel and
forming each turtle shell. Let the turtles set at room temperature
until firm, or place them in the freezer for about 3 minutes to set
the chocolate.

Note: Store the candies at room temperature in an airtight container.

It takes a little patience
to sort through a bag of
pecans to find the most
attractive nuts, but it's part
of making a good turtle.
These classic candies use
a creamy caramel body to
hold the pecan legs and
head of a turtle in place.
A chocolate glaze, kept
shiny by the use of oil,
completes the shell.

toasting nuts p. 138

melting chocolate p. 242

VARIATION

Cashew and Cranberry Clusters

Substitute 40 toasted whole cashews (about ½ lb) and 1¼ cups
dried sweetened cranberries for the pecans. Instead of shaping into
a turtle, mound the cashews and cranberries in small "hills" before
adding the caramel mixture. Cover with chocolate as described above.

Soft Caramels

Flourless cooking spray
for greasing

2 cups sugar

1 cup heavy cream

¾ cup whole or low-fat milk

Large zest strips from ½ orange

½ vanilla bean, split lengthwise

⅓ cup light corn syrup

1 Tbsp unsalted butter

Makes 1½ pounds

Lightly coat a 9-inch square baking pan with cooking spray. Cut two 9 x 16–inch rectangles of parchment paper. Lay one strip of the parchment in the baking pan, pressing it to the bottom and sides. Lightly coat the parchment with cooking spray. Lay the second parchment rectangle across the pan in the opposite direction to form a cross. Press the parchment to the bottom and sides of the pan and lightly coat with cooking spray. You should have a few inches of paper overhang on each side of the pan.

Combine the sugar, cream, milk, zest, and vanilla bean in a large, heavy saucepan. Bring the mixture to a boil over medium heat, stirring constantly. Once the mixture begins to boil, add the corn syrup while continuing to stir. Continue cooking until the mixture reaches a medium golden brown, 245°F on a candy thermometer, the firm ball stage.

Pour the mixture immediately into the prepared pan, remove the vanilla bean and orange zest, and cool to room temperature. Using greased kitchen shears or a greased sharp knife, cut into squares.

Caramels should be very smooth and rich, the result of adding cream, butter, and corn syrup to sugar as it cooks. These soft candies can be cut into a variety of simple shapes like disks, cylinders, rectangles, and diamonds. Wrap them individually in twists of waxed paper or colorful cellophane and stack them in tins or boxes for gift giving. Check in craft shops and stores that carry cake- and candy-making supplies for wrappers and boxes.

cooking sugar to stages
p. 244

Toffee

Flourless cooking spray for greasing, if needed

3 cups sugar

1½ cups heavy cream

⅓ cup light corn syrup

½ vanilla bean, split lengthwise

Makes about ¾ pound

Place a 12 x 17–inch silicone baking mat on a work surface or line a jelly roll pan with parchment paper and grease lightly.

Combine the sugar, cream, corn syrup, and vanilla bean in a large, heavy saucepan and stir to evenly moisten the sugar. Heat over medium heat, stirring constantly and occasionally washing down the sides of the pan with a pastry brush dipped in cool water, until the mixture reaches hard crack stage, 300°F on a candy thermometer.

Remove the vanilla bean and immediately pour the toffee onto the silicone baking mat or prepared pan and spread into an even layer about ⅛ inch thick with an greased palette knife.

Cool the toffee until it is rather firm but not brittle, 20–30 minutes. Use a sharp knife to score it into pieces. Cool to room temperature before breaking the toffee into pieces along the scored lines.

Toffee is a crisp confection that gets its main flavoring from sugar that is cooked until it becomes brittle. Added fat, in the form of heavy cream, keeps the candy tender enough to break apart. Toffee can be dipped in chocolate, crushed and added to parfaits and ice creams (pp. 201 and 206), or scattered beneath a custard for a hint of something both pleasantly sweet and pleasantly bitter.

cooking sugar to stages
p. 244

tempering chocolate
p. 243

Nut Brittle

Vegetable oil for greasing,
if needed

2 cups sugar

1 cup light corn syrup

¾ cup water

3½ cups unsalted cashew or
hazelnut pieces

1 Tbsp fine sea or kosher salt

2 Tbsp unsalted butter

1 Tbsp vanilla extract

1 tsp baking soda

Makes 2 pounds

Lightly oil a marble work surface or line 2 jelly roll pans with silicone baking mats.

Combine the sugar, corn syrup, and water in a heavy saucepan and stir to evenly moisten the sugar. Attach a candy thermometer to the side of the pan, making sure that the bulb is submerged but not resting on the bottom of the pan.

Bring the mixture to a boil over medium heat, stirring constantly. As soon as it reaches a boil, stop stirring and skim the surface to remove any foam. Continue to cook without stirring until the mixture reaches 265°F, the soft crack stage. Add the nuts and salt. Stir the mixture gently with a nonmetal spoon over high heat until it is a rich golden brown. Remove the brittle from the heat and immediately stir in the butter and vanilla extract. Once they are thoroughly blended into the brittle, stir in the baking soda.

Pour the hot mixture onto the prepared marble or pans and, working quickly, spread the brittle into as thin a layer as possible using a heat-resistant silicone spatula.

Let the brittle cool just enough so you can handle it. (You may want to wear heavy, lined rubber or latex gloves, such as clean dish-washing gloves, to protect your hands.) Stretch small areas around the edge of the brittle out, and then cut away from the whole mass using a pair of scissors. Continue to stretch the edges until all of the brittle has been stretched and cut.

Note: If you have another pair of hands available when it is time to stretch the brittle, each person should grasp one end of the slightly cooled brittle and pull in opposite directions to stretch the entire slab of brittle at once. Then cut or break the brittle into pieces.

Brittles are sugar-based candies studded with nuts. There is no need to toast the nuts before you make brittle, since the sugar mixture's heat will toast them enough for a rich flavor and aroma. Adding a little baking soda to the candy creates tiny bubbles for a slightly waffled texture after the candy has cooled. Brittles call for a slow, steady stir after the nuts are added to keep the mixture from becoming grainy. One of the hallmarks of a good brittle is that it is pulled into thin sheets as it cools for a more delicate texture.

Silicone baking mats or lightly oiled marble slabs make it easier to spread the brittle; it tends to stick like glue to everything else.

cooking sugar to stages
p. 244

Pecan Diamonds

1 doubled recipe Tart Dough
(p. 117)

All-purpose flour as needed

2 cups (4 sticks) unsalted
butter, diced

2 cups tightly packed light
brown sugar

½ cup granulated sugar

1 cup honey

½ cup heavy cream

9 cups whole shelled pecans

Makes 120 diamonds

Preheat the oven to 350°F. Line a jelly roll pan with parchment paper. Scatter the top and bottom of the tart dough lightly with a little flour and place it between sheets of parchment or waxed paper. Roll the dough out into a rectangle of ⅛-inch thickness just slightly larger than your pan. Transfer the dough to the pan and press it into the bottom and up the sides of the pan. Prick the dough in several places with the tines of a fork. Line the dough with parchment paper and weight with dry beans or rice. Bake until the dough is firm but has no color, 10–12 minutes. Remove the weights and let cool completely on a wire rack.

Combine the butter, sugars, honey, and cream in a heavy saucepan. Attach a candy thermometer to the side of the pan, making sure that the bulb is submerged but not resting on the bottom of the pan. Heat over medium-high heat, stirring constantly to prevent scorching, until the mixture reaches 240°F. Add the nuts to the boiling mixture, stir until fully incorporated, and then return the mixture to a boil, stirring frequently. Immediately pour into the prepared crust and spread into an even layer.

Bake until the entire surface of the mixture is evenly covered with bubbles or foam and the crust is brown on the edges, 40 minutes.

Cool thoroughly in the pan on a wire rack. To cut into diamonds, first make straight cuts at 1-inch intervals lengthwise. Holding the knife blade so that it intersects the first cuts at a 45-degree angle, make an initial cut as close to the lower left-hand corner of the pecan pastry as possible. Continue to make cuts parallel to the first cut at 1-inch intervals to make regular-shaped pieces, then lift the diamonds from the pan.

Any time you combine more than one sugar in a confection, you also change the way the sugars behave when they are cooked. Syrups are used in confections because they have a different structure from granular sugar, one that is less likely to become a crystal. You could substitute other syrups, such as maple syrup, cane syrup, or dark corn syrup, for the honey in this recipe, as long as you add enough syrup to keep the pecan filling smooth.

blind baking p. 115

cooking sugar to stages p. 244

Fruit Gelées

Flourless cooking spray for greasing

¾ cup frozen juice concentrate, thawed

¾–1¼ cups water

Two 1¾-oz packets (8 tsp) powdered fruit pectin

1 tsp baking soda

2 cups sugar plus extra for coating

1⅓ cups light corn syrup

½ tsp fruit extract or oil

¼–¾ tsp citric acid, or as needed

Food coloring as needed (optional)

Makes about 120 pieces

Lightly coat a 9 x 13–inch rectangular cake pan with cooking spray, line with parchment paper, and coat the parchment lightly with cooking spray.

Put the juice concentrate in a large saucepan. If using frozen cranberry juice cocktail, add ¾ cup water; for other frozen juices, add 1¼ cups water. Add the pectin and baking soda.

In a second large saucepan, combine the sugar and corn syrup.

Bring the contents of both saucepans to a boil over medium-high heat. The pectin mixture will foam up as it comes to a boil. Reduce the heat to medium and stir both mixtures for 8 minutes. Gradually add the juice-pectin mixture to the sugar mixture, stirring constantly. Continue to boil for 1 minute more.

Remove the saucepan from the heat and stir, adding a few drops of fruit flavoring (extract or oil) and/or about ¼ tsp citric acid for tartness, and a few drops of food coloring, if desired. Spoon a little of the mixture onto a plate and taste it when it has cooled slightly. Adjust the flavor with a few more drops of flavoring or citric acid, if desired. Pour into the prepared pan. Set the pan on a level surface and let cool until the candy is firm enough to cut into pieces, about 2 hours at room temperature.

Scatter a thin layer of sugar on a jelly roll pan. Coat a pizza cutter, kitchen scissors, a slicer, or aspic cutters with cooking spray so the candies won't stick. Invert the slab of candy onto a work surface and cut into strips about ¾ inch wide. Cut each strip into pieces and set them on the sugar-coated pan. Turn the candies so that all sides are evenly coated, rubbing the sugar into the candy. Set the sugar-coated candies on a wire rack lined with waxed paper and let air-dry for at least 8 hours.

Note: To store, pack in an airtight container, lined with waxed paper. These candies are sensitive to humidity and may become sticky.

Fruit gelées are candies that are made from fruit juices or purées. Fruit extracts and oils may be added in small amounts to boost the candies' flavor. While extracts are available in many supermarkets, you may wish to experiment with oils to expand your repertoire. Many natural-food stores carry food-grade oils, but be sure to ask if you aren't sure if an oil or extract is meant to be eaten.

Some good juice-extract combinations are apple juice with mint, orange or cranberry-orange with cinnamon, cranberry with lime, limeade with lemon, and orange juice with lime. A good neutral-flavored juice that pairs well with many extract flavors is white grape.

Citric acid may sound like an exotic ingredient, but it is what gives sour candies their pucker. You can find it in drugstores (ask the pharmacist) or in stores that specialize in candy-making supplies. If you have trouble locating citric acid, you can try crushing a vitamin C tablet.

using pectin p. 242

Hard Candies

Vegetable oil for greasing

2 cups sugar

1 cup water

⅔ cups light corn syrup

Liquid food coloring as needed

½ tsp oil of peppermint,
cinnamon, orange, or lemon

Makes 1¾ pounds

Place a 12 x 17–inch silicone baking mat on a work surface or lightly oil a marble work surface.

Combine the sugar and water in a heavy saucepan with tall sides. Attach a candy thermometer to the side of the pan, making sure that the bulb is submerged but not resting on the bottom of the pan. Bring the mixture to a boil over medium heat, stirring constantly. Add the corn syrup and enough food coloring to give the candy the appropriate color for the intended flavoring (green for mint, yellow for lemon, and red for cinnamon, for example).

As soon as the mixture returns to a boil, stop stirring and skim the surface to remove any foam. Continue to cook over medium heat, occasionally washing down the sides of the pan using a pastry brush dipped in cool water, until the mixture reaches 295°F, the hard crack stage.

Remove the mixture from the heat and add the flavoring oil. Pour the candy onto the silicone baking mat or oiled marble. Cool until it can be handled but is still warm. (You may want to wear heavy, lined rubber or latex gloves to protect your hands.) Cut the candy into 1-inch-wide strips using oiled kitchen scissors, then pull and stretch the strips lengthwise until they are about ½ inch wide. Use the oiled scissors to cut the pulled candy into pieces about 1 inch long. Cool the pieces completely before layering them with waxed paper in airtight containers for storage. They will keep for about 4 weeks at room temperature.

For a more elaborate version of these candies, you can prepare the sugar mixture as directed, but omit the coloring. When you take the mixture from the heat to add the flavoring, first pour it into separate bowls, and then add the different food colorings and flavors to the separate batches. For example, you can keep one half uncolored, color the other red, and flavor both with either peppermint or spearmint for classic candy canes. Once you've stretched the strips (which will turn the clear strips white), twist the different colors together, cut them into lengths, and curl one end to make a cane. Or, use bright colors with fruit flavors to make fruit twists—try lime with lemon, cherry with grape, mango with pineapple.

cooking sugar to stages
p. 244

VARIATION

Lollipops

Pour the colored and flavored sugar mixture into greased small molds and add a lollipop stick, available through shops that carry candy-making supplies and some craft shops. Let the lollipops set up completely before unmolding.

Marshmallows

Flourless cooking spray for greasing

1 cup granulated sugar

¼ cup honey

¼ cup light corn syrup

¾ cup cold water (divided use)

2 packages (4½ tsp) powdered unflavored gelatin

2 tsp vanilla extract

2 cups confectioners' sugar

Makes 49 marshmallows

Cut two 8 x 16–inch rectangles of parchment paper. Lightly coat an 8 x 8 x 2–inch baking pan with cooking spray. Lay one strip of the parchment in the baking pan, pressing it to the bottom and sides. Lightly coat the parchment with cooking spray. Lay the second parchment rectangle across the pan in the opposite direction to form a cross. Press the parchment to the bottom and sides of the pan and lightly coat with cooking spray. You should have a few inches of paper overhang on each side of the pan.

Combine the granulated sugar, honey, and corn syrup with ¼ cup of the water in a heavy saucepan and stir until the sugar is evenly moistened. Bring the mixture to a boil over high heat, stirring constantly. As soon as it reaches a boil, stop stirring and skim the surface to remove any foam. Continue to cook without stirring until the mixture reaches 240°F on a candy thermometer. Remove the sugar mixture from the heat, pour it into the bowl of a stand mixer fitted with the whisk attachment, and let cool undisturbed until it reaches 210°F.

Meanwhile, sprinkle the gelatin over the remaining ½ cup cold water in a small bowl and stir to break up any clumps. Let the gelatin soften for about 2 minutes. Heat the softened gelatin over simmering water or in a microwave for about 20 seconds on low power until the granules melt and the mixture is clear. Stir in the vanilla extract. Mix the gelatin into the cooled sugar mixture.

Beat the sugar mixture on high speed until it is white and foamy and holds a medium peak when the whisk is turned upright. The bottom of the bowl should still feel very warm.

Pour the mixture into an even layer in the prepared pan. Spread it gently with a small offset spatula or palette knife if necessary to level it. Freeze the marshmallow mixture until set, about 30 minutes.

Lift the parchment paper from the pan to remove the slab of marshmallow. Sift 1 cup of the confectioners' sugar over a large piece of parchment or waxed paper. Peel the parchment from the sides of the marshmallow and cut the slab into 1-inch squares with a lightly oiled knife. Place the marshmallows on the coated parchment paper, sift the remaining 1 cup confectioners' sugar over the marshmallows, toss to coat completely, and shake off the excess.

Marshmallows were once made from the root of the mallow plant. The Egyptians are known to have cooked the sap from this root with honey and nuts to make a confection that was deemed fit only for gods and royalty. Today, gelatin is used instead of the mallow plant. This homemade version is noticeably less rubbery and more flavorful than packaged marshmallows. Feature these marshmallows in your best hot chocolate, dot some over the surface of brownies before you bake them, or toast or broil them to sandwich with a piece of chocolate and some graham crackers for s'mores, the classic childhood favorite.

working with gelatin
p. 170

cooking sugar to stages
p. 244

Marzipan Shapes

One 7-oz tube or box marzipan

Confectioners' sugar as needed

Liquid or paste food coloring as needed

Vegetable oil as needed

Lightly beaten egg white as needed

Makes enough to cover an 8-inch cake or form a variety of shapes

Gently knead or roll the marzipan, still in its packaging, on the counter a few times. Dust the work surface lightly with the confectioners' sugar. Remove the marzipan from the package. To make more than one color, divide the marzipan into smaller pieces. Squeeze a few drops of food coloring onto the marzipan. Knead it by hand just until the color is evenly distributed and the marzipan is soft enough to roll out or mold into shapes. Keep any portion of the marzipan that you aren't working with well covered to prevent drying.

To cover a cake, working on a surface lightly dusted with confectioners' sugar, roll the marzipan into an evenly thin sheet about 1/16 inch thick. Turn the marzipan as you work to keep it from sticking and tearing. Cut to cover small cakes, or transfer the entire marzipan to the cake. Allow the sheet to drape over the sides and press them gently onto the sides of the cake. Pinch off any excess marzipan and rub the seams to seal and smooth them.

To make cutout shapes, dust your work surface and rolling pin lightly with confectioners' sugar. Roll the marzipan into a very thin layer, about 1/8 inch thick. Use cutters of various shapes. Transfer the marzipan shapes to a plate and cover to keep them pliable.

To make flowers, use a flower-shaped cutter or a knife to create the petals. Roll a small ball of marzipan. With the handle of a wooden spoon, make a small depression in the center of the flower petals, and press the ball into the depression. To make fruit and vegetable shapes, roll the marzipan into a ball of the approximate size you'd like for the finished shape, then mold or sculpt as you would clay. To make coffee beans, color the marzipan a deep brownish black. Break off small pieces and roll them into bean shapes. Press the blade of a paring knife lengthwise down the center of each bean.

Dip a toothpick into vegetable oil and use it to press any seams or depressions into the shape for a more natural look.

To attach smaller pieces, such as stems, centers, or leaves, use a toothpick to make a small depression at the point where you want to attach something, such as in the top of an apple shape. Use your fingertip to very lightly moisten the attachment (a small ball for the center of a flower, cutout leaves, longer cylinders for stems, for example) at the place where it should join the marzipan shape and press it gently in place. Use egg white to glue if necessary.

In many parts of the world, sweet shops produce dazzling marzipan confections shaped and colored to look like fruit fresh from the tree and an array of other tempting shapes. Although the town of Lübeck in Germany is credited with making some of the best marzipans in the world, it is likely that this candy originated long ago in the Mediterranean, perhaps in parts of Italy where almonds were a mainstay of the diet, inspiring someone to invent this fragrant paste of almonds and sugar.

Kneading marzipan softens it and distributes any coloring you add. Once it is easy to work, you can roll the marzipan into sheets and cut out shapes. Or, roll marzipan by hand into small balls or cylinders to create three-dimensional candies or decorations. Fanciful fruit and vegetable shapes turn out best if you use a delicate touch with food coloring; vivid colors may look unnatural.

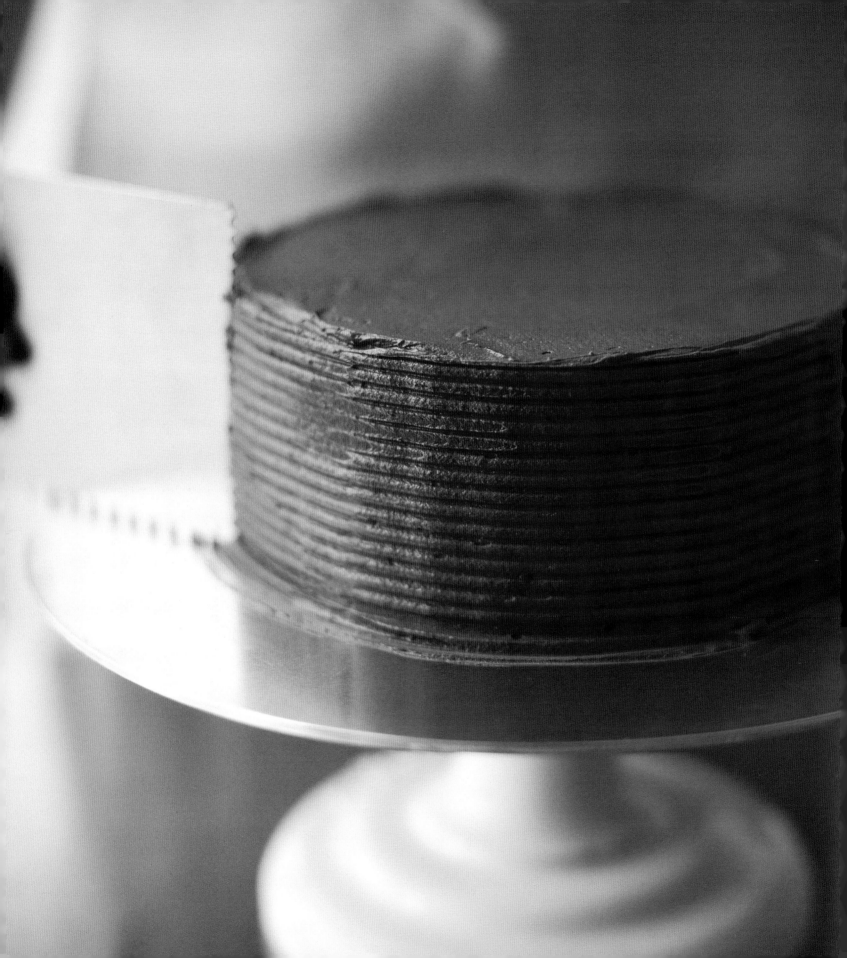

Icings, Glazes,
10 and Sauces

The desserts you order in a restaurant are known to chefs as "plated desserts," indicating a special presentation or plating. The difference between a plain piece of cake and a plated dessert may be the use of an icing, filling, or glaze. Sometimes, a sauce is included on the plate; perhaps a mellow custard sauce is used to lighten the intensity of a dark chocolate torte. Other desserts may get a splash of color and flavor by adding a sauce or glaze with a lot of contrast, like a tart lemon curd with a spicy ginger cake or a warm caramel sauce with vanilla ice cream. To give your desserts a special polish, we've assembled a number of recipes that can transform a plain chocolate sponge cake into a Chocolate Sabayon Torte (page 162), for instance, or add that elegant finishing touch to dessert soufflés or apple pie.

If you were to pick the single most versatile sauce in this chapter, you might choose the basic Custard Sauce (page 274). This elegant and rich sauce marries beautifully with other flavors, including chocolate, orange, nuts, coffee, and liqueurs. A warm spoonful drizzled into an ethereal soufflé adds both flavor and substance. Drizzled cold over a warm piece of pie or served with a cobbler, it transforms those simple, homey favorites. It can even be used as the basis of ice cream (page 199).

A close second would have to be the classic chocolate-and-cream combination called ganache. You can vary the ratio of chocolate to cream and substitute different types of chocolate or dairy to make an intense, light-textured Chocolate Sauce (page 270), a more full-bodied soft Ganache (page 284) that can be whipped to serve as a mousse or a filling, or a Chocolate Glaze (page 284) to pour over cakes and cookies for a shiny coating.

Add some special fruit sauces, such as coulis and curds, to your repertoire and you will be able to capture the essence of raspberries, strawberries, mangoes, pineapple, lemons, limes, or oranges to add a potent jolt of color and flavor to a dessert. Coulis are purées made from fresh or poached fruits. Curds, on the other hand, share some characteristics with custard sauce; they have a cooked egg-and-juice base finished with butter instead of the cream you would use for custard sauce. The fresh flavors and slight acidity of these sauces complement rich chocolate cake as well as buttery tart dough.

Caramel sauce, yet another classic in the dessert repertoire, is perfect as a topping for ice cream. You can also swirl it into ice cream for a rippled frozen dessert, or pair it with fresh fruit. Caramel, fudge, and chocolate sauces are perfect to put in fondue pots and enjoy with plenty of fresh fruit and chunks of cake for dunking.

One advantage of some of these sauces, especially ganache, fudge sauce, caramel sauce, and fruit coulis, is that you can make them ahead when you have time, or when berries are at the peak of their season, and then store them until you are ready to use them. Kept in the refrigerator, most chocolate and caramel sauces last up to 2 weeks. Fruit coulis will hold for at least 10 days, in most cases, and some, especially those made from berries, freeze well for up to 3 or 4 months. Even curds, pastry cream, and custard sauce—relatively perishable because of the eggs they contain—can be made a day or two ahead of time. In some cases, the additional time to mellow in the refrigerator actually improves the sauce's flavor.

One of the simplest of all icings, fillings, and sauces is whipped cream. Add a touch of sugar and a drop or two of vanilla extract and you have Chantilly Cream (page 281). You can whip cream a few hours ahead of time to avoid last-minute work, but since it takes only a few minutes with a handheld or stand mixer, and not much longer if you use a balloon whisk, a freshly whipped topping is always at hand if you keep heavy cream stored in your refrigerator. (Heavy cream usually lasts up to 3 weeks if unopened, and 3 days once you open the carton.) Light, fluffy whipped cream makes a great textural contrast to a crunchy phyllo dessert or warm baked fruit.

A simple buttercream (page 276), made by creaming softened butter with confectioners' sugar, has the familiar texture children and grown-ups alike enjoy on cupcakes and simple layer cakes. A more silken, elegant rendition (page 279) calls for the butter to be creamed into a meringue. Both types of buttercreams can be used to fill, frost, and decorate cakes and tortes.

If you introduce a filling with a flavor and color that is distinct from the cake or pastry you are serving, these desserts become more complex. For example, a raspberry curd lends sophistication to a simple chocolate cake. Sauces and fillings can also be combined to great effect; for example, you can fold sauces such as fruit coulis or lemon curd into Chantilly cream or pastry cream. Glazes add a glossy sheen to cakes and other pastries. Be generous with glaze for a luxurious look.

Sauces for serving

Some sauces are best served warm or even hot (think hot fudge sundae). You can use the microwave on low or medium power to warm most sauces; the high sugar content makes them heat up quickly. You can also warm them in a saucepan over direct heat or in a double boiler over simmering water (page 167). If you've made a large batch, heat up only what you need rather than the entire amount. Other sauces are most effective when served very cold. Sometimes a cool sauce is desired so that the main dessert element will stay cool. Other times, a cold sauce is chosen for the contrast it provides with a hot or warm dessert, as when a cool dollop of Chantilly cream melts slowly on a piece of pie or cobbler.

Using a starch slurry

Starch slurries are simply pure starches such as cornstarch or arrowroot blended with a little water. They give body to sauces and fillings.

1 Making a starch slurry

Both cornstarch and arrowroot thicken a sauce or other mixture by trapping liquid in a network of softened starches. Arrowroot is slightly more translucent than cornstarch and has the ability to maintain its texture after cooling without "weeping" or separating, but cornstarch is more readily available. They can usually be substituted for one another in equal amounts.

Blend an equal quantity of cold water into the measured starch to produce a consistency similar to that of heavy cream. You can safely leave the mixture at room temperature as you work on the rest of the recipe. As the slurry sits, the starch will settle on the bottom, so stir the slurry just before you add it to a mixture. Adding cold water to the starch helps it disperse so you can add it without causing lumps to form.

The liquid should be at a simmer when the slurry goes into the dish, and will thicken very quickly; as soon as the liquid returns to a boil you will be able to gauge how thick the sauce or filling is. While you can always add a bit more slurry to a too-thin preparation, it is harder to thin out a thick one. If you are making a recipe for the first time, add the slurry gradually and stop at the thickness you prefer. For a relatively stiff, sliceable filling, add enough slurry so that the hot filling holds soft peaks.

Whipping cream

Whipped cream is used alone as a filling or topping and is folded into other ingredients in desserts such as mousses.

1 Chilling equipment

For the best results when you whip cream, be sure that it is very cold. The bowl and beaters can also be chilled; place them in the freezer for a short time. If whipping by hand, choose a deep and wide bowl and a balloon whisk to incorporate the most air. Use the whisk attachment for a stand mixer, or use a handheld mixer for small amounts of cream.

2 Adding sugar

Start whipping at medium speed and keep whipping until the cream just starts to thicken. At this point, gradually add sugar. Superfine and confectioners' sugars dissolve more quickly than granulated.

3 Whipping to desired thickness

Increase the speed to high and keep whipping the cream until it holds soft, medium, or firm peaks, according to your recipe's requirements. Turn the whisk upright to check the peaks. Soft peaks will gently slump over to one side, while firm peaks will remain more pointed and upright. Soft-peak whipped cream is typically used as a sauce to pool under or spoon over desserts. Medium peaks are suitable for using as the lightener for mousses or for folding into pastry cream. Cream whipped to firm peaks is best for icing cakes or piping. (Cream should not be whipped to stiff peaks, since it can easily turn into butter.)

Making buttercream

A good buttercream icing has a rich taste and a silky texture.

1 Making butter-based buttercream

To make a simple buttercream, good-quality unsalted butter at room temperature is whipped until it is very light, and sifted confectioners' sugar is added to make a thick icing. You can thin the icing as desired by beating in a little water or cream.

2 Making meringue-based buttercream

Buttercreams based upon sweetened beaten egg whites are very smooth, because the sugar in the buttercream dissolves into the egg whites. The first step is to prepare a Swiss or Italian meringue (page 234) that you whip to stiff peaks. Cubes of room-temperature butter are then added to the meringue. At first the icing may look thin or even curdled, but as you continue to add butter, the icing becomes thick and creamy.

3 Flavoring buttercreams

Allow flavoring ingredients, such as fruit curds, fruit purées, cordials or liqueurs, melted chocolate, and extracts or essences, to come to room temperature in order to incorporate them easily. Hot ingredients may melt the icing, whereas cold ingredients could stiffen it. Blend about one-third of the icing with the flavoring, then combine the flavored portion with the unflavored portion. Fold together until the mixture is very smooth, with no streaks.

Glazing a cake

For the best results, make enough glaze to be lavish as you pour the glaze over the cake.

1 Setting up

Soaking glazes are applied to cakes as soon as they cool enough to remove from the pan, to intensify the cake's flavor and add moisture. Icing glazes are applied to cooled cakes. The glaze should be at the correct consistency—liquid enough to pour easily, but thick enough to adhere properly. To get ready for glazing, set the cake on a rack in a baking sheet. To glaze a molded cake with layers that have been trimmed, first apply a crumb coat (page 265) of either whipped ganache or jam.

2 Pouring the glaze

Pour or ladle the glaze evenly and generously over the top of the cake. For the top and sides, make two or three strokes with an offset spatula over the top of the cake to level the glaze and send it cascading down the sides. Work quickly and don't overdo this step; otherwise, the glaze will retain the marks.

3 Finishing

There is something appealing about a scalloped curtain of glaze on the sides of a Bundt cake, but if you want to touch up the sides of a cake to make an even coating of glaze all around, scoop up a bit of glaze with the tip of your palette knife and delicately apply it to the bare spot. Use a skewer or the tip of a small knife to break any air bubbles trapped in the glaze. This should be done before the glaze sets up.

Icing a cake

Icings give a finishing touch to cakes. For more about assembling and filling cakes, see page 142.

1 Applying the crumb coat

A crumb coat is an initial coat of icing or jam spread on the cake to keep cake crumbs from showing in the finished icing. After the cake has been filled and assembled, brush away loose crumbs from the tops and sides of the cake. Set the cake on a decorating turntable, cardboard round, or a cake plate. If you are using a cake plate, put strips of waxed or parchment paper under the edges of the cake to catch drips that would otherwise fall on the plate. (Remove the strips from under the cake once the cake is fully iced.) Spread the icing or jam evenly but thinly over the tops and sides of the cake. This coating needn't completely cover the cake; its function is to glue any loose crumbs onto the cake and hold them in place. Let the coating set up for about 1 hour in the refrigerator.

2 Applying icing to the cake top

Once the crumb coat is set, spoon a goodly amount of icing onto the cake's top. Using a back-and-forth stroke with a level palette knife, spread the icing in an even layer that extends over the top edge of the cake.

3 Applying icing to the cake sides

Scoop up the icing with your palette knife and hold the knife vertically to spread icing on the sides; again, use a generous amount so that you create a layer thick enough to completely coat the cake. Use as many strokes as necessary, turning the cake to apply an even coat and scooping up more icing as you work. Once you have applied the icing all the way around the cake, hold your palette knife straight up and down with the blade at a 45-degree angle to the side of the cake. Turn the cake against the knife to smooth out the icing. The excess will rise above the top of the cake. After the edge is smooth, hold your palette knife horizontally and parallel to the top of the cake and smooth the excess from the edge toward the center of the cake. This makes a sharp edge all around the cake and a very level top.

4 Finishing touches

Use a cake comb (page 266) or the teeth of a serrated knife to make a design on the sides of the cake if you like, or create scallops and swirls with the tip of your palette knife or the back of a spoon. Any remaining icing can be piped (page 266) in rosettes on the top.

Using a cake comb

A cake comb can be used to create a decorative pattern in the icing on the sides or top of a cake.

1 Preparing the cake or torte

The iced cake should be on a fairly flat surface before you start to comb it. A turntable is ideal, but you can use any plate that has a level surface. The icing should be at room temperature and soft enough to spread easily.

2 Using the comb

Select the side of the comb you want to use and hold it so that the teeth just barely dig into the icing or glaze without reaching all the way to the cake underneath. Keep it at a 45-degree angle to the side of the cake to avoid digging the teeth in too far. Make a light stroke, always working in the same direction. If using a turntable, hold the comb still against the cake's side as you rotate the cake with the other hand. If the comb is not tall enough to decorate the side of the cake in one pass, make another pass, just overlapping the strokes. Instead of holding the comb so that the teeth run through the icing in a straight line, you can use a zigzag motion for a different look. This works especially well for the top of a cake.

Piping

Pastry bags and tips have many uses in dessert making, from filling to shaping to decorating.

1 Filling the bag

To use a pastry bag to portion out batters like pâte à choux or to add fillings and toppings like meringue or mousse, you can use it without any tip at all. For decorating, pastry tips are available in a wide array of shapes and sizes. To fill a pastry bag, position the tip securely in the bag's opening or in a coupler or tip holder. Fold down the bag's top to create a wide cuff, then transfer the ingredient to the bag with a large spoon. Support the bag under the cuff with your free hand while filling it with the other. Use a tall container to support the bag if you need to use both hands, folding down the cuff around the edge of the container.

2 Closing the bag

Fill the pastry bag only two-thirds full. Twist the bag to close it, compressing the mixture and releasing any air pockets.

3 Piping

Holding the bag at a 45-degree angle to the surface you're piping onto, use your dominant hand to slowly and steadily squeeze the bag and your other hand to guide and steady the tip. Release the pressure on the bag as you lift it away to make clean lines without thin tails. For decorative work, you may want to test the piping on parchment or waxed paper first. After each use, wash tips and reusable pastry bags thoroughly in warm, soapy water and dry them completely inside out.

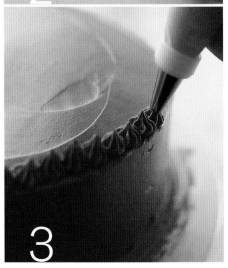

a small tip (page 266) or a parchment paper cone (page 268) to pipe the neatest lines.

3 Flooding with icing

To adjust the consistency of royal icing in order to fill in an outline (called "flooding"), add water a little at a time. To test the consistency, drop a small amount of the royal icing from a spoon back into the bowl. If the icing flattens out in 10 seconds, it is ready to use for flooding. Pipe the diluted royal icing to fill outlines by piping it into the center of the design and letting the icing run to the edges of the border on its own so that it sets to a smooth, shiny finish.

4 Finishing the design

While the icing is still moist, you can add various decorations. Scatter colored or decorating sugars or sprinkles over the icing and shake off the excess. Small candies, nuts, dragées, or dried fruits can be pressed into still-soft royal icing. As the icing dries, it holds these decorations in place. The icing dries quickly in a warm, dry environment, but to speed the drying process and retain a shiny gloss, use a hair dryer set on low speed.

Working with royal icing

Royal icing is a mixture of confectioners' sugar and egg whites, often used to decorate cookies.

1 Mixing and coloring the icing

Royal icing can have different degrees of thickness. A royal icing used to create outlines or filigrees should be relatively stiff. As you mix the icing, look for it to develop peaks and lose some of its glossiness. Once mixed, royal icing can be tinted by adding food coloring. Divide the icing among as many bowls as you need for the different colors you want. Use the tip of a toothpick to add a small amount of food coloring paste or add liquid food coloring a few drops at a time, mixing after each addition. You will need very little food coloring, so start with a small amount and add more as needed.

2 Piping outlines with icing

When you are ready to use royal icing for outlines or borders, use a pastry bag with

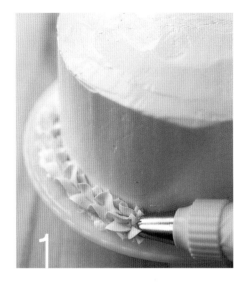

Piping a shell border

A border gives an attractive finish to an iced cake.

1 Piping shells

To make a shell border, use a pastry bag with your choice of plain or star-shaped tip. The larger the opening of the tip, the larger the shells will be. Fill the bag (page 266) and press out any air bubbles before you begin to avoid blowouts of icing as you work. It is always a good idea to practice on parchment paper before working on a cake surface. Hold the tip of the pastry bag at a 45-degree angle close to the surface. Use even pressure to squeeze the icing out with one hand. Use your other hand to guide the tip of the bag. As you squeeze, lift the tip very slightly to allow the icing to fan forward in a rounded shape. When the shell is the size you want, ease the pressure on the bag and pull the tip toward you and down toward the cake, cutting it off. Continue making shells all the way around the cake, starting each new shell at the end of the previous one.

Making a paper cone

Use a paper cone for piping fine lines.

1 Cut a triangle from parchment paper

Fold a large sheet of parchment to make a square. Fold the square in half and crease it, then use a sharp knife to slice the square into two triangles.

2 Begin to roll the cone

Hold the longest side of the triangle, positioning your fingers at its midpoint. With the other hand, roll one corner in so that you have a cone shape. Continue until the cone is completely rolled up. When you look into the cone, the opening should appear closed or as just a pinhole opening.

3 Secure the cone and fill

Fold the corners down into the cone, creasing them well to keep the cone from unrolling. Set the cone in a glass and spoon the ingredient to be piped into the cone, filling it only halfway. Fold the upper edge down to seal the cone and press the filling down toward the tip to work out any air pockets. If the opening is too small, use scissors or a sharp knife to nip off a small piece from the tip; the larger the opening, the wider the piping will be.

For more details on piping, see page 266.

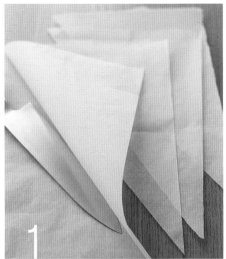

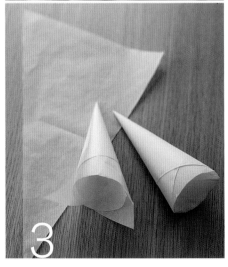

Making chocolate shavings and curls

To create chocolate shavings and curls, you need a good-sized block of chocolate at room temperature.

1 Setting up

Choose or cut a piece of room-temperature chocolate that is at least 1 inch thick. Set the chocolate on a piece of parchment or waxed paper on a baking sheet. Stabilize the baking sheet by placing a very lightly moistened towel under it and brace the sheet against a wall or other sturdy backing.

2 Making shavings

Hold a chef's knife or a vegetable peeler so the blade is at a 45-degree angle to the surface of the chocolate, then scrape the blade across the surface without digging into the block or gouging it. To make short shavings, use a short stroke. Longer strokes will produce longer shavings; they may curl slightly. If the chocolate block is cold, the shavings will be powdery.

3 Handling chocolate shavings

Chocolate shavings are quite thin and should not be touched with bare hands. The heat of your hands could easily melt them. Instead, use a spatula, preferably offset, to lift the shavings and scatter or pile them on top of a dessert. If you make shavings in advance, use the spatula to transfer them to a parchment paper–lined container. Make relatively thin layers so the shavings don't fall apart from their own weight.

Plating desserts

A large part of a dessert's appeal is in the artful arrangement of colors, shapes, textures, and temperatures on a plate.

1 Chilling or heating plates

Refrigerate dishes for cold or frozen desserts for 20 minutes or so. Warm or hot desserts stay at their ideal temperature longer if you warm plates in a low (200°F) oven for 10 minutes before plating. You can also rinse or soak plates in very hot water; dry them completely before using them.

2 Adding a sauce

The color of a sauce and its placement on the plate can change the look of a dessert. You can make a pool of sauce, setting a slice of cake, torte, tart, or pie on top. Or, drizzle the sauce over the top of the dessert. If you have two sauces with flavors and colors that work well together, such as a custard sauce and a raspberry coulis, use a spoon to deposit a few droplets of one sauce over the surface of the other. Dragging a toothpick or skewer through drops creates heart or paisley shapes.

3 Adding a garnish

A scattering or dusting of finely chopped nuts, confectioners' sugar, cocoa powder, or chocolate shavings is a lovely finishing touch. You can use a stencil to create a pattern or simply sift or sprinkle these garnishes over the dessert or the entire plate. A sprig of a fresh herb or an edible flower is an appealing element as long as the flavor complements the dish.

Chocolate Sauce

¾ cup half-and-half

2 Tbsp sugar

2 Tbsp unsalted butter

5 oz bittersweet, semisweet, milk, or white chocolate, coarsely chopped

2 Tbsp dark rum, brandy, Grand Marnier, framboise, Kahlúa, Tia Maria, amaretto, or Frangelico, (optional)

Makes about 2 cups

Combine the half-and-half, sugar, and butter in a heavy saucepan and bring to a boil over medium-high heat. Remove the pan from the heat, add the chocolate, and let the mixture rest for 2–3 minutes.

Stir until the chocolate is completely melted and the sauce is very smooth. When the sauce is cool, stir in the liquor, if desired. Transfer the sauce to a clean bowl or jar and cover tightly. Store, refrigerated, for up to 1 week. Rewarm the sauce over low heat or in the microwave before serving.

Use this sauce to make a chocolate fondue. Select ripe but firm fruit to cut into pieces: pineapple, bananas, strawberries, cherries, plums, or pears. Or, warm the sauce and serve it drizzled over sliced pound cake (p. 145), Cream Puffs (p. 231), or Profiteroles (p. 231).

melting chocolate p. 242

Hot Fudge Sauce

6 oz unsweetened chocolate, melted

½ cup cocoa powder

⅔ cup water

1 cup sugar

½ cup light corn syrup

8 Tbsp (1 stick) unsalted butter

¼ tsp salt

2 tsp vanilla extract

Makes about 2 cups

Combine the melted chocolate, cocoa powder, and water in a saucepan over low heat and stir gently until fully combined, about 2 minutes. Add the sugar, corn syrup, butter, and salt to the mixture and simmer over medium heat, stirring constantly, until thick and very smooth, 5 minutes.

Remove the pan from the heat and add the vanilla extract. Use the sauce at once, or stir it occasionally as it cools to room temperature. To store the fudge sauce, transfer it to a clean bowl or jar, cover tightly, and refrigerate for up to 2 weeks. Reheat the sauce over low heat or in the microwave before serving.

The classic hot fudge sundae brings together vanilla ice cream and a dense, chocolate sauce. Whipped cream falls halfway between the temperature extremes of hot fudge and frozen ice cream and adds lightness. Don't forget the cherry on top for color!

melting chocolate p. 242

Caramel Sauce

1½ cups heavy cream

¾ cup sugar

½ cup light corn syrup

2 Tbsp unsalted butter

Makes about 2 cups

Prepare an ice bath. Bring the cream to a boil in a saucepan over medium heat. Remove from the heat.

Combine the sugar and corn syrup in a heavy saucepan over low heat and stir until the sugar dissolves. Slowly cook to a golden brown without stirring, 8–9 minutes. Remove from the heat and put the saucepan in the ice bath for 20 seconds to stop the cooking. Remove from the ice bath and stir in the butter.

Carefully stir in the hot cream, mixing until fully blended. To store the caramel sauce, transfer it to a clean bowl or jar, cover tightly, and refrigerate for up to 2 weeks. Reheat the sauce over low heat or in the microwave before serving.

Always popular as an ice cream topping, caramel sauce can also be served drizzled over fresh fruit or as a topping for crêpes, waffles, or pancakes. If you make your own ice cream, you can add it as a swirl (p. 197).

making an ice bath
p. 169

caramelizing sugar
p. 171

Lemon Verbena Sauce

¾ cup water

6 Tbsp freshly squeezed lemon juice

2 Tbsp sugar

1 Tbsp light corn syrup

12 large lemon verbena leaves (divided use)

1 stalk lemongrass, soft inner core only, minced

2 tsp cornstarch or arrowroot

2 tsp white wine or water

Makes about 2 cups

Combine the water, lemon juice, sugar, corn syrup, 6 of the lemon verbena leaves, and the lemongrass in a saucepan and bring to a simmer over low heat, stirring until the sugar is completely dissolved.

Remove the pan from the heat. Cover the pan and steep for 10 minutes. Transfer the mixture to a storage container and refrigerate overnight.

Strain the cooled mixture into a saucepan and return to a boil over medium heat. Create a slurry by mixing the cornstarch with the wine. Gradually add just enough of the slurry to the boiling sauce to thicken it lightly. Let the sauce cool to room temperature, then cover and store in the refrigerator for up to 2 days. (If you are making this sauce in advance, use arrowroot so that the sauce will not thin or weep during storage.) Just before serving, mince the remaining 6 lemon verbena leaves and stir into the sauce.

This sauce has a tart, vibrant flavor that pairs well with sweet and nutty pastries, like Date and Pistachio Kataifi (p. 228). It would also be a good choice to serve with Warm Gingerbread Pudding (p. 184).

making simple syrup
p. 244

using a starch slurry
p. 263

Raspberry Coulis

1 lb fresh or frozen raspberries
(3½ cups)

¾–1 cup sugar

1–2 Tbsp freshly squeezed
lemon juice

Makes about 2 cups

Combine the raspberries, ¾ cup of the sugar, and 1 Tbsp of the lemon juice in a saucepan and bring to a simmer over medium heat. Simmer until the sugar has dissolved, about 10 minutes. Taste the mixture and, if necessary, add more sugar. Continue to heat until any additional sugar is dissolved.

Strain the coulis through a fine-mesh sieve.

Adjust the flavor by adding additional lemon juice if necessary. The coulis can be served warm or cold; it will thicken slightly when stored in the refrigerator, and keeps for up to 10 days.

Note: If you find that your sauce separates after you have finished it, you can add a cornstarch slurry (2 tsp cornstarch blended with 2 tsp cold water) to thicken it. To add the slurry to a cooled sauce, pour the coulis in a saucepan, bring to a boil, and gradually whisk in enough slurry to thicken the sauce slightly. Bring the sauce to a boil a second time after adding the slurry, then allow the coulis to cool.

Coulis are made by puréeing something—often a fruit or vegetable—until it is liquid enough to serve as a sauce. Good-quality frozen berries make delicious coulis, so you can enjoy summer fruit flavors year-round. Pastry chefs often store fruit coulis in a squeeze bottle so that they can easily squirt the sauce in a pattern on a dessert, pool it onto plates, or add a few droplets to garnish another sauce.

zesting and juicing citrus
p. 69

using a starch slurry
p. 263

VARIATIONS

Strawberry Coulis

Substitute fresh or frozen strawberries for the raspberries and prepare as directed above.

Blueberry Coulis

Substitute fresh or frozen blueberries for the raspberries and prepare as directed above. After straining the coulis, return it to a simmer. Make a slurry by blending 2 tsp cornstarch with 2 tsp cold water. Drizzle the slurry into the simmering coulis gradually, adding just enough to lightly thicken the coulis.

Mango Coulis

Substitute diced fresh mango for the raspberries. If desired, substitute lime juice for the lemon juice. Prepare as directed above.

Lemon Curd

6 large egg yolks

¾ cup sugar (divided use)

¾ cup (1½ sticks) unsalted butter, diced (divided use)

¾ cup freshly squeezed lemon juice

1 tsp grated lemon zest

Makes about 1½ cups

Prepare an ice bath. Blend the egg yolks with ¼ cup of the sugar and set aside.

Combine ½ cup of the butter, the remaining ½ cup sugar, the lemon juice, and lemon zest in a heavy nonreactive saucepan and bring to a boil over medium heat, stirring constantly. Temper the egg yolks by gradually adding about one-third of the hot butter mixture, whisking constantly. Add the remaining hot butter mixture and return the tempered mixture to the pan; continue cooking over medium heat, stirring constantly. As soon as the mixture comes to a boil, reduce the heat to low, and whisk in the remaining ¼ cup butter.

Pour the curd through a fine-mesh sieve into a clean bowl and cool over the ice bath. Stir the sauce occasionally as it cools. Store in the refrigerator for up to 3 days.

Lemon curd is wonderful as a spread on scones and biscuits. You can use it to make a quick and simple mousse or filling by just folding in some whipped cream. We feature it as a filling in tarts and tartlets, often using a different fruit juice for a special flavor. Use curds instead of jams to spread between cake layers when you build a torte or layer cake.

making an ice bath p. 169

tempering eggs p. 167

Custard Sauce

1 cup whole milk

1 cup heavy cream

½ vanilla bean, split lengthwise

½ cup sugar (divided use)

4 large egg yolks

Makes about 2 cups

Combine the milk, cream, vanilla bean, and ¼ cup of the sugar in a large, heavy nonreactive saucepan. Bring to a simmer over medium heat.

Prepare an ice bath if you plan to serve the sauce cooled. In a medium bowl, combine the remaining ¼ cup sugar with the egg yolks. Whisk until thoroughly combined. Temper the eggs by gradually adding about one-third of the hot cream mixture, whisking constantly. Add the remaining cream mixture, return to the pan, and gently cook over low heat, stirring constantly, until it is thick enough to coat the back of a spoon, 6–8 minutes.

Strain the sauce through a fine-mesh sieve into a pitcher to serve warm, or into a bowl set over the ice bath to serve chilled. Stir the sauce occasionally as it cools. Refrigerate for at least 2 hours or up to 2 days.

Custard sauce is a perfect partner for a bowl of fresh berries, a soufflé, a steamed pudding, or fruit-filled pies and tarts, whether you serve the sauce warm or cold. To keep it safe, be sure that you don't let it stay warm for too long. If possible, make it at the last moment and serve it warm from the stove. If you make the sauce ahead of time, cool it quickly over an ice bath and rewarm it just before using if desired.

making an ice bath p. 169

tempering eggs p. 167

Bavarian Cream

2 packages (4½ tsp) powdered unflavored gelatin

½ cup cold water

2 cups Custard Sauce (p. 274), cooled but not chilled

1 cup heavy cream

Makes about 4 cups, or enough to fill an 8-inch cake

Sprinkle the gelatin over the water in a small bowl and stir to break up any clumps. Let the gelatin soften for about 2 minutes. Heat the softened gelatin over simmering water or in a microwave for about 20 seconds on low power until the granules melt and the mixture is clear.

Stir the melted gelatin into the custard sauce and continue to cool, either over an ice bath or in the refrigerator until the mixture mounds when dropped from a spoon, about 20 minutes.

Whip the cream in a chilled bowl until it holds a medium peak when the whisk is turned upright. Working by hand with a spatula, fold the whipped cream into the slightly gelled custard sauce until evenly blended.

The Bavarian cream should be used as soon as possible to pipe or spoon into a cake-lined mold or individual molds. Chill for at least 2 hours or up to 2 days before serving.

This rich custard, lightened with whipped cream and stabilized with a touch of gelatin to keep its shape after you unmold it, has been part of the classic dessert repertoire since the eighteenth century. It's a wonderful cake filling when used to layer together a plain or flavored sponge cake (p. 149) or when it replaces the whipped cream in a jelly roll (p. 159).

working with gelatin p. 170

whipping cream p. 263

VARIATIONS

Chocolate Bavarian Cream

Prepare the Custard Sauce as directed on page 274, and before cooling stir in 4 oz of melted bittersweet chocolate. (Blend about one-third of the warm custard sauce with the melted chocolate, then blend the chocolate mixture into the remaining custard sauce.) Cool the custard sauce, but do not chill it, and continue with the recipe as directed above.

Raspberry or Strawberry Bavarian Cream

Replace 1 cup of the custard sauce with 1 cup raspberry or strawberry purée (page 190) combined with ¼ cup sugar.

Lemon Bavarian Cream

Replace 1 cup of the custard sauce with 1 cup Lemon Curd (page 274).

Simple Buttercream

1 cup (2 sticks) unsalted butter, at room temperature

4 cups confectioners' sugar, sifted, plus extra as needed

1 tsp vanilla extract

⅛ tsp salt

¼ cup heavy cream or whole milk plus extra as needed

Makes about 4 cups, or enough to fill and ice an 8- or 9-inch cake

In a stand mixer fitted with the paddle attachment, cream the butter on medium speed until it is very light in texture, 2 minutes. Add the confectioners' sugar, vanilla extract, and salt and mix on low speed until the sugar and butter are blended, scraping down the bowl with a rubber spatula as needed. Increase the speed to medium and, with the mixer running, add the cream in a thin stream. Increase the speed to high and whip the buttercream until very smooth, light, and a good spreading consistency. Adjust the consistency if necessary by adding a bit more confectioners' sugar or cream. Use to fill, ice, and decorate a cake.

Note: Once blended, buttercreams can be stored in the refrigerator for up to 2 weeks. To use after refrigeration, let the buttercream soften at room temperature for about 15 minutes. Transfer it to the bowl of a stand mixer and beat with the paddle attachment until it is a smooth, light spreading consistency, 3–4 minutes.

This is a relatively simple, virtually foolproof icing. It has a rustic texture and an assertive flavor, relying heavily upon the quality of the butter you choose, of your flavorings, and even of your sugar. Adjust the texture of this icing to make it as firm or flowing as you like by adding more sugar to make it stiffer or a bit of warm water or cream to make it softer. Italian Buttercream (p. 279) has a smoother, almost mousse-like, consistency; it also has a somewhat more complicated technique.

using a cake comb
p. 266

piping p. 266

VARIATIONS

Citrus Buttercream

Add 2 Tbsp finely grated lemon, lime, or orange zest and 1–2 Tbsp fresh citrus juice, to taste. You may need to increase the amount of confectioners' sugar slightly to balance the tartness of the juice.

Mocha Buttercream

Make a coffee paste by blending 2 tsp powdered instant coffee with 2 tsp boiling water. Melt 2 oz bittersweet or dark chocolate and stir together with the coffee paste. Cool to room temperature and add this mixture to the creamed butter. Blend on medium speed before continuing with the recipe above.

White Chocolate–Cream Cheese Icing

8 oz white chocolate

1 cup (2 sticks) unsalted butter, at room temperature

8 oz cream cheese, at room temperature

½ tsp vanilla extract

1 pinch salt

Makes about 2½ cups, or enough to ice 14–16 cupcakes or fill and ice an 8-inch cake

Chop the white chocolate and melt in a double boiler over barely simmering water or in the microwave on low power in 15- to 20-second increments, until it is barely softened. Stir the chocolate until it is smooth, returning it to the microwave if necessary. (White chocolate can overheat quickly, so keep the power low and the time short.) Let the chocolate cool to room temperature.

Cream the butter and cream cheese in a stand mixer fitted with the paddle attachment on medium speed until very smooth and light, about 3 minutes. Scrape down the bowl as needed to blend evenly. Add the chocolate, vanilla extract, and salt; continue to mix until very smooth, 1–2 minutes more.

Use the icing immediately or transfer the icing to a storage container, cover tightly, and refrigerate for up to 2 weeks. Before using, allow the refrigerated icing to soften slightly and then use the paddle attachment of a stand mixer to whip the icing until it is soft, smooth, and spreadable.

Select a good-quality white chocolate for this recipe. The icing has an extremely smooth texture and pairs well with flavorful cakes like our Carrot Cake (p. 152). It would also make a good filling and frosting for an 8-inch layer cake made with either a sponge cake (p. 149) or a butter cake (p. 146).

melting chocolate p. 242

Devil's Fudge Icing

1½ cups unsweetened cocoa powder

½ cup (1 stick) unsalted butter, at room temperature

½ cup light corn syrup

1 tsp vanilla extract

½ tsp salt

½ cup hot water

2¼ cups confectioners' sugar, sifted

Makes about 5 cups, or enough to fill and ice an 8- or 9-inch cake

In a stand mixer fitted with the paddle attachment, cream together the cocoa powder and butter on low speed until blended, scraping down the bowl with a rubber spatula as needed, until very smooth, about 2 minutes. Add the corn syrup, vanilla extract, and salt and continue to mix until evenly blended, 1–2 minutes. Add the hot water and mix on low speed until evenly blended.

Add the confectioners' sugar, mix on low speed until blended, then increase the speed to medium and whip until the icing is very smooth and light, 2–3 minutes.

Use immediately or transfer to a storage container, cover tightly, and refrigerate for up to 1 week. Allow the icing to return to room temperature before using it. If necessary, beat the icing using the paddle attachment on low speed until it is smooth and spreadable.

When you make a fudge icing, you add hot water to help dissolve the cocoa powder so that its flavor spreads evenly throughout the texture. This technique also results in a thick and creamy icing. The Devil's Fudge Cake (p. 151) is an obvious pairing, but this intensely chocolate icing also works well as the finishing touch for a butter cake (p. 146), filled with jam or Bavarian Cream (p. 275).

making buttercream p. 264

sifting p. 71

Italian Buttercream

1 recipe Italian Meringue
(p. 234)

2 cups (4 sticks) unsalted
butter, diced, at room
temperature

1½ tsp vanilla extract

Makes about 4½ cups, or enough to
fill and ice an 8- or 9-inch cake

Just before you are ready to make the buttercream, prepare the Italian meringue. Once the meringue cools to room temperature and reaches stiff peaks, add the butter a few pieces at a time while continuing to whip on high speed. Once all the butter has been incorporated and the buttercream is thick and very smooth, blend in the vanilla extract. The buttercream is ready to use now, or store covered in the refrigerator for up to 1 week. Let the buttercream soften at room temperature before beating it on low speed with the paddle attachment to make it warm and soft enough to spread.

There are advantages to an Italian buttercream—a silky smooth texture and a refined taste. There are some extra steps involved, however. To make an Italian meringue, you need to cook sugar syrup to a specific temperature and blend it into egg whites that you've just beaten to medium peaks. Let the meringue cool enough that it won't melt the butter as you add it. When you first start to add the butter to the meringue, the icing may appear curdled or very thin. This is normal, and as you continue to whip it the icing will thicken and become smooth and fluffy.

making buttercream p. 264

cooking sugar to stages p. 244

VARIATIONS

Chocolate Italian Buttercream

Melt ⅓ cup chopped bittersweet chocolate (page 242), let cool to room temperature, and add to the buttercream just after the vanilla extract has been added by stirring about 1 cup of the buttercream into the chocolate to lighten it, then adding the lightened chocolate to the remaining buttercream.

Coffee Italian Buttercream

Dissolve 2 Tbsp powdered instant coffee with 1 Tbsp boiling water and let cool to room temperature. Add to the buttercream along with the vanilla extract.

Adding coffee to the chocolate variation above will result in Mocha Italian Buttercream.

Royal Icing

2 large egg whites

⅛ tsp cream of tartar

2½ cups confectioners' sugar, sifted

Liquid or paste food coloring(s) as needed (optional)

Makes about 1 cup

In the clean, grease-free bowl of a stand mixer fitted with the whisk attachment, beat the egg whites on low speed just until they become loose, about 1 minute. Add the cream of tartar and continue mixing on low speed until the whites become frothy, 2 minutes. Add the confectioners' sugar gradually with the mixer on low speed. Continue to mix until the icing holds a soft peak and is dull in appearance, about 2 minutes. The icing is ready to use for piping lines. Or, add a small amount of water until the icing reaches a looser consistency for flooding, or filling in, an outline. If desired, divide the icing among smaller bowls and add coloring(s).

If you won't be using the icing right away, take the following steps to keep the icing from drying out: Clean the sides of the bowl or container to remove any drips; if a dry crust develops on the bowl, small pieces can drop into the icing and clog the tip of your pastry bag or parchment paper cone. Place a dampened paper towel directly on the surface of the icing and then cover the bowl very tightly with plastic wrap. Refrigerate for up to 5 days.

Note: You may prefer to use pasteurized egg whites in this recipe to eliminate any food safety concerns.

Royal icing, plain or colored, can be used to decorate Gingerbread Cookies (p. 100) as well as Petits Fours (p. 105). The egg whites in the icing dry into a smooth, lustrous shell. If you scatter the icing with finely chopped nuts, sprinkles, or decorating sugar before it dries, the decorations will stick.

working with royal icing p. 267

whipping egg whites p. 139

Chantilly Cream

1 cup heavy cream, chilled

¼ cup confectioners' sugar

½ tsp vanilla extract

Makes about 2 cups

Chill a stainless-steel bowl and the beaters of a handheld mixer, the whisk attachment of a stand mixer, or a balloon whisk.

Pour the cream into the chilled bowl and whip on medium speed until thickened, about 3 minutes. Increase the speed to high and gradually add the confectioners' sugar while whipping. Add the vanilla extract and continue to whip until the cream has the desired peak according to its intended use. Soft peaks are good for dolloping cream, while firmer peaks are better if the cream is to be piped, used for topping, or folded into another mixture.

Note: If your cream starts to turn slightly yellow while you are whipping, it is close to being overwhipped and turning into butter. Fold in a small amount of unwhipped cream, if you have it, to rescue the texture.

Ultrapasteurized heavy or whipping cream contains a stabilizer. Many bakers prefer to use pasteurized (not ultrapasteurized) creams if they are available, for their flavor and better whipping quality.

whipping cream p. 263

Pastry Cream

¼ cup cornstarch

¾ cup sugar (divided use)

2 cups whole milk (divided use)

4 large egg yolks, lightly beaten

1 pinch salt

2 tsp vanilla extract

2 Tbsp unsalted butter

Makes about 2 cups

Combine the cornstarch with ¼ cup of the sugar in a mixing bowl, then stir in ½ cup of the milk. Blend the yolks into the cornstarch mixture, stirring with a wooden spoon until completely smooth.

Prepare an ice bath. Combine the remaining 1½ cups milk with the remaining ½ cup sugar and the salt in a nonreactive saucepan over medium heat and bring to a boil. Remove the pan from the heat.

Temper the egg mixture by gradually adding about one-third of the hot milk mixture, whisking constantly. Add the remaining milk mixture to the eggs. Return the mixture to the saucepan and continue cooking over medium heat, vigorously stirring with a whisk, until the mixture comes to a boil and the whisk leaves a trail in the pastry cream, 5–7 minutes. As soon as the pastry cream reaches this stage, remove the pan from the heat and stir in the vanilla extract and the butter. Transfer the pan to the ice bath. Stir occasionally until the pastry cream is cool, about 30 minutes.

Transfer the pastry cream to a storage container and place parchment or waxed paper directly on the surface to prevent a skin from forming. Cover the storage container tightly and refrigerate until needed, up to 3 days.

Pastry cream is an extremely versatile item. It can be used as the filling for simple fruit tarts (p. 129), an an ice-cream base, and as the base for a dessert soufflé (pp. 190–91), as well as to fill pastries made from pâte à choux, such as Cream Puffs (p. 231) or Chocolate Éclairs (p. 233).

making an ice bath p. 169

making stirred custards and puddings p. 169

Diplomat Cream

1 package (2¼ tsp) powdered unflavored gelatin

¼ cup cold water

2 cups Pastry Cream (above)

1 cup heavy cream

Makes about 4 cups

Sprinkle the gelatin over the cold water in a small bowl and stir to break up any clumps. Let the gelatin soften in the water for about 2 minutes. Heat the softened gelatin over simmering water or in a microwave for about 20 seconds on low power until the granules melt and the mixture is clear. Stir the gelatin into the pastry cream by hand with a rubber spatula until evenly blended.

Whip the cream in a chilled bowl until it holds a medium peak when the whisk is turned upright. Working by hand with a spatula, fold the whipped cream into the pastry cream in 2 or 3 additions, folding just until evenly blended. Use at once.

Diplomat Cream, a blend of pastry cream and whipped cream, can be used in place of crème légère as a filling for Cream Puffs (p. 231), Chocolate Éclairs (p. 233), or Berry Napoleon (p. 223). The pastries should be baked and cooled before you make the diplomat cream; once the ingredients for this filling are mixed, you should pipe or spoon it immediately.

working with gelatin p. 170

whipping cream p. 263

Crème Légère

1/3 cup plus 2 Tbsp sugar (divided use)

2 Tbsp cornstarch

2 Tbsp all-purpose flour

1 cup whole milk (divided use)

3 large egg yolks

1 Tbsp dark rum

1 tsp vanilla extract

2 cups heavy cream

Makes about 4 cups

Prepare an ice bath. Blend 1/3 cup of the sugar, the cornstarch, and the flour in a bowl with 2 Tbsp of the milk. Add the egg yolks and stir to blend evenly. Bring the remaining milk to a boil in a saucepan over medium heat. Add about one-third of the hot milk to the egg mixture in a stream, whisking constantly. Return the yolk mixture to the remaining hot milk and cook over medium heat, stirring constantly with a whisk, until the mixture comes to a boil. Reduce the heat to low and simmer until thick enough to mound slightly when dropped from a spoon, about 3 minutes, stirring constantly. Transfer to a bowl and set in the ice bath. Stir in the rum and vanilla extract. Let cool, stirring occasionally, until very cold.

Whip the cream and remaining sugar in a chilled bowl to medium-stiff peaks. Gently fold the whipped cream into the cooled mixture in 2 or 3 additions. Use at once.

Crème légère is the classic filling for napoleons. It is similar to Pastry Cream (p. 282) except that flour is used to thicken it in addition to cornstarch. It is also similar to Diplomat Cream (p. 282), since it is lightened with whipped cream (hence the name, which means "light cream").

making an ice bath p. 169

whipping cream p. 263

Chocolate Sabayon

1 1/4 cups heavy cream

1 package (2 1/4 tsp) powdered unflavored gelatin

1/4 cup cold water

5 large egg yolks

1/3 cup sherry wine

1/4 cup sugar

4 oz semisweet or bittersweet chocolate, chopped

Makes about 4 cups, or enough to fill a 9-inch cake

Whip the cream in a chilled bowl until it holds a firm peak when the whisk is turned upright (page 263). Cover and refrigerate.

Sprinkle the gelatin over the cold water in a small bowl and stir to break up any clumps. Let the gelatin soften in the water for about 2 minutes. Heat the softened gelatin over simmering water or in a microwave for about 20 seconds on low power until melted.

Prepare an ice bath (page 169). Whisk together the egg yolks, sherry, and sugar in a heatproof mixing bowl and set over simmering water. Continue to whisk as the eggs cook. They will thicken, triple in volume, and become a pale yellow, about 15 minutes. The mixture should fall from the whisk in ribbons that hold their shape on top of the sabayon. Remove from the heat and set directly in the ice bath.

Melt the chocolate in the microwave or over simmering water and let cool slightly. Add about one-third of the sabayon mixture to the cooled melted chocolate to lighten it, then add the chocolate mixture to the remaining sabayon. Stir in the melted gelatin. Continue to whisk over the ice bath until the sabayon is cool. Fold the whipped cream into the sabayon and use immediately.

This filling is featured in Chocolate Sabayon Torte (p. 162). You can also use it to make a dramatic version of a chocolate cream pie: pipe or spoon the sabayon into a fully baked pie or tart crust (pp. 116–17). Or, serve it on its own in a slender glass, topped with a puff of whipped cream. The quantity of gelatin is just enough to let the sabayon hold its shape, not so much that it turns out rubbery.

working with gelatin p. 170

melting chocolate p. 242

making molded cakes p. 141

Ganache

10 oz semisweet or bittersweet chocolate, finely chopped

1¼–1⅔ cups heavy cream

2 Tbsp unsalted butter (for soft ganache)

Makes enough for 24 truffles or 2¼ cups soft ganache or about 4 cups after whipping

Place the chopped chocolate in a bowl. Heat 1¼ cups cream for a hard (truffle) ganache or 1⅔ cups for a soft ganache in a heavy saucepan over medium heat, just to a boil. Pour the hot cream over the chocolate and add the butter (if making soft ganache). Let the mixture rest for 2–3 minutes and then stir until the chocolate is completely melted and the ganache is very smooth. Cool the ganache to room temperature, then cover and refrigerate at least 8 hours and up to 2 weeks.

To make truffles from hard ganache, see the recipe on page 246. To make a whipped filling or frosting from soft ganache, transfer the chilled ganache to the bowl of a stand mixer fitted with the paddle attachment. Beat the ganache on low speed until it softens and lightens, about 3 minutes. Change to the whisk attachment and whip on medium speed until the ganache thickens and lightens in color; it should hold soft or medium peaks, 2–3 minutes. The ganache is ready to use as a filling or icing now.

By changing the amount of cream in the ganache, you can vary its consistency from soft to hard. A soft ganache is soft enough to whip, using the paddle attachment of your mixer to make an icing or filling that spreads or pipes easily. A hard ganache for truffles will hold its shape even at room temperature. If you want a filling or topping with a light texture, more like whipped cream, add ⅓ cup of chilled heavy cream to cool ganache before whipping.

assembling a layer cake p. 142

Chocolate Glaze

½ cup plus 2 Tbsp heavy cream

1 Tbsp corn syrup

8 oz semisweet or bittersweet chocolate, finely chopped

Makes about 1½ cups, or enough to glaze a 9-inch cake

Combine the cream and corn syrup in a heavy saucepan and bring to a boil over medium heat. Remove the pan from the heat and add the chocolate. Let the mixture rest for 2–3 minutes. Stir until the chocolate is completely melted and the sauce is very smooth.

The glaze may be used at this point, or it may be cooled to room temperature, poured into a clean, dry container, covered tightly, and refrigerated for up to 2 weeks. To reheat chilled chocolate glaze, warm it over very low heat or in the microwave until it is warm enough to flow easily.

This chocolate glaze stays shiny but soft and is a perfect topping for Cream Puffs (p. 231) or Éclairs (p. 233). Use it to glaze a cake or to drizzle into vanilla ice cream for a chocolate ripple effect (p. 197).

glazing a cake p. 264

Café au Lait Glaze

1½ tsp powdered instant espresso

1 Tbsp boiling water

¾ cup heavy cream

1 Tbsp light corn syrup

8 oz milk chocolate, finely chopped

Makes about 1½ cups, or enough to glaze a 9-inch cake

Stir together the instant espresso and boiling water until smooth. Set aside.

Combine the cream and corn syrup in a heavy saucepan and bring to a boil over medium heat. Remove the pan from the heat and add the chocolate and the dissolved espresso. Let the mixture rest for 2–3 minutes. Stir until the chocolate is completely melted and the sauce is very smooth.

The glaze may be used at this point, or it may be cooled to room temperature, poured into a clean, dry container, covered tightly, and refrigerated for up to 2 weeks. To reheat chilled glaze, warm it over very low heat or in the microwave until it is warm enough to flow easily.

This glaze is good for a sponge or layer cake that was filled with soft ganache, mousse, or ice cream; you can also warm it and serve it as a sauce with ice cream. If you can't find powdered espresso, use powdered instant coffee instead. In that case, you can increase the amount of powdered coffee by another ¼ tsp for a more intense coffee aroma.

glazing a cake p. 264

Lemon Soaking Glaze

1½ cups confectioners' sugar, sifted

4 Tbsp freshly squeezed lemon juice

2 Tbsp grated lemon zest

Makes about 1½ cups, or enough to glaze a 9-inch cake

Combine the confectioners' sugar, lemon juice, and zest in a bowl. Stir until blended.

To use the soaking glaze, remove a warm cake from its pan and set on a rack in a larger baking pan or baking sheet to catch the overflow. If the glaze has been sitting for more than 10 minutes (or if you have made it ahead and stored it in the refrigerator) warm it over very low heat or on low power in the microwave just until it is liquid enough to flow easily, 10–15 seconds. Use a toothpick or wooden skewer to poke very small holes over the top of the cake. Pour, spoon, or ladle about half of the glaze over the cake. Let the glaze set, about 1 hour, and repeat with the remaining glaze, warming the glaze again if necessary. Let the glaze set before slicing and serving the cake.

The idea behind a soaking glaze is essentially the same as that of brushing a cake with simple syrup. The glaze soaks into the cake for extra moisture and sweetness, especially nice with cakes like Lemon Buttermilk Cake (p. 148) and Sweet Polenta Cake (p. 144). Since most of the glaze's flavor comes from the zest, you can easily adjust the amount of zest to make the glaze more or less tart.

glazing a cake p. 264

zesting and juicing citrus p. 69

CONVERSIONS AND EQUIVALENTS

Useful measures

3 tsp = 1 Tbsp

4 Tbsp = ¼ cup

16 Tbsp = 1 cup

1 cup = ½ pt = 8 fl oz

2 cups = 1 pt

2 pt = 1 qt

4 qt = 1 gal

1 stick butter = 8 Tbsp = 4 oz = ½ cup

To convert Fahrenheit to Celsius

Subtract 32. Divide result by 9. Multiply result by 5 to get Celsius.

To convert Celsius to Fahrenheit

Divide by 5. Multiply result by 9. Add 32 to get Fahrenheit.

Useful temperatures

Water freezes at 32°F, 0°C.

Water boils at 212°F, 100°C.

Baking is an exacting craft; therefore, accuracy in measuring is an important first step. The temperatures of your ingredients, your oven, and your refrigerator or freezer each play a specific role in how successful your baked goods and pastries can be. If you are having trouble getting the results you hoped for, it may be the result of discrepancies in how you measured ingredients or read a temperature. Or, you may be reading and using these recipes in a kitchen outside the United States, so you will need to convert to metric measurements for weight, volume, and temperature. The unit of measure for oven temperatures in some areas also differs from those in the U.S.; "gas marks" are used instead of a Fahrenheit or Celsius temperature. The information in the following charts allows you to make a variety of conversions—pounds to kilograms, ounces to grams, cups to milliliters and liters, and Fahrenheit to Celsius.

In addition to information about converting temperatures from one measuring system to another, you will find charts that help to convert volume measurements into weight, as another way to increase accuracy. And don't forget that baking pans hold differing volumes of batter or dough; with the chart on pages 294–95, you can substitute a different pan than the one suggested in the recipe.

Temperature conversions

GAS MARK	FAHRENHEIT	CELSIUS	DESCRIPTION
½	250	120	very slow oven
1	275	135	very slow oven
2	300	150	slow oven
3	325	160	slow oven
4	350	175	moderate oven
5	375	190	moderate oven
6	400	200	hot oven
7	425	220	hot oven
8	450	230	very hot oven
9	475	250	very hot oven

Key temperatures

DESCRIPTION	DEGREES FAHRENHEIT	DEGREES CELSIUS
Freezing (water)	32	0
	40	4
	100	38
Egg whites coagulate	140	60
Egg yolks coagulate	150	65
	160	70
	170	75
	180	82
	190	88
	200	95
Boiling (water)	212	100
Simple syrup	212	100
Thread stage (sugar)	215–230	102–110
Soft ball stage (sugar)	240	116
Firm ball stage (sugar)	245	118
Hard ball stage (sugar)	250–260	121–127
Soft crack stage (sugar)	265–270	129–132
Hard crack stage (sugar)	295–310	146–154
Caramel*	320–350	160–177

*Do not use a cold water test for caramel. Since caramel changes rapidly once color changes begin, these temperatures are provided for information. By the time you could take the temperature of a caramelized sugar, it would continue cooking to the next stage.

High-altitude baking

As indicated in the chart at left, at sea level, water boils at 212°F. As you increase the altitude at which you are baking, increase the oven temperature by 15 to 25 degrees and decrease baking time by about 5 minutes.

At 2,000 ft above sea level, it boils at 208°F

At 5,000 ft above sea level, it boils at 203°F

At 7,500 ft above sea level, it boils at 198°F

At 10,000 ft above sea level, it boils at 194°F

Taking a room's temperature

A room thermometer indicates when your kitchen is hot or cool, so that you can adjust the temperature of your ingredients appropriately. If your kitchen is warmer than usual on a bread-baking day, you can use slightly cooler water so that the rising times will stay the same. If you are working with pastry or pie doughs, finding a cooler area in which to work or chilling your equipment is helpful.

Checking a thermometer's accuracy

To check a probe or candy thermometer's accuracy, let it stand in boiling water for 10 minutes. It should read 212°F, assuming that you are at sea level. (See above for boiling temperatures at various altitudes.) If it doesn't read 212°F, add or subtract the appropriate number to make allowances when using the thermometer. For example, if the water is boiling and your thermometer reads 208°F, it registers 4 degrees cooler than the actual temperature, so you would add 4 degrees to the number showing on the thermometer when measuring the temperature of an ingredient.

American bakers tend to use standard volume, or household measures. Useful, inexpensive, and universally available, they are great tools to have on hand. Our recipes have been written using that system. Volume measures are relatively accurate for liquid ingredients. The truth is, however, that these measuring tools are not produced to any specific or enforced standards. As long as you are familiar with your measuring tools and as long as you fill them the same way each time you use them, your results will be consistent. Professionals prefer to use weight measures for even greater consistency,

To convert ounces and pounds to grams

Multiply ounces by 28.35 to determine grams; divide pounds by 2.2 to determine kilograms.

To convert grams to ounces or pounds

Divide grams by 28.35 to determine ounces; divide grams by 453.59 to determine pounds.

Weight conversions

U.S. UNIT	METRIC (ROUNDED)
½ oz	15 g
1 oz	30 g
2 oz	55 g
3 oz	85 g
4 oz (¼ lb)	115 g
8 oz (½ lb)	225 g
16 oz (1 lb)	455 g
2 lb	910 g
3 lb	1.3 kg
4 lb	1.8 kg
5 lb	2.25 kg
6 lb	2.75 kg
7 lb	3.15 kg
8 lb	3.6 kg
9 lb	4 kg
10 lb	4.5 kg

critical to maintaining the quality of the goods they offer for sale. They weigh almost all ingredients, even liquids, whenever possible because of the greater accuracy they can achieve with a scale. Knowing what the ingredients in the original recipe weigh makes it much easier to accurately increase or decrease a recipe for your needs. Another advantage to working with a scale is that you can weigh directly into a container, adding one ingredient on top of another in many cases, and cut down on the measuring cups and spoons cluttering your workspace and needing washing up as you work.

Volume conversions

VOLUME MEASURE	U.S. VOLUME	METRIC (ROUNDED)
1 tsp	1/6 fl oz	5 ml
1 Tbsp (3 tsp)	1/2 fl oz	15 ml
1/8 cup (2 Tbsp)	1 fl oz	30 ml
1/4 cup (4 Tbsp)	2 fl oz	60 ml
1/3 cup	2⅔ fl oz	80 ml
1/2 cup	4 fl oz	120 ml
2/3 cup	5⅓ fl oz	160 ml
3/4 cup	6 fl oz	180 ml
1 cup	8 fl oz	240 ml
3/4 pt (1½ cups)	12 fl oz	360 ml
1 pt (2 cups)	16 fl oz	480 ml
1¼ pt (2½ cups)	20 fl oz	590 ml
1½ pt (3 cups)	24 fl oz	710 ml
1 qt (2 pt; 4 cups)	32 fl oz	950 ml (1 L)
2 qt (4 pt; 8 cups)	64 fl oz	1.89 L (2 L)
1 gal (4 qt; 16 cups)	128 fl oz	3.8 L

To convert fluid ounces to milliliters

Multiply fluid ounces by 29.58 to determine milliliters.

To convert milliliters to fluid ounces

Divide milliliters by 29.58 to determine fluid ounces.

Ingredient equivalents

INGREDIENT	VOLUME	WEIGHT (U.S.)	WEIGHT (METRIC)
Apple			
1 medium	1 cup sliced	4.2 oz	119 g
Baking powder	1 tsp	.15 oz	4 g
Baking soda	1 tsp	.18 oz	5 g
Bread crumbs			
5 slices bread	1 cup crumbs	3.5 oz	100 g
Butter			
1 stick	8 Tbsp	4 oz	113 g
Cheese			
hard (e.g., Parmesan cheese)	1 cup grated	3.75 oz	106 g
medium (e.g., Cheddar cheese)	1 cup shredded	3 oz	85 g
soft (e.g., fresh goat cheese)	1 cup crumbled	4.75 oz	135 g
Chocolate chips	1 cup	5.5 oz	156 g
Coconut (fresh)	1 cup	2.75 oz	78 g
Coconut (dried)	1 cup	2.4 oz	68 g
Cornstarch	1 Tbsp	.3 oz	8.5 g
Eggs			
5 large eggs	1 cup		
4 extra-large eggs	1 cup		
7 large egg whites	1 cup		
14 large egg yolks	1 cup		
Flour			
all-purpose	1 cup	4.4 oz	125 g
cake	1 cup	3.9 oz	111 g
bread	1 cup	4.8 oz	136 g
Gingerroot	1 tsp grated	.15 oz	4 g

Ingredient equivalents (continued)

INGREDIENT	VOLUME	WEIGHT (U.S.)	WEIGHT (METRIC)
Herbs (dried)	1 Tbsp	.08 oz	225 mg
Herbs (fresh)	1 Tbsp minced	.115 oz	3 g
Honey	1 Tbsp	.75 oz	21 g
Jalapeño	1 tsp minced	.10 oz	3 g
1 medium	2 Tbsp minced (approx.)	.5 oz	14 g
Lemon			
1 medium, juiced	3 Tbsp	1.5 oz	43 g
1 medium, zested	2 tsp	.10 oz	3 g
Lime			
1 medium, juiced	3 Tbsp	1.5 oz	43 g
1 medium, zested	2 tsp	.10 oz	3 g
Nuts	1 cup chopped	4 oz	113 g
Orange			
1 medium, juiced	½ cup	4 oz	113 g
1 medium, zested	1 Tbsp	.25 oz	6 g
Raisins	1 cup	6 oz	170 g
Salt (table)	1 tsp	.25 oz	7 g
Seeds (sesame, cumin, fennel, etc.)	1 tsp	.20 oz	6 g
Spices (ground)	1 tsp	.07 oz	2 g
Sugar			
brown	1 cup	7.75 oz	220 g
confectioners' (sifted)	1 cup	4 oz	113 g
granulated	1 cup	7.1 oz	201 g
superfine	1 cup	7.5 oz	213 g

Scaling recipes up and down

Doubling or tripling recipes or cutting them in half successfully requires more than simple multiplication. Recipes for baked goods rely upon a number of "sensitive" ingredients, such as leaveners, flavorings, seasonings, and thickeners. These ingredients don't scale up or down directly in proportion with other ingredients.

If you are planning to triple a cake recipe, and simply multiply the amount of baking powder it calls for by three, the cake could easily rise up and over the sides of the pan. A mousse might either set into a rubbery consistency or not set at all if you haven't properly adjusted the amount of gelatin from the original. If a cookie recipe calls for ⅛ tsp ground cloves and you quadruple the recipe, the resulting amount of cloves could overpower the other flavors in your cookies.

Changing from one size batch to another may also call for different equipment, mixing times, baking temperatures, or baking times. Scaling a recipe up or down often requires a test run to determine whether the new recipe works well, which means it is rarely a good idea to make a first attempt at doubling a recipe for cakes or puddings when you have dinner guests.

The first step of scaling recipes is to calculate the basic "recipe factor," which results when you divide the desired yield by the original yield. For example, if you want to change a recipe for muffins so that it makes 4 dozen muffins instead of 1 dozen:

48 muffins (desired yield) divided by 12 muffins (original yield) = 4 (recipe factor).
Or, if you want to make just one loaf of bread instead of two:

1 loaf (desired yield) divided by 2 loaves (original yield) = .5 (recipe factor).

Once you figure out the recipe factor, multiply the measurements for each ingredient by the recipe factor. You may need to round the result or convert it to a more logical unit of measure; 4 tablespoons, for example, is easier to measure as ¼ cup. Pay special attention to ingredients used for leavening, flavoring, coloring, or thickening. If a pudding to serve 4 calls for 3 tablespoons of flour as a thickener, it is not necessarily true that you will need 12 tablespoons (or ¾ cup) of flour to thicken the same pudding when you prepare it to serve 16. And since many baked goods cannot be adjusted once they are mixed and in the oven, you may need to retest the recipe, using different amounts each time, until the correct texture or flavor is achieved.

The more you know about how foods behave when you cook or bake them, the more success you will have. For scaling up the amount of thickeners and leaveners such as cornstarch, arrowroot, gelatin, and yeast, start with about 75 percent of the amount you calculated using the recipe factor. For flavorings, you might want to lower that to about two-thirds of the amount calculated with the recipe factor. The best advice we can offer, however, is that you make a test batch when you are increasing or decreasing a recipe and make the necessary adjustments to get the results you want.

Substituting pans

You may want or need to substitute one pan for another when you bake cakes, pies, or muffins. Maybe you need to make cupcakes for a party or gathering. Perhaps you only have a 9-inch tube pan and the recipe calls for a 10-inch tube pan. There are plenty of good reasons to substitute one pan for another, and there are a couple of factors to keep in mind.

First, fill all pans using the guidelines below. Second, monitor baking temperatures and times. If you use a larger pan than called for in the original recipe, lower the oven temperature 15–25 degrees and increase the baking time. (Jot this information down so you'll have it handy next time.) Conversely, using smaller pans generally calls for slightly higher temperatures and shorter baking times.

If you want to replace the pan called for in a recipe with something larger or smaller, it's helpful to know about how much batter your recipe makes. You can determine this by looking at the volume capacity for the original pan in the substitution chart. Then, figure out if the pan you want to use holds significantly more or less batter than the original. For example: A recipe that makes enough batter for an 8-inch round cake will fill that pan by about two-thirds, but if your put it in a 10-inch Bundt pan, there won't be enough batter to fill the pan and the cake won't rise properly. Increase the recipe quantity using the charts and information in this appendix, or make more than one batch.

Although the sizes in the chart on pages 294–95 are considered standard, the actual size of your pan may vary slightly because different bakeware manufacturers may have slightly different specifications. To measure the dimensions of a pan, measure from inside edge to inside edge of the pan, ignoring any central tubes. To determine pan volume, measure the amount of water needed to fill the pan to the rim.

You can substitute one pan for another using the following guidelines:

To substitute a glass or nonstick pan, reduce the baking temperature by 25°F.

To substitute a pan that is shallower than the one specified in the recipe, reduce the baking time by 25 percent.

To substitute a pan that is deeper than the one specified in the recipe, increase the baking time by 25 percent.

Use the following guidelines for filling pans:

Fill cake pans at least one-half full but no more than two-thirds full. (Deep pans like tube pans and Bundt pans are typically filled half full.)

Fill loaf pans and muffin tins two-thirds full.

Fill soufflé dishes and steamed pudding molds to within 1 inch of the rim.

Fill jelly roll pans at least half full or to within ¼ inch of the top.

Add fruit fillings to the top of a pie pan, mounding them slightly higher in the center.

Pan dimensions and volume

PAN SHAPE OR NAME	APPROXIMATE PAN DIMENSIONS	APPROXIMATE TOTAL VOLUME CAPACITY*
Round cake pan	6 x 2 inches	4 cups
Round cake pan	8 x 1½ inches	4–5 cups
Round cake pan	8 x 2 inches	5–6 cups
Round cake pan	9 x 1½ inches	6 cups
Round cake pan	9 x 2 inches	7–8 cups
Round cake pan	10 x 2 inches	10–11 cups
Heart-shaped cake pan	8 x 2½ inches	8 cups
Springform cake pan	8 x 3 inches	12 cups
Springform cake pan	9 x 2½ inches	11 cups
Springform cake pan	9 x 3 inches	13 cups
Springform cake pan	10 x 2½ inches	13 cups
Tube pan	7½ x 3 inches	6 cups
Tube pan	8 x 3 inches	9 cups
Tube pan	9 x 3 inches	12 cups
Tube pan	10 x 4 inches	16 cups
Bundt pan	7½ x 3 inches	6 cups
Bundt or fancy tube pan	9 x 3½ inches	9 cups
Angel cake pan	9 x 3½ inches	12 cups
Angel cake pan	10 x 4 inches	16 cups
Square cake pan	8 x 8 x 2 inches	8 cups
Square cake pan	9 x 9 x 1½ inches	8–9 cups
Square cake pan	9 x 9 x 2 inches	10 cups
Square cake pan	10 x 10 x 2 inches	12 cups
Rectangular cake pan	11 x 7 x 2 inches	6 cups
Rectangular cake pan	13 x 9 x 2 inches	14 cups

*Total volume refers to capacity of the pan when filled to the rim with water, not the volume of batter or dough that can be baked in the pan.

Pan dimensions and volume (continued)

PAN SHAPE OR NAME	APPROXIMATE PAN DIMENSIONS	APPROXIMATE TOTAL VOLUME CAPACITY*
Pie pan	7 x 1¼ inches	2 cups
Pie pan	8 x 1½ inches	4 cups
Pie pan	9 x 1½ inches	5 cups
Pie pan	10 x 1½ inches	6 cups
Deep-dish pie pan	9 x 2 inches	6 cups
Deep-dish pie pan	10 x 2 inches	8 cups
Round tart pan	11 x 1 inches	4 cups
Quarter sheet pan	9 x 13 x 1 inches	8 cups
Jelly roll pan	15 x 10 x 1 inches	10 cups
Jelly roll pan	17 x 12 x 1 inches	14 cups
Half sheet pan	18 x 13 x 1 inches	16 cups
Full sheet pan	26 x 18 x 1 inches	32 cups
Loaf pan	8 x 4 x 2½ inches	5 cups
Loaf pan	8½ x 4½ x 2½ inches	6 cups
Loaf pan	9 x 5 x 3 inches	8–9 cups
Mini muffin tin	1¾ x ¾ inches	2 Tbsp
Muffin tin	2¾ x 1½ inches	½ cup
Giant muffin tin	3 x 1¼ inches	½ cup plus 2 Tbsp
Extra-small soufflé dish	5 x 2 inches	1¼ cups
Small soufflé dish	5½ x 2½ inches	2½ cups
Medium soufflé dish	6¾ x 3 inches	6 cups
Large soufflé dish	7½ x 3½ inches	8 cups
Extra-large soufflé dish	8½ x 3¾ inches	8 cups
Charlotte mold	6 x 4¼ inches	7½ cups
Brioche mold	9½ x 3¼ inches	8 cups

*Total volume refers to capacity of the pan when filled to the rim with water, not the volume of batter or dough that can be baked in the pan.

WHAT WENT WRONG?

Sometimes, despite the baker's best efforts at care and consistency, a baked good does not turn out as expected. While this is a frustrating experience, you may be able to learn something from it. Certain faults in a baked good indicate that ingredients were measured improperly, mixtures were not cooled properly, or the oven temperature was incorrect. The charts below examine some common faults and what might have gone wrong.

Common baking problems

TYPE OF BAKED GOOD	EFFECT	CAUSE
Yeast bread	Didn't rise well	Improper mixing; too much salt; not enough yeast; dough underproofed or too cold; pan too large; oven temperature too high
	Crust pale	Not enough salt or sugar; oven temperature too low; dough overproofed
	Crust dark	Too much sugar; oven temperature too high
	Crust too thick	Not enough sugar; baked too long; oven temperature too high
	Uneven grain	Dough proofed too long or at too high a temperature
	Coarse grain	Improper mixing; dough too cold; improper shaping technique; pan size too large
	Poor taste and flavor	Not enough salt; dough insufficiently risen; dough allowed to rise at too warm a temperature; dough overproofed
Quick breads and cakes	Crust dark	Too much sugar; oven too hot
	Cake shrinks	Mixed too long; batter too wet; cake overbaked
	Crust bursts	Mixed too long; batter too dry; oven too hot; wrong type of flour
	Cake falls	Not enough flour; cake underbaked
	Coarse or irregular crumb	Undermixed; not enough eggs
	Dense texture	Not enough leavener; batter too warm; wrong type of flour
	Tough texture	Not enough sugar; not enough fat; not enough liquid; batter beaten too long
	Fruit sinks	Too much leavener in batter; not enough flour in batter; fruit not dried enough
Cookies	Crumble	Removed from the pan while hot; let cookies cool before lifting from pan
	Dry or hard	Too much flour; baked too long; dough or batter overmixed; dried fruits not properly plumped before mixing; too much salt; not enough fat

Common baking problems (continued)

TYPE OF BAKED GOOD	EFFECT	CAUSE
Cookies	Spread too much	Dough not chilled; pans overgreased; batter portioned onto warm or hot pans; butter too warm during creaming step
	Baked unevenly	Dough not rolled out to even thickness or not portioned evenly; cookies placed too close to each other on the baking sheet
	Stick to the pan	Pan not properly greased or lined with parchment paper; too much sugar; oven too hot; cookies overbaked
	Too crisp	Used all white sugar
	Too soft	Wrong type of baking fat; too much brown sugar, honey, or molasses
Pies and tarts	Dough stiff	Not enough fat; not enough liquid; wrong type of flour; mixed too long
	Dough crumbly	Mixed too long; not enough shortening or butter; not enough liquid; wrong type of flour
	Dough shrinks	Dough mixed too long or overbaked
	Filling boils over	Hot filling added to crust; failed to vent crust; too much acid in filling; oven temperature too low (requires longer baking)
	Bottom crust soaked	Mixed too long; bottom heat in oven not working; wet pie pan; too much sugar in filling
	Meringue topping "weeps"	Sugar not dissolved; oven temperature too low; humid atmosphere
	Meringue topping tough	Oven temperature too high; too much sugar
Baked custards	Surface cracks	Overbaked; left in water bath too long
	Curdled	Overbaked; high-moisture ingredients (fruits and vegetables) insufficiently cooked before adding to custard or quiche
	Does not unmold	Not enough eggs, especially whites; underbaked; unmolded before cooling
Stirred custards and puddings	Skin forms	Not properly wrapped before refrigeration
	Weeps	Wrapped before completely cooled
	Soft or runny	Not enough eggs; not cooked long enough; not chilled long enough; for starch-thickened puddings, mixture did not reach a full boil after adding eggs
	Lumpy or curdled	Cooking time too long, temperature too high; was not strained

INDEX